SECURITY AID

Canada and the Development Regime of Security

JEFFREY MONAGHAN

Security Aid

Canada and the Development Regime of Security

UNIVERSITY OF TORONTO PRESS
Toronto Buffalo London

Toronto Buffalo London
www.utppublishing.com

ISBN 978-1-4875-0118-1

Library and Archives Canada Cataloguing in Publication

Monaghan, Jeffrey, 1980–, author
Security aid : Canada and the development regime of security / Jeffrey Monaghan.

Includes bibliographical references and index.
ISBN 978-1-4875-0118-1 (cloth)

1. Humanitarian assistance, Canadian – Developing countries – Case studies. 2. National security – Developing countries – Case studies. 3. Canada – Foreign relations – Developing countries – Case studies. 4. Developing countries – Foreign relations – Canada – Case studies. I. Title.

FC244.T55M65 2017 327.710172'4 C2016-908255-5

This book has been published with the help of a grant from the Federation for the Humanities and Social Sciences, through the Awards to Scholarly Publications Program, using funds provided by the Social Sciences and Humanities Research Council of Canada.

University of Toronto Press acknowledges the financial assistance to its publishing program of the Canada Council for the Arts and the Ontario Arts Council, an agency of the Government of Ontario.

Canada Council for the Arts Conseil des Arts du Canada

Funded by the Government of Canada Financé par le gouvernement du Canada

Contents

Figures

Acknowledgments

Many friends and colleagues have assisted in making this book possible, including some I have likely/regrettably overlooked when writing this note. It's worth starting with those from Queen's University at the Department of Sociology, and more notably the Surveillance Studies Centre (SSC). I am greatly indebted to David Lyon, director of the centre, and David Murakami Wood, my PhD supervisor. In his work establishing and running the centre, David Lyon has crafted a unique and inspiring program. From the high calibre of students and researchers to the biweekly seminar series, the SSC is a thriving hub of activity and creativity. As my link to the broader surveillance studies network, having a position at the SSC was an exceptional opportunity, and both Davids have been tremendous sources of knowledge and inspiration. From the first time I met him, David Murakami Wood has been an uncompromising supporter of my work and a great mentor. I was also fortunate to have an excellent PhD committee, who were supportive as well as challenging. Many thanks to Elia Zureik, Marcus Taylor, and my external, Didier Bigo. I should also mention Abigail Bakan, whose participation on my committee was short-lived yet had a significant impact on the direction of my research.

During my time at Queen's I was fortunate to meet many scholars and friends. Special thanks go to Jennifer Matsunaga, Natasha Saltes, Ozgun Topak, Sachil Singh, Lucas Melgaço, Adam Molnar, Midori Ogasawara, Ciara Bracken-Roche, Alana Saulnier, Scott Thompson, Mohammed Masoodi, Alicia Horton, Steven Richardson, Debra Mackinnon, as well as Michelle Ellis, Joan Sharpe, and Emily Smith. It has also been a pleasure to meet a number of scholars within the broader surveillance studies community, along with several who have mentored me in the process, including Torin Monahan, Peter Fussey, Valerie Steeves, and Kevin Haggerty, among others. In addition to wonderful colleagues from Queen's, I've been fortunate to have many good friendships during my faculty positions at University of Ottawa and now at Carleton University. From uOttawa, I am grateful for the support and encouragement from Justin Piché, Steve Bittle, Maritza Felices-Luna, Sandy Lehalle, David Moffette, Carolyn Côté-Lussier, Patrice Corriveau, Jon Frauley, Bastien Quirion, Prashan Ranasinghe, and of course Val Steeves, who has been an exceptional source of inspiration and encouragement. Having started an exciting new chapter at Carleton's Institute of Criminology and Criminal Justice, I have three colleagues in the Institute with whom I hope to share in long and fulfilling collaborations: Nicolas Carrier, Lara Karaian, and Evelyn Maeder. In addition to my specific unit colleagues, there are a number of people at Carleton who have long been colleagues and friends including Dawn Moore, Augustine Park, Aaron Doyle, William Walters, Dale Spencer, Erik Stephenson, Randall Germain, and Stacey Douglas. Of course, I look forward to fostering many more friendships and collaborations with folks at Carleton in the years to come.

With particular reference to the research and writing that made this book possible, I have some very important people to thank. Ajay Parasram has read and reread several chapters. His comments and keen eyes have been invaluable in shaping my arguments. I am also very grateful to other friends who have read chapters and provided much encouragement, including Kevin Walby, Nicolas Carrier, Augustine Park, Maddy Santos, Matthew Hoye, Jamie Brownlee, and Etienne Turpin. A number of those chapter readers are dear friends, whose influences have marked far more than these pages, with special thanks going to Turps, Wibber, DT, Maddy, Tubbs, Gord, KE, Yavar Hameed, Pat Williams, Peter Vance, Uncle Denis, and Andy Crosby. I would also like to thank Greg Szabo for helping bring my Excel 2000 graphs out of their Atari aesthetics and into more respectable form. Al Kratina's attentive eyes were instrumental in editing my initial manuscript, and Sarah Lawrance was exceptionally helpful assisting with my data entry. I would also like to thank Heather Anderson and her colleagues from the Carleton University Art Gallery for their assistance in finding the cover art used for this book, *Bridge* by Joseph Drapell. Special thanks to Mr Drapell for allowing the use of his piece. Daniel Quinlan, the editors and staff at UTP, as well as the copy editing of Ian MacKenzie, were superb in their managing of the manuscript and bringing it to fruition. I am very grateful to both anonymous reviewers for their attentive and thoughtful engagements with my work. Their constructive and challenging comments were of great assistance in shaping and improving the analysis and argumentation of the manuscript.

Finally, finishing school and figuring out teaching has been a collective project that would not have been possible without my family. My parents have been unconditional supporters and have had (for a long time) been nothing short of exemplars of patient parenting. Thank you. The Mooney family have also been tremendously reliable and supportive. Most importantly, my partner Angela has provided much needed encouragement and support. In addition to being supportive and encouraging of my work, Ange has been the rock for our family, filling in many, many gaps. Ange and the kids sometimes have no idea what the hell I'm working on, but they provide the most important support I have: an escape from the drudgery of the academy and a reminder of what matters most.

Many others have contributed, including participants in this study and the many writers whose works I've learned from and engaged with. My work builds from the insights of many others and I hope the following text offers readers a useful narration of the social realities of security aid and Canada's participation in it.

Abbreviations

ACCBP	Anti-Crime Capacity Building Program
ATIA	Access to Information Act
CANSOFCOM	Canadian Special Operations Forces Command
CBSA	Canadian Border Services Agency
CCC	Canadian Commercial Corporation
CDS	Chief of Defence Staff
CF	Canadian Forces
CIDA	Canadian International Development Agency
CPA	Canadian Police Arrangement
CPC	Canadian Police College
CSC	Correctional Services of Canada
CSEC	Communications Security Establishment Canada
CSIS	Canadian Security Intelligence Service
CTAG	Counter-terrorism Action Group
CTCB	Counter-terrorism Capacity Building
DFAIT	Department of Foreign Affairs and International Trade
DFATD	Department of Foreign Affairs, Trade, and Development
DND	Department of National Defence
DoJ	Department of Justice
DPSA	Defence Production Sharing Arrangement (Canada-U.S.)
FINTRAC	Financial Transactions and Reports Analysis Centre of Canada
GES	Global Engagement Strategy (DND)
GPSF	Global Peace and Security Fund

HNP	Haitian National Police
IOM	International Organization for Migration
IRTC	International Recommended Transit Corridor
JIPTC	Jordan International Police Training Center
MENA	Middle East and North Africa
MTCP	Military Training and Cooperation Programme
NTC	National Transitional Council (Libya)
OAS	Organization of American States
ODA	Official Development Assistance
OGD	other government departments
OIC	Office of the Information Commissioner
PA	Palestinian Authority
PADF	Pan American Development Foundation
PCO	Privy Council Office
PCP	Palestinian Civilian Police
PIU	Port Intelligence Units
PKO	Peacekeeping Operations (United Nations)
PMO	Prime Minister's Office
PSC	Public Safety Canada
RCAF	Royal Canadian Air Force
RCMP	Royal Canadian Mounted Police
RLG	Roma–Lyon Group
SEA	Southeast Asia
START	Stabilization and Reconstruction Taskforce
START-GPSF	Stabilization and Reconstruction Taskforce, Global Peace and Security Fund
UNDP	United Nations Development Program
UNODC	United Nations Office on Drugs and Crime
UNOPS	United Nations Office for Project Services
USSC	United States Security Coordinator (Palestine)

SECURITY AID

Canada and the Development Regime of Security

Security Aid: An Introduction

Security aid refers to assistance projects that aim to develop security capacities most commonly associated with, though not limited to, institutions such as police, prisons, borders, and the military. Put forward most prominently by the world's wealthy and most powerful countries, this type of assistance aspires to develop security with a mind towards stability and social control in the Global South. As research on the security-development nexus has demonstrated, perceptions of globalized threats stem from a view that the "underdeveloped" world is a major source of insecurity and instability. This perspective elicits a desire to control the broad and heterogeneous sources of insecurity (Aas 2013; Aas and Gundhus 2015; Bigo 2008; Dillon 2007; Duffield 2001, 2007; McCulloch and Pickering 2013; Mitchell 2010). Scholarship on the intersection of security and development has identified how the discursive structure of "security" blends (and extends) with discourses of "development," in effect functioning as dominant rationalities that support the geopolitical interests of the Global North (Duffield 2005, 2010; Essex 2013; Reid-Henry 2013; Sovacool and Halfon 2007; Stern and Öjendal 2010; Taylor 2009). Framed as a form of humanitarian support, a common response to perceptions of insecurity are practices to enhance underdeveloped governance regimes through "aid," "assistance," and "capacity building." In the subsequent chapters, I offer a conceptual framework to classify this particular articulation of "development assistance," which I call security aid.

Practices of security aid are not new but their contemporary incarnations are pervasive (Chandler 2010; Duffield 2001, 2007; Hettne 2010;

Hills 2009, 2010). This book provides a wide-ranging account of Canada's sprawling aid regime that aims to enhance the security, border control, policing, and surveillance capacities of insecure states. As a venue of foreign assistance funding, the programs that are rationalized as a form of security humanitarianism have become increasingly central to Canada's relationship with the world. Animated as a humanitarian responsibility to assist the populations of the Global South, I demonstrate that claims to provide security development have become a dominant framework for Canadian foreign assistance – whether sending fighter jets to participate in NATO bombing campaigns; providing equipment to security forces in Kurdistan, Palestine, Jordan, or Pakistan; facilitating the shipment of Light Armour Vehicles (LAVs) for Colombia to fight the drug war; or developing complex police, military, or counter-terrorism training programs for countries of the Trans-Sahel, Mexico, or Haiti. Within all these endeavours, claims of providing "assistance" serve to rationalize Canadian security development throughout the geographies of (in)security in the Global South.

As a product of late modernity's tendencies towards efficiency and orderly social control, efforts to manage (in)security are intimately bound to what is commonly referred to as "governance." A term that has gained considerable traction, thanks to the contributions of Michael Foucault (1978, 2003, 2007; see also Foucault et al. 1991), the notion of governance has been described as "a kind of catch-all to refer to any strategy, tactic, process, procedure or program for controlling, regulating, shaping, mastering or exercising authority over others" (Rose 1999, 15). By employing the concept of "security governance" (Krahmann 2003; see also Dillon and Lobo-Guerrero 2008; Valverde 2001, 2011), scholars have emphasized how agencies and actors have worked to systematize transnational "best practices" in the realm of security. This scholarship includes the reform of policies internal to security and policing agencies themselves to adopt "best practice" regimes (Goldsmith and Sheptycki 2007; Scherrer 2009), as well as the role of policing and crime control in the management of populations (Rose 2000; also see Mitchell 2010; Neocleous 2011). Focused on what have traditionally been referred to as "hard security" aspects of governance, a major component of the enhancements provided to the Global South are intended to improve the capacities of police, courts, correctional services, and border controls, as well as build their abilities to effectively participate in what Bigo (2002, 2008) calls the "management of unease."[1] My work contributes to this line of argumentation by demonstrating how security aid is used as a reformatory project to develop the security governance practices in what Aas (2013, 30) has called "deviant states" – countries that are deemed insecure as the result of their inability "to respond to issues on the international crime control agenda." Unlike literature that uses the term *failed states*, my borrowing of Aas's notion of deviant states underlines how the Global North expects countries of the Global South to participate in reformatory undertakings that correct and improve their contributions to global security governance.

With insecurities having eclipsed the singular responsibility of domestic states, the responsibilities for governing (in)security have globalized into an integrated and layered webs of actors. A number of scholars have commented on the collapse of "internal" and "external" aspects of security by highlighting the contemporary "transversal" character of threats (Bigo 2006; Eriksson and Rhinard 2009; Huysmans 2014; Pickering and Weber 2013). My focus is on state-based actors involved in the management of these transversal security threats, in which Canada is only one (small) actor among an increasingly competitive field. Notwithstanding its marginal status, Canadian contributions within this milieu are the focus of this book, and I suggest Canada's practices of security aid are shaped by what I describe as the transversal security community. Security communities have been used to theorize shared normative imperatives among like-minded countries who "desecuritize" from relations of enmity and form governance regimes based on "mutual identification, transnational values, intersubjective understandings, and shared identities" (Adler and Barnett 1998, 59; see also Kitchen 2010a; Pouliot 2010; Wæver 1995). While emphasizing the fluidity of the transversal security community in terms of membership and coexistence with a plurality of other communities (Adler and Greve 2009), I argue that the practices of the transversal community are centred on an aspirational drive for global security governance. As participants within the transversal security community, countries desecuritize – in the sense that they no longer imagine wars against each other – while entering into cooperative,

1 Much of the literature on security proliferations – particularly those scholars using bio-political frameworks – has noted that the term *security* discursively encompasses a growing field of activity, from counterterrorism to health care and food scarcity. My contention here is not to dispute this claim, but to focus on activities that were (and still are) the traditional domain of "hard" security.

transnational practices that aim to collectively manage global insecurities. As a process of governing these contingencies, I suggest that the transversal security community can be characterized by an overarching focus on the development of transnational cooperation and integration, while simultaneously anchoring its reformatory interventions in tropes of global humanitarianism. Through practices of *assistance*, security aid projects aim to develop regimes of security cooperation and integration in the deviant states of the Global South.

Built on the presumption that "development and security are inextricably linked,"[2] governments of the Global North and international organizations – the UN, most notably – have fully institutionalized contemporary discourses of security into their traditional development paradigm of economic growth. As the interconnectedness of security and development is becoming the dominant theme of foreign assistance strategies pursued by donor nations and international organizations, the convergence has prompted a rise in critical scholarship that gives substantive, empirical accounts of the negative consequences of security and policing development projects. In what Davis (2006) calls the "dark side" of security development, these programs – and their negative consequences – are often removed from donor countries (Abrahamsen 2005; Davis 2006; Hills 2009; Kessler and Daase 2008; Macaulay 2007; Mitchell 2010; Sovacool and Halfon 2007; Walby and Monaghan 2011; L. Zanotti 2010). Impacts are rarely subject to public debate, and the oversight functions administered by donor countries are often preoccupied with "effectiveness" and risk equations (Hyndman 2009), as opposed to questioning relationships between the fragmented rewards of globalization and efforts to "securitize" the Global South.

To explain the concept of security aid, I highlight a minor but important distinction from security-development literature on the "securitization of development" (Carbone 2013; Del Biondo et al. 2013; Howell and Lind 2009a; Mawdsley 2007; Watson 2011; Wilkinson 2015). Scholars such as Howell and Lind (2009b, 719) have detailed the "securitization of development and aid policy," which they define as the "absorption of global and national security interests into the framing, structuring and implementation of development aid." Similarly, Brown and Grävingholt (2016) have provided a detailed volume that analyses changes in Official Development Assistance funding and offers a unique exploration into how the "security lens" has (and has not) impacted

2 Kofi Annan, in 2004, quoted in full in Stern and Öjendal (2010, 5).

development programming in wealthy donor countries. Insomuch as the scholarship on the security-development nexus and the "securitization of aid" highlights how security discourses have crept into development discourses, I suggest that security aid regimes are specific projects that target security. Furthermore, these projects are enacted by security experts within security-related departments, which, in delivery, are divorced from development bureaucracies that traditionally administer foreign aid. While complementing other trends in foreign assistance, security aid is not just the securitization of aid but *the development regime of security*. As an expanding field of transversal security governance, I contend that "security aid" – while not entirely new – has a particular contemporary characterization that pairs a humanitarian spirit of providing assistance to the vulnerable with the normative imperative of developing security capacities (police, surveillance, prisons, border control) to maintain social order. Complementary to the securitization of aid, practices of developing security have become increasingly coordinated to integrate deviant states into collaborative security governance practices. Focusing on Canadian practices as a donor country in the regime of security aid, I demonstrate how efforts to enhance security techniques and technologies in the Global South contribute to expanding control infrastructures of transversal security governance.

Types of Security Aid

Practices of security aid can be categorized by three types: interventions, infrastructures, and techniques. Distinguishing between these three types of aid allows practices to be sorted and compiled, thereby clarifying the exploration of my empirical materials. Though the categories can be flexible, they offer solid enough boundaries to distinguish between three different spheres of security aid practices. In this book, each category of security aid is addressed with a standalone chapter, which provides for detailed theoretical and empirical explorations. The chapters engage with relevant literature to demonstrate how Canadian practices complement or contrast with trends in the development of security governance. Like other efforts to globalize policing or surveillance (Murakami Wood 2013), there are coexisting tensions between the aspirational pursuits of security aid and the realities of these practices. I will explain how strategic interests, and Canada's particular position as a norm-supporter, have a certain strategic unity in directing practices of security development in the Global South. Yet this unity can be disrupted by the heterogeneity and complexity of so many actors, agendas, and fields of engagement. Though this can result in highly diverse and unpredictable outcomes, the types of security aid detailed throughout the book illustrate the aspirational drives that rationalize security aid programs and Canada's engagements in them.

Security Interventions

Often appearing under the discursive framing of "humanitarian interventions," security interventions relate to direct forays into contested territories most often in the form of military offensives, bombing campaigns, drone strikes, multinational occupations, regional build-ups for rapid deployment, border enforcement, and deterrence, as well as other multinational collaborations that foster forms of transnational policing. Frequently described as policing operations, security interventions are most often military in orientation and rationalized by universalistic discourses of human rights, human security, the "responsibility to protect," and the protection of civilians. Unlike a Foucauldian discourse of intervention – which places emphasis on indirect forms of power that cultivate voluntary inducements and responsibilization – security interventions are far more direct. As forms of assistance grounded in the post–Cold War environment, security interventions involve activities by foreign countries or international actors directly within other countries in response to governance failures, threats to civilians by forces of violence (state or non-state), actors deemed threats to Western countries, civilians, or interests, or the fortification of governments facing the possibility of collapse in response to social or environmental forces. Chandler (2016, 1) has concisely defined security interventions as "projections of external power in or over another state in order to direct or influence the security behaviour of actors within that state." I do not place a limit on the categorical rationalizations for these interventions, other than that they do not include transnational private security entities and therefore must be grounded in overt state-based activities. Using the case study of NATO's 2011 intervention in Libya – but equally relevant in recent interventions in Iraq, Syria, Afghanistan, Haiti, and Mali – I argue that this category is an important aspect of security development precisely because of its rationalization as "assistance" to needy and vulnerable global populations. In a context where sovereignty is increasingly contingent and fragmented, security interventions represent the contemporary reconceptualization of military conflicts as forms of transversal "policing" operations under norms of human security and humanitarian responsibilities. Moreover, as a component of the security aid regime, I detail how security interventions provide gateways to initiate more comprehensive security development programming defined in the subsequent types of aid.

Security Infrastructures

Aid for security infrastructure is best illustrated by the technological analogy of "hardware." This form of assistance is focused on procurement of technologies for policing and surveillance, as well as the construction of buildings and infrastructures of prisons and border management, in effect providing the materials that enable the practices (i.e., "software") of security. As a very specific materialization of "aid," the category of security infrastructure includes direct efforts to provide materials for policing and security agencies in the Global South. In addition to demonstrating the priority enhancements given to agencies in the "developing" world, the category of security infrastructures illustrates the political economy of security aid. As I detail with the activities of the Canadian Commercial Corporation (CCC), security aid packages are often announced as monetary assistance projects. As an example, in 2012, Prime Minister Harper announced $12 million[3] to combat human smuggling in Southeast Asia (discussed in chapter 5). But the countries of Southeast Asia have yet to receive any monetary assistance. When these assistance packages are structured to include infrastructure enhancements, the government of Canada uses the "assistance" funding to contract security companies (often Canadian) through CCC. As a Crown corporation, CCC acts as an intermediary, offering a "suite of services" to broker deals between the Canadian government, a recipient government, and private corporations. The net outcome of the "aid" announcements are in-kind donations of security infrastructure to recipient countries, a source of revenue for security economy (with a privilege status to Canadian companies), and flashy press availabilities to celebrate the humanitarianism of Canadian security aid projects. Through a host of channels like the CCC, Canadian aid is mobilized to develop the material capacities needed to manage transversal insecurities. Using the case study of Haiti, I detail in chapter 4 how Canada

3 All figures in this text are in Canadian dollars, unless otherwise noted.

funded over $100 million in security infrastructures aid. While publicized to the Canadian public as aid, much of this funding was directed towards infrastructures like prisons, police stations, and border checkpoints. Often efforts to develop the material infrastructures of security work in tandem with aid projects to develop security techniques.

Security Techniques

To continue the technological analogy, security techniques are the "software" of security development. As knowledge practices, the techniques of security provide the roadmap for "doing" security governance. Contributing to an already rich literature on techniques of security governance (Amoore and de Goede 2008; Bigo 2008; Muller 2010; Salter 2008), chapter 5 explores how the development of security techniques aim to enhance – or "capacity build" – the abilities of deviant states in risk management, policing, border control, prison operations, surveillance, and security governance. As efforts to develop security governance practices on a global scale, these development regimes stem from an interest in both fortifying "international security" and articulating a humanitarian reason to assist the vulnerable, at-risk populations of the Global South. In addition to a focus on security sector reform, which has traditionally emphasized building on the basic capacities of security actors, a characteristic of transversal security development is an emphasis on cooperation, integration, and interoperability. Focusing on contributions of Canadian security experts in developing policing and border controls, in chapter 5 I demonstrate the priority given by the transversal security community to developing capacities in the Global South to control global "illegal" mobilities. To illustrate how Canada plays a supportive and technical role in developing security governance, I emphasize throughout this book that Canadian security aid funds are especially effective when functioning to integrate "recipient countries" into the transversal security community.

Practices within these three types of security aid – and especially programs to develop technologies and techniques – can be contemporaneous and complementary. But they nonetheless categorize approaches for the development regime of security governance. As I demonstrate through case studies, there are often multiple projects with these programs of security aid. There are dozens of projects detailed over the course of this text, and I provide detailed case studies of security aid practices in Libya (chapter 3), Haiti (chapter 4), and Southeast Asia (chapter 5) to demonstrate how these efforts weave together in the development of transversal security practices. These case studies represent larger projects of security aid undertaken by Canada, both in financial commitments and number of programs. In each case, I underline how Canadian security aid has been positioned within reformatory projects that provide concrete and practical steps to support development of transversal security best practices in the Global South, thereby leveraging assistance programming to increase the reputation and visibility of Canadian aid programming.

Although my collection of security aid practices is only partial, the annual security aid programs in Canada amount to hundreds of millions of dollars and include hundreds of projects and initiatives involving thousands of employees and actors from dozens of government entities. While major departments like Global Affairs Canada (GAC),[4] the Department of National Defence (DND), the Canadian International Development Agency (CIDA), the Royal Canadian Mounted Police (RCMP), and Public Safety Canada (PSC) figure prominently throughout this book, it should be noted that a host of other federal departments – Correctional Services Canada (CSC), Canadian Border Services Agency (CBSA), Department of Justice (DoJ), and Transport Canada, among others – have active international assistance programs to enhance the abilities of recipients (or "beneficiaries") in the Global South. Very little systemic research has explored practices of Canadian security aid, which is an evolving domain of foreign assistance. My research aims to provide a conceptual apparatus to analyse these contemporary realities and thoroughly map Canadian "security aid" practices. Given the impact that security development has in arming, training, and enabling policing and security forces throughout the world, exploring these practices raises significant ethical questions for society, as well as logistical questions for researching these opaque and expanding fields of Canadian internationalism.

4 From 2013 to late 2015, the department was named the Department of Foreign Affairs, Trade, and Development (DFATD). From 1993 to 2013, it was named the Department of Foreign Affairs and International Trade (DFAIT), but changed to DFATD when it merged with the Canadian International Development Agency (CIDA). Both acronyms DFAIT and DFATD were used during my research, though I have updated all references to use GAC unless used in quotations from participants or to denote a specific temporal reference.

Accounting for Security Aid

Accounting for practices of security aid is very difficult. Much like traditional development assistance programs, the actual funding mechanisms are obscured by national and international bureaucracies, myriad press releases, overt and covert funding arrangements, and a host of other political contingencies that render the accounting of the actual funding mechanisms complex and unreliable (Brown and Sinclair 2011). Since security aid does not exist within a unified concept or category – like the development assistance category of Official Development Assistance (ODA) – accounting for the vast array of these projects becomes even more difficult.

To engage in a structured, systematic exploration of secretive and sensitive social worlds of security aid, my research has relied on two primary methods to produce data: semi-structured interviews with security development experts, and the use of the Access to Information Act (ATIA) to gather declassified documents. The interview component of this research project included sixteen anonymized interviews with Canadian experts in fields related to security and/or development.[5] Interviews were conducted with senior level officials as well as expert practitioners from most of the major departments and branches discussed herein. Participants include individuals currently in their posts, as well as individuals who had recently left their positions. My questions guides were constructed to remain abstract, but presented opportunities for participants to offer specific details about projects. For example, staple questions were: How do you measure "success"? What have been the ingredients of a "successful" project? What are prominent barriers to security development programming? What are unique features of Canada's role in providing security assistance?

While interview participants provided informative discussions on "success" and barriers to security development, the format of semi-structured interviews limits in-depth discussions on specific projects. Given the extensive scope of security aid practices, interviews themselves cannot provide much in dates, figures, timelines, procurements, training, and the mechanics of security aid. To address this significant empirical gap, my research design included an ambitious data production using the ATIA. In using a mosaic-effect strategy for ATIA data production

5 Interviews quoted were randomized numbers that do not reflect chronological order.

(Hameed and Monaghan 2012; Monaghan 2015b), I have made over 150 ATIA requests,[6] as well as using the "informal" requests provision to receive previously disclosed requests. I have read, coded, and analysed contents from 276 ATIA requests, which include over 12,500 pages of documentary materials. The text quotes from documents contained across many ATIA requests, all of which have been itemized in the references section. A number of researchers have made significant contributions to contemporary policing scholarship using the ATIA (Dafnos 2012; Kinsman and Gentile 2010; Larsen and Piché 2009; Luscombe and Walby 2014; see also Larsen and Walby 2012). I believe this research project is the largest use of the ATIA in Canada, and the results illustrate the power of ATIA as a data production practice.

Given the scope of foreign assistance funding, as well as the secretive inclinations of government, accounting for specific programs and practices is a complex undertaking. While accounting for security aid is difficult work for non-governmental organizations and the research community, it has also been an untenable task for governments. A case in point is the UN Counter-Terrorism Action Group (CTAG). Established in July 2003 at the G8 Summit, CTAG was a committee of the UN Security Council Counter-Terrorism Committee (CTC) with the explicit purpose of "coordinating donations" of security assistance to the Global South.[7] Despite being a UN subgroup, the CTAG has become managed and administered largely by the G8, itself a transfer of authority that demonstrates the norm-making powers of the transversal security community. As one of myriad security aid networks, the CTAG underlines that counter-terrorism capacity-building assistance is "the provision of training, funding, expertise, equipment, technical and legal assistance to developing countries and economies in transition to enable them to prevent and respond to terrorist activity in a manner consistent with international norms and standards" (GAC 2012-2009, 8). At one point,

---

6 Since no academic style guides have developed a standard regime for ATIA/FOI citations, I use a citation style that denotes ATIA requests using an in-text citation (department year–request number, page in file). For example, a 2011 request with DND will quote the provision of "2000 military vests to Belize" as (DND 2013-701, 21). Since the citation of ATIA materials that I detail are extensive, and often only a summary of records, this citation style allows readers and other researchers to use the informal requests provision of the ATIA to access and find all documents cited.

7 Canada's GAC maintains a website exclusively for Canadian involvement in the CTAG (http://www.international.gc.ca/crime/ctag-gact.aspx?lang=eng), which lists the "most recent meeting" having taken place in April 2007.

the CTAG maintained a technical assistance "matrix" to aggregate the assistance programs from donor countries. Intended as a database that would assist with "gap analysis" and help coordinate delivery of counter-terrorism capacity-building assistance, the compilation of the "matrix" became excessively difficult. Responsibility to maintain the matrix fell under the annual G8 host state ("chair"), but because substantial resources were required to maintain the complex database, it "quickly became a several-hundred page document that suffered from lack of editing, consistency, and reliability and gradually became less and less relevant to the CTAG's work" (ibid.).

When researching the CTAG matrix, I submitted ATIA requests to get the matrixes for the years 2005, 2007, 2010, and 2012. Disclosures from my ATIA efforts are telling of the difficulties associated with accounting for security aid. A preface letter to the records states, "Notwithstanding searches and confirmation with our information management group, we were unable to locate records for 2005 and 2010. Furthermore it should be noted that CTAG ceased to exist after 2010." Apparently, not even the Canadian government could find the matrixes. Adding an element of mystery is that Canada was the G8 chair in 2010 and held the two-year presidency from 2009 to 2011 (PSC 2012-466). Not surprisingly, the list for 2007 contained heavy redactions, yet nonetheless displayed at least 150 pages of itemized security assistance projects. Despite many substantive redactions related to the programs, the lists' overall size illustrates the expansive scope of the Global North's security aid. Moreover, since the matrix effort was abandoned by the governments who control security aid, its discontinuation illustrates the methodological difficulties for exploring these practices. Giving evidence of the sheer magnitude of security aid practices, the efforts of CTAG underline the importance of giving a conceptual architecture to the social universe of "security aid," as well as what Aradau et al. (2015) have called an experimental approach to critical security research.

Though I do not provide a definitive calculation of security aid funding, I do map Canadian security aid bureaucracies in chapter 2. In this mapping exercise, I differentiate between two spheres of the security aid bureaucracy. One sphere is referred to as "security aid hubs." Functioning as information and management experts, the hubs detailed in this book have become main centres for strategic development of security aid programming since their establishment in 2004. The other sphere has been called "security innovators," which represents the practical and creative dimension for implementing security development. Their expertise is in technical "capacity building" and security-sector reform, which increases the abilities of recipient countries to interoperate in the transversal security community's practices of surveillance, policing, and border management.

To illustrate the "hubs" of security aid, I comprehensively detail the funding mechanisms provided by three of Canada's security aid funds: the Global Peace and Stability Fund (managed by the Stabilization and Reconstruction Taskforce, hereafter called START-GPSF), the Anti-Crime Capacity Building Program (ACCBP), and the Counter-Terrorism Capacity Building (CTCB) program. All three hubs are housed within the GAC department of the federal government. While there are other hubs for security aid – such as the Global Partnership Program – I have focused on these three for their global focus, availability of documents, and relevance of the interview data with Canadian experts in security development.[8] Although I do provide a significant overview of the funding mechanisms, my efforts to "account" for the spending of security aid hubs remains incomplete. In addition to redactions and layers of complexity encountered exploring these three funds, spending figures from another major funding hub of security aid – the Department of National Defence (DND) – are not available. Nonetheless, I do detail spending from various branches and programs of DND, but my calculations remain partial. A similar problem arises with calculating costs from other prominent security innovators, such as RCMP, CBSA, and CSC, which do not have formal budgets for foreign "programming," but nonetheless have branches that engage in regular international security development. Therefore, figures from the many departments providing technical assistance are not easily accessible, nor are the enormous staff, labour, or material costs that sustain the network of the bureaucracies supporting these security development efforts. Doing "international relations" is not cheap and, given the prominence of security aid to Canadian internationalism, the aggregate costs of supporting such work are far beyond my ability to report.

Security Aid and Canada's "Place in the World"

A study of Canadian security development practices is timely, particularly given the transformations to Canadian internationalism under the

8 There are other security aid hubs within GAC that I have not examined. For example, the Global Partnership Program is a fund of $367 million (2013–18) to assist former Soviet states with weapons controls, demilitarization, and anti-terrorism training.

Harper government (2006–15). Among the significant changes have been Harper's idealization of Canada as a warrior nation (McKay and Swift 2012), and the government's distain for all things related to the United Nations and cultural representations of peacekeeping. In practical terms, the Conservatives implemented two major reformulations of Canadian internationalism. First was the Harper administration's explicit linking of foreign assistance to trade. Under the Global Markets Action Plan (Canada 2013), the Harper government promoted new policies of tied-aid, by placing trade and commercial success for Canadian firms as the dominant focus of Canada's foreign policy. In aiming to coordinate delivery of international assistance with broader Canadian objectives, the strategy included an explicit push to deliver foreign aid in tandem with private sector activities abroad (Mackrael 2013). As former minister of international cooperation Julian Fantino (2013) wrote, "Doing so helps foster sustainable economic growth in developing countries while advancing Canada's own long-term prosperity and security." Scholars have long noted that foreign assistance is calibrated according to domestic interest (Chin 2009; Cowen and Shenton 1996; Lancaster 2007; see Brown 2007, 2013 on Canada), and the twinning of commercial interests with the Global Markets Action Plan should be regarded as an intensification of these trends.

A second major component of the Harper reorientation of Canadian internationalism was an ideological adherence to "principled" foreign policy, which some pundits have called the Harper Doctrine (see Ibbitson 2011). Though it was not an explicit doctrine, the central components of the Tories' "principled" foreign policy included the unequivocal support for "allied and like-minded nations" (Israel being a prominent example), increased military funding, attention to northern sovereignty, defunding of development assistance groups that do not align with more socially conservative principles, and, finally, a pronounced distancing and de-prioritization of multilateral institutions (notably the UN). Many critics – including several participants in this study – point towards the Harper Doctrine as diminishing Canada's standing as a respected figure in the realm of international relations. Though some have focused on the role of the Harper government in the decline of Canadian internationalism (Heinbecker 2011; Mulroney 2015), debates regarding a decline from an era of more "spirited internationalism" (Cohen 2003, 2) long predates the Harper administration (see Hart 2008; Nossal 1989; Welsh 2004; see also Nossal 1988). While the Harper government has disrupted aspects of Canada's traditional foreign policy, my central contention is that trends in transversal security governance are globally driven and, in this context, Canada – and Canadian influence – is negligible.

Though Canada is a peripheral and marginal actor, I argue that an analysis of security aid practices offers a critical lens in long-standing debates regarding Canada's "place in the world." Through a comprehensive analysis of security aid programs, I detail how these mechanisms of foreign assistance are parlayed in highly strategic measures to maximize the visibility and reputation of Canadian expertise within the transversal security community. I focus on Canadian expertise that is provided as assistance to deviant states to advance the interoperability and cooperation of surveillance, policing, and security governance. Through practical and tangible security development that increases the visibility and reputational value of Canada within the transversal security community, I demonstrate that the marshalling of security aid has been met with substantive investment and reward, advancing a number of organizational, economic, and political interests through the aspirational practices of transversal security governance.

In exploring the practices of a donor country in the field of security aid, it is important to identify the crossroads at which the dominant themes of this research converge. Security aid is an expression of humanitarian governance existing within a convergence of globalization, development, and security, giving it a universalistic rationality that aims to enhance and develop a shared global communion. Given that the deployment of assistance is an enterprise in what Fassin (2012) calls humanitarian governance, this study is intimately tied to broader understandings of culture and place, as well as fundamental questions of inequality separating much of Canadian society from the geographies of (in)security that require "assistance." As reformatory projects, Canadian security aid aims to transform the governance regimes of recipient countries yet, not un-paradoxically, I suggest that practices of security aid reveal more about Canada than they do about the insecure world.

In exploring inequality and global governance, there are many similarities between security development and traditional development. As critical development scholars have long noted, development strategies – regardless of their humanitarian intentions – have functioned to sustain global power hierarchies, not challenge or transform them (Escobar 1995; also Duffield 2005). In large part, the development regimes of the Global North have done little to address poverty and inequality – fundamentally a problem of wealth distribution, not wealth creation – which continue to plague our global lived experiences. Security aid cannot be separated from the poverty of development, as nothing sustains the status quo more than systems of surveillance, police, border, prisons, and social sorting sciences of security governance.

When faced with the tragic violence afflicting too much of the world, a desire for safety and well-being is a fundamental element of the human condition. Yet "security" as a discursive technology of nation states has traditionally been a device in the service of power, not human dignity (Dillon 1996; Neocleous 2008). A number of the security development projects undertaken by Canadian agents have provided immediate safety to vulnerable populations. Many of these Canadian funded and directed projects – and many more that are similarly structured around the discourses of human security – are not featured in the following pages and chapters. While these projects are composed within the overall package of security aid funding offered by Canadian agencies, they are peripheral to the central rationale of developing "hard" security capabilities that integrate recipient countries of the Global South.

In the chapters that follow, I demonstrate the scope and shape of Canadian security aid practices. While I assess how the aspirational character of security assistance is always circumscribed by challenges and barriers, I focus on the significant impacts of security aid in contributing to transversal security governance regimes. In trying to develop the regimes of policing, surveillance, and social control in the insecure world, I argue that security aid also produces a particular relationship between Canada and rest of the world – primarily between Canada and members of the transversal security community. Canada has long aspired to "punch above its weight," as one participant put it (Interview 5). I argue that security development is a particular domain for an international lightweight and has allowed Canadian security experts to marshal small but strategic contributions to the development regime of transversal security governance, thereby increasing the country's visibility as a reliable player on the security stage.

Since security aid is primarily a vehicle for Canadian strategic interests, the secondary relation is one of tragedy, since global society is at crossroads. The avarice of the wealthy – not exclusive to the Global North, but an assemblage linked to it – has far eclipsed human or environmental carrying capacities. Although security aid is a relationship animated by humanitarian sentiments, the materialities of these relations are structured by growing inequalities. Given that aid regimes themselves are gifts between unequals, the extent to which Canada has invested in developing the security regimes of the Global South reflects a desire to step away from underlying question of global (in)justice. Not only is Canada avoiding these questions at the peril of those living in closest proximity to the thresholds of bare life, but it is doing so in a manner that is increasingly provincial and self-serving. Developing the regimes of security governance in the Global South may benefit in the immediate management of crime or unease but, given trajectories towards more extreme practices of global exclusion and fragmentation, security aid risks amplifying inequality and insecurities as opposed to alleviating them.

Chapter One

Canada and the Transversal Security Community

Introduction: Characterizing Canadian Internationalism

A major theme for understanding the "globalizing" practices of security comes from a foregrounding of their *transversal* dimensions. Scholarship exploring the transversality of contemporary security underline that traditional distinctions between "internal" and "external" threats have blurred, as have the institutional formations that relied on these firm boundaries of inside/outside (Bigo 2008; Bowling and Sheptycki 2011; Burgess 2009; CASE Collective 2006; Coleman 2007; Ericson 2007; Eriksson and Rhinard 2009; Huysmans 2014; Muller 2010; Pickering 2010; Pickering and Weber 2013; see also Bigo and Walker 2007; Walker 1993). The co-penetration of the internal and the external has meant that external threats are now always internal threats and, for prosperous countries of the Global North, has resulted in transformations to the governing practices associated with security. Transformations provoked by the transversality of security governance have meant that militaries are integrated into domestic surveillance and crime control; domestic agencies (including but not limited to police) are increasingly involved in global partnerships and international "stabilization" efforts as a response to political and environmental crises; external intelligence agencies are increasingly involved in surveillance of domestic groups and individuals; and foreign military interventions are reframed as "policing" operations. It is the globalization of internal and external security threats along with the blurring of internal/external security agencies that characterizes transversal security governance. In this globalizing process, prosperous countries set the governance agenda on (in)security issues, prioritizing a need to reform the deviant states of the Global South who are perceived as sources of transversal threats. This chapter details how security aid characterizes a particular role of Canadian internationalism within these dramatic transformations to global governance.

A number of scholars have tried to explain the limited role of Canadian internationalism, which includes a field of foreign policy scholarship that has long lamented the nation's limited and marginal international role. Although the contemporary rise of non-traditional actors in the international field has further isolated and marginalized Canadian influence, I suggest that security aid is an important outlet to understand both the character of Canadian internationalism and how Canada has positioned itself in managing the transversality of contemporary security governance. To explain Canada's participation in these transforming domains of security and globalization, I argue that security aid illustrates how Canada is a *norm-supporter* of efforts to develop transversal security governance. Positioning this argument in literature that details norm-makers and norm-takers of global governance trends, my characterization of Canada as a "supporter" highlights that the Canadian state is subordinate to norm-makers – primarily, although not exclusively, the United States – and mobilizes "aid" programming in a manner that tends to curry favour and recognition by more powerful actors. Canadian participation in transversal security governance is not about "setting an agenda," but providing highly catered technical support for advancing the efforts of norm-makers to develop more integrated and coordinated capacities to manage (in)security. Through the use of foreign assistance practices, I develop the theme of Canada as a norm-supporter by showing the practice-committed field of security expertise in which Canadian actors support the norms of the transversal security governance through an impressive realm of technical security development programming.

In addition to detailing how security aid has been mobilized strategically to advance Canadian visibility and reliability as a supporter of efforts to develop transversal security governance, I follow the argument in security governance literature that suggests trends in transversal security governance are driven primarily by experts in the management of (in)security (see Bigo 2008). I contribute to scholarship that explores how practices of security are driven by an assemblage of experts, innovators, networks, and heterogeneous forces (Bigo 2011b; Kauppi and Madsen 2014; Muller 2010; Salter 2010; Scherrer 2009). Transversal governance regimes exist under a framework established by legislators and political executives, yet their practices far exceed the controls or intelligibility accorded to political authorities. Beyond the oversight of political authorities, an array of security "best practices" focused on integration, cooperation, and development represent what I call the transversal security community. As I detail below, the transversal security community is a cooperative and voluntary regime of transnational practices that have an overarching objective in coordinating the management of global (in)security. Though securitization might be influenced by the securitizing moves of politicians, I underline how the knowledge practices of "doing security" within this collaborative community of actors are produced and circulated by security experts within policing agencies, prison services, border authorities, intelligence networks, public security, and foreign affairs departments. To provide an account of Canadian participation in the transversal security community, I detail how – beginning in 2004 and accelerating over the course of the late 2000s – Canadian security development was systematically reorganized around funding hubs for security aid. These hubs have been created explicitly to maximize the "strategic" use of Canadian aid resources. As an expert node for marshalling security aid, the hubs are central in Canada's strategic norm-supporting within the transversal security community.

In focusing on the bureaucracies of security aid and the strategic orientation of what I define as security aid hubs, this chapter highlights the role of security development experts in furthering cooperation in transversal security governance. Using the notion of Canada as a norm-supporter, I contribute to the literature on security governance by highlighting how the practical orientation of Canadian security aid is positioned towards furthering norms of integration, cooperation, and development, through forms of expertise that I call security innovation. Norm-supporting is contingent on security innovation in that Canada's role in the transversal security community is defined through modest but strategic marshalling of expertise in the knowledge practices of security governance. These can include policing sciences, surveillance techniques, border controls, and prison management, all of which are mobilized to support the broader development regime of transversal security. Given that "doing security" has become a powerful normative logic of contemporary governance (Huysmans 2014), Canadian security aid contributes to transversal efforts to enhance the security governance of deviant states in the Global South, while enhancing the visibility and reputation of Canada as a norm-supporter.

Norm-Making and the Transversal Security Community

Ubiquitous referencing to the importance of sharing "best practice" regimes as the norms of global regulation indicates the fluidity, travel, and isomorphism of contemporary governance. Spanning all fields of global governance, norms of security and criminal justice are also prone to transnational travels (Melossi, Sozzo, and Sparks 2011; also Eski 2011). Literature on norm-making has emphasized how regimes of practices are transferred or distilled across organizations, particularly across policy fields between countries. Scholars have argued that these practices, often produced by expert knowledge of policymakers, are projections of the normative power of powerful states who influence interlocutors through cooperative, not coercive, relations (Krahmann 2013; Scherrer 2009; Scherrer and Dupont 2010). Manners (2002, 253) has defined normative power by saying it is representative of actors who can "shape what can be 'normal' in international life." Although norms are always being (re)defined and contested (Acharya 2011; Krahmann 2013), they nonetheless constitute "appropriate standards of behaviour" (Finnemore and Sikkink 1998, 89) that bind collective actions (and shared values) between countries. Debates on norm-making (and norm-taking) have been particularly fruitful for theorizing how security governance norms have transferred over the past decade-plus. Scholars have noted the normative (and norm-making) power of the United States in the "war on terror" (Argomaniz 2009; Kempin and Mawdsley 2013; Pawlak 2009). Other authors have explored the decline of U.S. influence as a norm-maker in the transatlantic and hemispheric security communities (Andreas and Nadelmann 2006), as well as Canada's movement away from the United States as its prominent ally (Kitchen and Sasikumar 2009; Nossal 2010; Shaw 2010; Welsh 2004). Some scholars have described how norms transfer from "the negotiations of value" between more- and less-influential countries within the European security community (Burgess 2009, 323; also Björkdahl 2005, 2007, 2013; Brommesson 2010; Horgby and Rhinard 2015; Rees 2008). Others have detailed the rising responsibility of the EU in promoting human rights norms as opposed to the exceptionalism of U.S. unilateralism (Andreas and Nadelmann 2006, 235–44; Manners 2006; Hettne and Söderbaum 2005). A central theme of the norm-making literature is an exploration of how norms can be negotiated and transferred through cooperative security communities. This reflects the notion that actors can practise influence through appeals to ideals of cooperation and principles of common governance, as well as fostering cooperative and collaborative engagements between security experts who manage security governance regimes.

Contemporary efforts to govern security threats have been transformed by these transversal practices, which have changed the relations between countries who cooperate on the grounds of "security." In the original formulation of the concept of "security community," Deutsch et al. (1957, 5–9) described "a shared community" of countries that would work towards "integration." Speaking specifically to North Atlantic countries during the Cold War, the central component of the shared community was a no-war principle in which the states forming the community could not imagine a war among each other, what Wæver (1998, 71) called the "identity-based no-war community." The concept of security community allowed for competition between member countries, yet conflicts are "dealt with as are normal political, economic, environmental, and societal problems – not as matters of security" (Buzan and Wæver 2003, 56; see also Adler and Barnett 1998). Koschut (2014, 342) has written that the "security community describes a 'zone of peace' by effectively transcending the security dilemma among its members through the attainment of mutual trust and a sense of community to resolve their disputes peacefully."

Theories of security communities have underlined how the notion of security contains a common reference, intersubjective meanings of threats are shared, and a collective approach is taken to confronting insecurities. In describing normative changes within security communities, Krahmann (2013, 55) has underlined that norms prescribe "how individuals or collectives ought to act because of ethical or moral concerns." Kitchen (2010a, 2010b) has argued that the transatlantic security community has fostered a common identity (Atlanticism) enabling members to act together in-the-world. Regarding the transatlantic community, it is not just "an alliance based on common interest, but also a values community which shares a common identity and behavioural norms" (Kitchen 2010a, 106; 2010b; see also Moore 2007). For the transatlantic security community, this value-identity formation has twinned with shared liberal values, and many post–Cold War security missions – particularly the "out of area" NATO missions – have been tied up with projections of human rights, the responsibility to protect, and promoting democracy (Kitchen 2010a; also Huysmans 2002; Rotmann, Kurtz, and Brockmeier 2014).

Breaking with the dominant characterization of security communities having a shared security identity (e.g., Adler and Barnett 1998), Pouliot

(2007, 606; 2010) examined the nascent Russian-Atlantic security community to demonstrate that security communities need not require a shared sense of values (or a genuine sense of we-ness). For Pouliot (2010), the practices of cooperation are what bind security communities, not necessarily a shared communion of values. This point is particularly relevant to the transversal security community, especially in regards to political liberalism, for the principal norms shared in the transversal security community are centred on practical concerns in the governance of (in)security, and valorize the importance of security within a spectrum of norms. Though other norms – like human rights – may appear, best-practice regimes of security governance are often presented in apolitical terms that focus on technical aspects of security governance. However, following Krahmann (2013), who warns that norms are always normative, the best practices of the transversal security community (even if represented as apolitical) rely on a normative prioritization of security that takes place against a prioritization of other principles, notably – as Huysmans (2014) argues – democratic norms. It is therefore through a shared communitarian value to normative imperatives of *integration* and *cooperation* that determines membership in the transversal security community. This membership, of course, is conditional on partaking in these cooperative practices of transversal security governance that are set by norm-makers.

Therefore membership of the transversal security community is contingent on cooperation engagement in efforts to govern (in)security, primarily through integrated approaches to manage crime, terrorism, instability, and unease. So long as countries comply with the security governance requirements of the norm-makers, these countries share in the main value-criteria for membership in the transversal. In using the term *like-minded nation*, Canadian security experts denote that these countries were "buying in" to the programs (and would therefore be more "successful"), as well as being aligned with broader geopolitical strategies. Only through the rationale of transversal cooperation can the persistent use of "like-minded nations" by Canadian security experts be explained. When applied to Saudi Arabia, Jordan, Bahrain, or Colombia, the term *like-minded nation* does not imply the shared liberal values of the NATO transatlantic community, yet it does articulate the prioritization of integration and cooperation norms shared within the transversal security community.

Unlike the NATO security community, the transversal is more fluid and conditional. I underline that countries can be members of multiple security communities at multiple stages of security community development (Adler and Greve 2009). For example, Canada participates in the mature NATO transatlantic security community and Five Eyes security intelligence community, as well as the hemispheric security community. Canada also cultivates a mature and unique bilateral security community with the United States (Charbonneau and Cox 2008; Hobbing 2010). Moreover, Canada is an active participant in the transversal security community, which influences aspects of other transnational security communities. While the NATO security community has been defined on the basis of its ability to transfer norms and shared political values (Kitchen 2010a), the transfer of political values within the transversal security community is peripheral to the primary norms of integration, cooperation, and interoperability.

As a conjoined dynamic of the broader "war on terrorism," the transversal security community is intimately paired with the norm-making powers of the Global North. However, it is not exclusive to the Global North. Russia and China are both participants in the transversal security community, though their status as normative influence is debatable.[1] As demonstrated in moments of cooperation between the United States and Iran in the military campaign against ISIL, even countries who have been deemed security-antagonists can participate in practical aspects of the transversal security community. Some countries may participate more fully than others, and generally the level of commitment can be associated with changing strategic interests. My purpose is not to chart the participation of member countries or the strategic interests that animate these engagements, but to stress that the norm-making powers of the transversal security community have focused on improving the coordination and interoperability of global security governance regimes in ways that allow the pragmatisms of immediate cooperation to trump taken-for-granted political norms.

Norm-Supporter and Security Innovator: Canada and the Transversal

Scholars have contested the polarity of norm-makers and norm-takers within literature on policy transfers. Detailing the normative influence

1 Contessi (2010) has demonstrated how China engages in what he calls "norm-brokering," a balancing of their strategic interests with an increasing coordination of security activities with the West.

of Sweden, Björkdahl (2013) argues that small states can engage in "norm entrepreneurship" to "punch above their weight," despite having less institutional power within transnational security communities. Acharya (2011) has contested the polemic by suggesting that policy transfers within transnational security networks are dynamic processes where the normative agenda of powerful states is often contested, particularly by the Global South. Attending to the lack of theorization and attention to sub-powerful countries in the norm-making literature, Acharya (ibid., 96) uses the term *norm subsidiary* to describe the "process whereby local actors develop new rules, offer new understandings of global rules or reaffirm global rules in the regional context." Giving a more nuanced and localized interpretation of norm diffusion in the Global South, Acharya's framework of norm subsidiaries also offers insights into the agency of middle-power countries who play a "subsidiary" role in the creation, mobilization, and recirculation of transversal security norms.

A significant distinction from the recent works of Björkdahl or Acharya is highlighted by Canadian participation within the transversal security community. Rarely is Canada a norm entrepreneur that, as a minority voice, acts to persuade others of the inherent value of a particular proposition.[2] Canada may well engage in security entrepreneurship, yet its creativity is not on a political-values terrain of advocacy and persuasion, but rather on the value-neutral terrain of technical practices. Similarly – and unlike countries of the Global South – Canada does not present significant contestation or notable reinterpretation of best practices established by norm-makers. Often a beneficiary of the entrepreneurialism of norm-makers, Canada accepts trends of harmonization as an aspect of international good governance and, in playing a supportive role, helps *to practise the norm*. As Kavalski (2013, 249) has noted, "Normative powers are in the business not of enforcing orders over other actors, but of engaging other actors in shared practices." As opposed to entrepreneurship based on prescriptive values (Finnemore and

2 Finnemore and Sikkink (1998) have developed the notion of norm entrepreneurs within international organizations. Some scholars have made strong arguments regarding Canadian practices of norm entrepreneurship within the human security agenda and the development of the Protect (R2P) doctrine (see Maclean, Beck, and Shaw 2006). Curle (2007) has made a claim of Canadian norm-making in the establishment of the UN Declaration. Price (2004) has made a similar argument about the Ottawa Convention on landmines.

Sikkink 1998), Canadian practices are focused on the technical terrain of developing regulatory norms. While all normative practices "embody a quality of 'oughtness' and shared moral assessment" (ibid., 891), the Canadian focus on regulatory norms makes the value-embeddedness of security aid an implicit form of value-transformation, as opposed to more explicit tact of norm entrepreneurship.

In developing the notion of norm-supporter, I argue that Canadian security aid is characterized primarily by the tangible, practical, and concrete practices to support the transversal security community. Such security development aims to integrate and coordinate recipient countries of the Global South into transversal practices of security governance. In providing practical and tangible security assistance, Canadian security aid can be presented sometimes as a value-neutral undertaking to develop security practices. Though sometimes appearing neutral, the implicit value proposition of Canadian security aid is that these norms are, in fact, normatively good. Critiques of the "liberal peace" have pointed out that representations of the "value neutrality" of rule-of-law regimes betray normative biases that privilege modes of governance based exclusively upon ideals of the Global North (Chandler 2010; Oliveira 2013; Park 2010; Sabaratnam 2013). As an active participant within the transversal security community, Canada has prioritized a practical orientation towards sharing, diffusing, and harmonizing security norms, and – although some security experts stress their apolitical and technical objectives – their practices support an agenda of security development set by norm-makers. Canadian participation in the norm cycle is less about advocating new norms and more about transmitting (cascading) new normative practices as "normal." Canadian security aid is focused instead on technical contributions to advance, perfect, and transfer the techniques and technologies that assist in the transversal management of (in)security. Adler (2005) has noted that security communities are best conceptualized as "communities of practice" and, as a norm-supporter, Canada assists in developing the rule of the norm through technical security development.

The practicalities of norm-supporting are marshalled by transmitting Canadian expertise in managing (in)security. I refer to this marshalling of expertise as *security innovation*. Through the specific domains of expertise in policing, prisons, borders, and risk management, Canadian experts contribute to the transversal security community through the practical transfer of innovative techniques and technologies of security governance. Scholarship on the role of experts in security governance has called attention to the need to study the levels, competing interests, and divergent priorities that comprise security communities. As Oelsner (2009, 196) notes, security governance literature forces "attention to the different levels in which security and security policy unfold, and to the multiplicity of actors and institutions that are involved in the process of defining" security policies (see also Bigo 2008; Bonelli 2008; Salter 2010; Scherrer 2009). A challenge for countries engaging within these transversal processes of governing security rests on their abilities to marshal their expertise to increase their visibility and influence. Engaging in security aid provides a norm-supportive function of cementing norms of security governance while simultaneously advancing what are termed Canadian "strategic interests" within the transversal security community.

A key component of Canadian security aid is increasing the visibility of Canadian security expertise within the highly competitive field of security governance. With the objective of improving the reputation and position of Canadian security expertise within the transversal community, security aid has been specialized through the development of program funding hubs. These funding hubs are pivotal in directing the "strategic" application of Canadian security aid. Functioning as a bridge between the security innovators in bureaucracies (such as corrections, policing, security, and borders) and the recipient countries where security development takes place, the funding hubs act as planners to align the security assistance projects with the broader trends of security governance established by norm-makers. As security governance is a crowded area of global governance, security aid hubs provide strategic vision that aims at matching Canadian security innovation with practical areas of norm-supporting. By identifying areas to deploy the technical and logistical creativity of Canadian security innovation, the hubs utilize "aid" funding to provide concrete support for transversal security development.

In the section that follows, I detail how security aid allows for strategic advantages. They include efforts to expand security governance capacities to the Global South, promote commercial interests, increase visibility of Canadian norm-supporting, and contribute positively to relationships with norm-makers, particularly the United States. Centrally, I detail how security aid is highly demonstrative of Canada as a norm-supporter. Aid regimes are not an exclusive means of norm-supporting, yet I argue the bureaucratic organization of security aid has been positioned to make practical, tangible contributions to the development of transversal security governance.

Strategic Interests and the Whole-of-Government Approach

Canada's Department of Foreign Affairs, now called Global Affairs Canada (GAC) is one of the large departments of the Canadian bureaucracy. In June 2013, Canada's international development agency – the Canadian International Development Agency (CIDA) – was formally rolled into the Foreign Affairs department.[3] Although proposals to combine CIDA and Foreign Affairs had been an issue of long-standing debate, the merger has coincided with a more vocal effort by Canadian politicians to combine development programming with its broader political and economic interests. While the hyperbole from the Harper government (and critics) emphasized the merger as a new form of "economic diplomacy" – developed in the Global Markets Action Plan (Canada 2013) – Canadian foreign affairs and development bureaucracies have a long-standing tradition of using development strategies to further commercial interests (Brown 2013; Morrison 1998; Spicer 1966). Moreover, economic development regimes and humanitarian assistance programs from Northern countries have – from their conception – been tied to self-interests, not altruism (Cowen and Shenton 1996). What is germane to my examination of security aid regimes is how the reorganization of the Canadian foreign affairs bureaucracy predates the Harper government and, particularly with the creation of security aid hubs in the mid-2000s, has been undertaken to promote Canadian security innovation as way to support the development of transversal security governance.

The most prominent funding mechanisms of security aid are three hubs administered by the GAC known as the Global Peace and Security Fund (START-GPSF), the Anti-Crime Capacity Building Program (ACCBP), and the Counter-Terrorism Capacity Building (CTCB) program. With the creation of the CTCB in 2004, the START-GPSF in 2005, and the ACCBP in 2009, all three hubs have been designed as foreign policy tools within the "war on terror." With each hub having prioritized themes and geographies of focus, as I detail next chapter, the reorganization of security aid to be managed through these hubs is a central element for understanding the character of Canada's "aid" contribution to the transversal security community.

3 I refer to CIDA only when addressing programs that ran under CIDA before the merger of DFATD and CIDA in July 2013.

Though elements of the Canadian bureaucracy have historically engaged in practices of security aid, much of this programming has been funded by internal budgets based on departmental priorities. Yet within the context of the Canada's war efforts in Afghanistan, the post-9/11 security aid regimes have been organized around the GAC as the manager of most security development programming. The creation of centralized security aid hubs resulted in a transformation within Canadian foreign assistance bureaucracies, where international work has become more reliant on GAC as the principal funder and manager of development programming. One participant described these dynamics as a broader strategic undertaking: "As years went by, and certainly as our ability to act, perhaps, as independently as had in the past – kinda changed a little bit – we became more aligned with what are the government priorities, started to get involved with DFATD, CIDA (before CIDA became part of DFATD) we started to engage more with them, it became more 'here's where the government is going, here are the countries where the government is interested in working with or assisting.' So it became a bit more *strategic* in terms of the countries we would become involved in" (Interview 14; emphasis added).

Budget cutbacks during the Harper government accelerated dependence on GAC-funded security aid hubs. One participant referred to the changes under the Harper government as a "transition period" (Interview 7). The participant also noted that the department was pursuing other third-party funding to enhance foreign capacity-building projects (listing the OAS, World Bank, IMF, UN). In describing the reduction of international work funded internally by the RCMP, one participant noted a combination of government-wide restructuring that corresponded with personnel changes in upper management (Interview 12). Yet the most illustrative element of this transformation to security aid programming was what became known as the new whole-of-government approach. Itself now an unavoidable buzzword in the Canadian development lexicon, the whole-of-government approach was first articulated in the 2005 International Policy Statement (IPS), written in the context of the war in Afghanistan. The objective of the IPS was to synergize the activities of DND, Foreign Affairs, and the development work of CIDA (Desrosiers and Lagassé 2009). As a Canadian version of the American "hearts and minds" framework, its intention was to eliminate programming duplication, advance a unified strategic vision, and assist the war effort with a counter-insurgency strategy that included development (Chin 2009; see also Patrick and Brown 2007,

56–78). Intertwined with DND's 3D (defence, diplomacy, development) counter-insurgency policy in Afghanistan, the whole-of-government approach has been critiqued for its explicit linking of development work to the war campaign (Charbonneau and Parent 2010; Fenton and Elmer 2013; Joya 2013; Stein and Lang 2007).[4] One participant referred to the 3D approach as an effort to "win the hearts and minds of Canadian soldiers," which had little to do with the Afghan population (Interview 16). Giving tremendous weight to the criticisms of Canada's Afghan strategy, the projects pursued by the whole-of-government approach have all failed.[5] Even its most signature development project, the Dahla Dam, has been abandoned by the Canadian government and now faces a slow withering away (Pugliese 2014). What is germane to the study of security aid, however, is not the failure of the whole-of-government approach in Afghanistan. Rather, it is what the whole-of-government approach represents in collapsing internal/external security binaries and the transformation to security aid bureaucracies to manage an assemblage of military, development aid, policing, borders, prisons, public security bureaucracies, etc., into practices of security aid.

Although critics of the whole-of-government approach have correctly pointed out its logistical and ethical shortcomings, the reorganization of aid (and security) bureaucracies has been under-explored. Some have celebrated the whole-of-government approach (Baranyi 2014), overlooking practical concerns that are raised by practitioners (Monaghan 2015c, 269–331). Notwithstanding disagreements on the efficacy of these changes, the bureaucratic transformations themselves have been profound. The most significant component of this has been

---

4 Stein and Lang (2007) provide an insider account of the organizational dysfunction incurred by the 3D doctrine. They quote an unidentified senior military official saying, "Three D was never anything more than Chris Alexander [Canada's first ambassador in Kabul] and General Andrew Leslie tearing around in a jeep" (279). While Stein and Lang remain supporters of the 3D approach – as well as the Afghan mission in general – their account details the strong animosities between CIDA, DFAIT, and DND.

5 One participant who worked on the Afghan file for several years noted, "They have left everything. If you go there, you would see. Everything is incomplete. Nothing is complete ... the whole work is a total loss" (Interview 15). Speaking of the poor process of assessments and prioritization, the participant added, "Seriously speaking, Jeff, if we analyzed properly, if we admitted, when we found out there were problems, and we worked to reform them, to modify them, we could have been successful. That's what bothers me most" (ibid.).

the centrality of GAC in managing foreign assistance projects, including, but not limited to, security aid. While my project does not directly address traditional ODA funding, the folding of CIDA into GAC in 2013 only accelerated the program of making GAC key to the whole-of-government approach. Throughout a wide range of programs, the whole-of-government approach has become a buzzword and, most often, revolves around GAC coordination of activities between agencies and governmental departments in security assistance projects.

An example of the whole-of-government approach is Canadian efforts to control migration in Southeast Asia, which include the Portable Intelligence Units (discussed in detail in chapter 5). Documents related to these security aid projects underline how the whole-of-government approach is an "integrated approach [that] draws on the full scope of Canadian law enforcement, migration and border management, defence, and foreign affairs expertise to work together both domestically and abroad" (GAC 2012-3267, 3). As a reorganization of the Canadian bureaucracy that is itself an articulation of the transversal, the whole-of-government approach began to harmonize only in the Afghan military mission. However, instead of understanding these transformations as the militarization of aid (Christie 2012; Pugh 2001), the whole-of-government approach – particularly post-Afghan war – has meant greater blurring between military and criminal matters, in many ways bringing the military into the governance of transversal crime. In particular, DND has maintained a large role for their technical security innovation, yet the reorganization of aid under the whole-of-government approach has centred GAC as the strategic director of Canadian foreign interests. As one participant described this transformation,

> We were never funded to do international work. It's not in our mandate. So there was no envelop of money put aside, you know. We would oftentimes be looking to work with CIDA to get some money. But then it changed, where DFAIT became a bit of a bigger player – or perhaps we became a player with DFAIT (is perhaps more of the case, than they became a bigger player [*laughs*]). We started working with them. They were the ones who came to the table with all of the money, and *we kinda became employees – contractors* if you will [*laughs*] – for DFAIT [GAC]. And that changed things … and that was really kind of with Afghanistan. That was the first time we got significant funds. I mean that was huge, huge, huge project. (Interview 14; emphasis added)

Under the umbrella of GAC, other departments – borders, defence, policing, prisons, transport, and public safety – have all become integrated as "contractors" into a framework for using security development as an avenue for strategic foreign assistance policies. It is within this organizational transformation that the "strategic" element of Canadian security aid regime assumes its principal characteristic of norm-supporting. It is through marshalling security expertise and foreign assistance resources controlled by the funding hubs that Canadian security aid can be mobilized more strategically to develop the practices of transversal security governance. In providing practical programming to increase cooperation, integration, and efficiencies of security governance in deviant states of the Global South, the whole-of-government framework has centralized security aid through the infrastructures of GAC as a mechanism for more strategic forms of norm-supporting in the transversal security community.

Strategic Norm-Supporting: Being a "Player on the Security Stage"

Canada is not alone in using security aid funds. Security assistance projects have provided a format for many countries of the Global North to allocate development funding under the banner of fighting terrorism or contributing to global security, particularly under the framework of security sector reform (Albrecht and Stepputat 2015; Bouris and Reigeluth 2012; Denney 2015; Jackson 2011). Contemporary emphasis on security sector reform from the international community, particularly norm-maker countries, has been a major focus of critique. Particularly within the literature on the "securitization of aid" (Howell and Lind 2009a, 2009b; Hyndman 2009; Shannon 2009; Wilkinson 2015), scholars have called attention to how security has solicited a larger focus from donor nations, hence holding a higher priority within North-South aid-funding mechanisms. Although I emphasize that security aid is a distinct form of assistance, critiques of the securitization of aid demonstrate how norm-makers have foregrounded the need to develop norms of security governance in the Global South, often at the expense of other needs. With the foregrounding of security and the all-encompassing scope of governance quagmires as components of security sector reform, Canadian security aid hubs have sought to fill a particular gap by focusing on specific security development programming in deviant states.

Many participants in my study referred to funding for security development as "sexy," because it has an international appeal and resonates with domestic Canadian interests. One participant stressed that the security aid regime in Canada accelerated in the mid-2000s because Canada had to "pony up" and "be a player on the security stage." The same participant noted that there were perceptions that the Canada "hadn't done enough on the security stage" (Interview 10). Another participant added that the new security aid programs offered "Canada an opportunity to play." Moreover, these funding arrangements provide an ability to "punch above our weight" and to "put money where our mouth is" (Interview 5). Although participants underlined that security aid funding provided an important gesture to other countries (particularly the United States), one participant added that the funding was "more about politics than substance" (Interview 10). Participants noted that, in creating security aid hubs, Canadian authorities could be counted upon by the international community (and particularly norm-makers) to provide a rapid response to international calls for assistance through direct program funding. Program funding is not simply a lump donation of "aid," but the creation of projects that focus on targeted areas of transversal security governance. These programs can cater to particular requests from recipient countries, filling gaps identified by Canadian security innovators or by norm-makers of the transversal security community. They can be immediate "crisis" environments like those in Haiti, Afghanistan, Libya, Mali, or – more recently – Ukraine, Iraq, Syria, as well as priority areas like Colombia, Mexico, Palestine, and other "hot spots" established by the transversal security community. As flexible hubs that would create programs catering to specific areas or issues, the START-GPSF, AACBP, and CTCB were originally created with preapproved funding authorities meant to eliminate the requirement for political (ministerial) approval and allow Canadian security innovators to engage in projects more efficiently and consistently.

Having a capacity to provide catered and timely security development programming is particularly valuable, since being seen as a "player on the security stage" is difficult in such a crowded theatre. Like other aid regimes, a key component for Canadian authorities is retaining influence. For a small player like Canada, funding security initiatives through non-directed funding with major entities like the UN Department of Peacekeeping Operations (PKO) means very little in bolstering Canadian influence or visibility on the international security stage. Nor does it particularly help to develop relationships with recipient nations, or advance Canadian interests. Instead, the use of funding hubs that direct security aid programming can allow Canada to influence the contents and outcomes of the assistance packages and build relationships in the process. One participant described the advantage of having domestic security programming by underlining the highly competitive field of international security assistance when administered through the UN:

> Whenever the Americans are in the same sandbox, good luck. The UN loses every time. Because what the Americans do, they focus on the hard materials. They have a lot of money. They produce quick results in terms of the mortar. As well as the weapons, all the cool, Gucci gear … It's often competitive among the member states. Sometimes I feel like we're often trying to sell ourselves, it's not a real relationship of "let's work together, we're here with some expertise and some money, and let's implement your vision – one that's expectable by the UN." [Instead], we're trying to sell ourselves just to stay involved so that we continue to get the funding to stay engaged. That's at a little more strategic level. (Interview 9)

Although some participants have noted that Canadian involvement through the UN is highly valued and "well regarded" (Interview 13), the comments above reflect officials' limited ability to marshal Canada's smaller institutional status within crowded international bodies. For these reasons, security aid is a mechanism to build bilateral relations with recipient states of the Global South and support specific security development initiatives developed by norm-makers. As demonstrated in major projects examined in later chapters (such as Haiti, Southeast Asia, Libya, as well as Palestine; see Monaghan 2016), security aid hubs have aimed to support norm-makers by focusing on practical and concrete security development. While many other countries are involved in security aid regimes, a number of participants in my research noted that the Canadian approach to security aid programming is distinct. Canada does not simply throw around "Gucci gear" like the Americans or, as another participant put it, "just dump money in projects like the EU and Spain [do] … that is not how we play" (Interview 1). Discussing the competitive field in supplying security aid programming, one participant noted "there is a lot of demand out there" (Interview 8) for security aid, and a number of participants used the term *shopping lists* to describe how recipient countries came to meetings with specific demands for security goods and services (Interviews 1, 4, 10, and 13). For Canadian officials who direct these funds, a key component to distinguish the Canadian approach to security aid from that of other countries is a strategic approach towards quality of programming.

Participants stressed the high reputation for Canadian assistance, and, as one participant put it, Canadian aid is "*more* strategic" than other countries', and we "take programming seriously" (Interview 1; emphasis added). Another participant noted that both the United States and the United Kingdom have adopted the security aid programming model of START-GPSF (Interview 3), while another senior director added that the specialization and attention provided by these security development hubs ensures more oversight than provided by other donor counties (Interview 1). The participant added, "Our accountability requirements make the Canadian approach different and better" (Interview 1). Moreover, having specific programming arms for security aid provides a "priority setting that helps focus" foreign assistance (Interview 10). Most interview participants stressed that programming funding is a distinguishing characteristic of Canadian security aid, as it gives substantial flexibility in advancing Canadian security innovation, increasing Canadian visibility and influence in security development. Given the crowded theatre of security aid, a heavy emphasis within the Canadian security assistance bureaucracy is placed on programming being *strategic*.

Meanings of *strategic* and *foreign interests* are often esoteric. As a flexible and highly popularized speech device, officials deploy *support strategic interests* as a type of catch-all category. Like other "buzzwords and fuzzwords" of governance, these terms "gain their purchase and power through their vague and euphemistic qualities, their capacity to embrace a multitude of possible meanings, and their normative resonance" (Cornwall 2007, 472; see also Cornwall and Brock 2005). The allure and popularity of buzzwords, argues Cornwall (2007, 474), is entirely in their ability to "fuzz" rationales and therefore articulate a broader purpose. Cornwall adds that "buzzwords aid this process, by providing concepts that can float free of concrete referents, to be filled with meaning by their users" (ibid.). High-profile fields like development and security governance constantly produce new buzzwords and fuzzwords, and the use of *strategic* as a buzzword has a particular salience for security experts themselves. While many government buzzwords are typically a communication device to external audiences – the general public, civil society organizations, other countries, or interlocutors – the buzzword *strategic* also functions as a self-referential device within security aid hubs that rationalizes the tying of aid to broader agendas.

Though sometimes romanticized as having more humanitarian sentiments than strategic interests, Canadian foreign policy has long combined "assistance" regimes with the advancement of foreign policy objectives. Brown (2007) has noted that in the decades following Canada's first "foreign assistance" programs – the first being the support of the 1950s Colombo Plan to combat communism in Asia (and promote Canadian business interests; see Morrison [1998] cited in Brown [2007]) – "international realism" has largely displaced "humane internationalism" and "Canadian security has become even more important in the foreign aid discourse" (Brown 2007, 215). Given the long-standing self-interests served by the Canadian aid regime, security aid programming is a recent technology for tying assistance funding to broader agendas of governance. When aid funding is criticized for only reflecting a state's "self-interests," it is often referred to as the economic interests of domestic corporations. But the meaning of strategic interests used by security experts is not related to economic interests. Certainly the Harper government's Global Markets Action Plan has received substantial scrutiny, yet it relates only (explicitly) to economic development projects that are funded through ODA. There is no explicit policy for tying security aid, which is not ODA-funded aid. In fact, I would suggest the profitable supply of security and surveillance materials through security aid funding (which I discuss further in chapter 4) is more appropriately described as an evolving, organic partnership between industry and Canadian security officials. When Canada looks to bolster the ballistics capacities of Central American countries, they are doing so as part of a broader initiative of the transversal security community to integrate information sharing and police collaborations, as well as export Canadian security technologies to Caribbean countries.[6] In doing so, security aid hubs do not need an explicit policy that sources Canadian technologies, since Canadian technologies are already deeply embedded into the operations of Canadian security bureaucracies. Though explicit tied-aid is not a component of security aid regimes, a senior programming official from one prominent security aid hub warned that while the

6 Between 2009 and 2011, ACCBP put $791,556 towards the Regional Integrated Ballistic Information Network (RIBIN) ballistics identification network in Barbados, Trinidad and Tobago, and Jamaica, developed by Canada-based Forensic Technologies Ltd. Another contract with Forensic Technologies Ltd. ($2,084,044) funded the Central American Ballistic Information Network (CABIN) for Belize and Costa Rica.

U.S. system is much more tethered to specific economic interests, "we are going that direction" (Interview 3). Though economic interests may be among the mix of interests that comprise the "strategic" direction of security aid, the rationalities underlined by security experts highlight the need to stand out. The strategic objectives that have been honed by GAC are grounded in advocacy for developing transversal security governance, while improving the standing and influence of Canadian expertise through reliable norm-supporting.

Though politicians may set an agenda for the "war on terror," the practices of developing security governance take place through programs, networks, agencies. These practices transpire in complex and competitive environments, far removed from the management of political representatives. In describing the strategic objectives of security aid, Canadian security experts underline the importance of being seen to support the transversal agenda of norm-makers. This strategic function of security aid allows Canada to be seen as "a player on the security stage" by providing practical development assistance to recipient countries in the Global South. By promoting concrete assistance programs that privilege transversal norms of integration, Canadian security innovation contributes modest but tangible support in the development of security governance. This articulation of what it means to be strategic is a major component of the reorganization of security aid bureaucracies under the whole-of-government approach and illustrates how security aid fits into Canada's "place" in the transversal security community.

The Development Regime of Transversal Security Governance

Scholarship on the dynamics of security has dramatically transformed over the past two decades, particularly given that theorization of "security" outside a very narrow field of "national security" is relatively new (Kinsman, Buse, and Steedman 2000). This transformation has had profound implications for how states "do" security, as well as how scholars research and theorize security practices. In contrast to the bipolarity of the Cold War, security governance literature has emphasized the emergence of "new threats" encompassing a far broader spectrum of security risks – including but not limited to failed states, famines, organized crime, cyber threats, "illegal" migrations, and, of course, terrorism. As a constellation of potential threats, the proliferation of security risks is associated principally with the Global South and concerns about these populations "importing their political disputes into the First World"

(Bigo, 2006, 387; see also Duffield 2001, 2007). Although threats from the Global South are not novel in themselves, the territoriality of "new threats" has erased the division between "external" threats in the colonies and "internal" threats within the wealthy countries of the Global North. Instead, the "new wars" are security operations that tend to "be mutual enterprises rather than contests of the wills" (Kaldor 2013, 13). Instead of enmities of warfare, security operations are coordinated, multinational efforts to ensure global stability with increasingly porous sovereignties.[7] A central focus of security governance studies has been an exploration of how these efforts in transversal management of (in) security are linked through nodes of experts and expertise that circulate and reproduce new practices of security across jurisdictional settings.

Although concerns about the governance of transversal threats can be identified in colonialism, Cold War counter-insurgency doctrines, and the wars on crime/drugs/terror, globalization has brought about an acceleration and intensification of these antecedents.[8] Central to the intensification of transversal security governance are the twinning of security aid as a humanitarian undertaking with the embedding of recipient states into security practices of the transversal governance. Underlining the humanitarian rationalities that animate the reformatory engagements in the Global South, I highlight how the transversal security community is characterized by its intense valorization of transnational cooperation and "global interoperability" (Lyon 2009; see also Andreas and Nadelmann 2006; Bowling 2010; Brunet-Jailly 2007; Deflem 2002; Sheptycki 1995). Mapping the contemporary terrains of transnational policing, Goldsmith and Sheptycki (2007, 11) have noted how exchanges and deeply embedded connectivities point "to processes of contact, communication, contagion, conversion, and convergence" across a global spectrum of security governance practices. I build on these observations regarding the cooperative and coordinated practices of security governance by demonstrating how aid regimes are

---

7 In announcing Canada's extension of the bombing campaign against ISIL, the Harper government revealed they did not even request the nominal consent of the Syrian government. Moreover, it became clear that questions about the formal legality of pursuing a bombing campaign within Syria had not even occurred to military planners or the executive (see Wherry 2015).

8 Several scholars have traced these historical antecedents/continuities; see, for example, Andreas and Nadelmann 2006; Duffield and Hewitt 2013; Kaplan 1995; Zureik 2010.

mobilized to advance the norms of "collaboration," "partnerships," and "global cooperation" with recipient countries of the Global South on transversal security.

It is precisely through a commitment to nurture, assist, collaborate, enhance, and develop that the norm-makers of the transversal security community have become moral entrepreneurs in the development of security governance. Though the norms themselves have, as Chandler (2016) has argued, assumed more post-liberal formations that no longer idealize democratic transformations, they are nonetheless normative – and reformatory.[9] The reformatory functions of Canadian security aid are not at an exclusively society level but remain tailored to developing the capacities of security apparatuses of recipient countries, to make these capacities more reliable in global governance directed by prosperous countries. It is the desire to reform the policing, prison, border, and military functions of these deviant states and integrate them into systems of security governance that are directed by the more powerful norm-makers of transversal security threats.

A final yet central component of my analysis of Canadian security aid demonstrates how the development of security governance is a regime fraught with failure. Despite the significant investment and investment by security innovators, my case studies of Haiti, Libya, and Southeast Asia all demonstrate elements – and varying degrees – of failed development strategies. These findings are not unique, given that, in parallel with the failures of economic development in general, a large body of scholarship has critiqued the effectiveness and lack of "successes" in security development (Abrahamsen 2005; Bouris and Reigeluth 2012; Bowling 2010; Davis 2006; Hills 2009, 2010, 2012, 2013; Jackson 2011; Jefferson 2007; Macaulay 2007; Maguire and King 2013; Marriage 2010; Rosga 2010; Samara 2010; Sayigh 2009; L. Zanotti 2008, 2010; and critiques of security sector reform in general: Albrecht and Stepputat 2015; Egnell and Haldén 2009; Eriksen 2011). The foregrounding of challenges,

9 I avoid framing this emphasis on security governance as a form of bio-politics because, in many respects, the assistance projects that I empirically detail lack the objectives of producing self-governing logics in the subjects of deviant states. I do detail aspects of bio-political management that contributes to literature on bio-politics and development (see Duffield 2007), and I frame my analysis of security aid by describing how rationalities of global humanitarianism are twinned with reformatory strategies to integrate security apparatuses in the Global South into control regimes directed by transversal norm-makers.

barriers, and failures of security aid is not to suggest that security aid does not work, but to demonstrate that failure is in fact an integral element in the acceleration of security aid work. In discussing similarities between neoliberal economics and the expansion of surveillance as a global model of control, Murakami Wood (2013) suggests both social entities are predicated on views that are simultaneously totalizing *and unrealizable*. They hold utopian ideals, yet unassailable practical limitations. He writes that, as policies, these efforts "are always incomplete and the failure of any particular policy is not seen as a reason for its abandonment rather as the conditions for a new wave of regulatory innovation" (321). In other words, efforts to develop security practices – like neoliberal globalization – absorb their own failures as rationalizations for further intervention and reformatory engagement. In this sense, my work follows a number of scholars who have highlighted that the "new" place of security within development have resulted from the inequalities and injustices accelerated by neoliberalism, which recirculate to produce calls for *more* security (Duffield 2007; Taylor 2009).

As the cycle of security development accelerates, the barriers and challenges will likely result in a continued drive towards more intense security development. Not despite failures but because of them, continued investment in efforts to reform deviant states will mean continued opportunities for Canadian norm-supporting. As beneficiaries of reproductions of (in)security, Canadian security innovators will – regardless of political parties in power – continue to hone the strategic characteristics of Canadian security assistance in providing tangible and practical support to the transversal security community. Canadian expertise in security development will never be "setting an agenda" as a norm-maker, but will be further refined to provide highly catered technical support to integrate and cooperate in practices of security governance.

Of course my research is focused on one actor within the transversal security community, and a very small one at that. Our world is beset with heterogeneous actors making significant investments to enhance systems of control, surveillance, and security governance. I aim to highlight one important trend within these trajectories of security, focusing on how aid regimes develop transversal security cooperation by integrating recipient agencies in the Global South into broader efforts of governance. Within a dynamic global regime of security cooperation and development, Canada remains a very small player – despite its strategic orientations – and my analysis provides an understanding of the norm-supporting character of Canadian security aid, as well as a sketch of the transversal character of global security aid regimes. Certainly, the United States, the United Kingdom, France, and the European Union have much more advanced programs of security assistance. However, these programs have not been categorized and chronicled comprehensively. Nor should we conclude that security aid is limited to only Western states. In parallel with a transformation to global donor regimes, a number of emerging powers are engaging in security development. So while actors like Canada, the United States, and the European Union have prominent and wide-ranging programs, countries like China, Colombia, Brazil, Pakistan, and Nigeria (to name a few) also participate in security aid.

My work underlines the fact that, even though Canada's security aid practices are only a small fraction of what transpires globally, the role played by Canadian norm-supporting is significant. And, as I underline, the relative smallness of Canadian contributions to transversal security is precisely how the strategic-orientation of security aid as a program of norm-supporting gains its character and value. With contributions of Canadian security expertise having been modelled to support the reproduction of transversal security norms, security aid is most *strategic* when providing practical, measured support that maximizes the reliability and visibility of Canadian innovation in the field of transversal security governance. Under a humanitarian rationale of "aid," I explore the theme of Canada as a norm-supporter by showing how the mobilization of Canadian security expertise is mobilized to support the norms of security cooperation, integration, and interoperability within the transversal security community. It is precisely at the intersection of humanitarian appeal and the norms of global security cooperation where "security aid" aims to develop the practices of transversal security governance – providing us an opportunity to critically assess both the character of Canadian security development practices and the broader contours of a globalization of control.

Chapter Two

Mapping Security Aid and the Geographies of (In)Security

Introduction: Mapping Canadian Security Aid

In February 2014 the Canadian Forces participated in a conference entitled "Places of Interest: The Canadian Army and the New Global Security Environment."[1] Sprinkled in with sympathetic academics, the CF command structure was also well represented. Presenters included Lieutenant-General Marquis Hainse, commander of the Canadian Army, on "Perspective on Future Challenges"; Major-General Christian Rousseau, commander, Canadian Forces Intelligence Command, on "Trends to Watch"; Commodore Darren Hawco, chief of Force Development on "Cyber Warfare"; a keynote from Brigadier-General Michael Pearson, commander of Task Force Jerusalem, on "Canada and the Middle East"; and Major-General Steve Bowes, commander Canadian Army Doctrine and Training System, chairing a panel titled "How Must the Canadian Army Prepare for the Future?" Also included was a roundtable with the representatives from the Canadian Army Land Warfare Centre on "The Army's Vision of the New Security Environment."

An excerpt of the presentation from Major-General Rousseau, chief of Defence Intelligence, outlines a catalogue of "new" global threats: Al-Qaeda's continuing threat "as a stateless army and as a social movement"; activities of over a dozen other listed terrorism entities; threats from other "homegrown violent extremist" groups; threats posed by "political transition and instability" in Africa; state support for

1 Annual Conference – Gregg Centre for the Study of War and Society at the University of New Brunswick; see: http://www.unb.ca/fredericton/arts/centres/gregg/study/conference/annual/places.html (accessed 8 April 2015).

terrorism (listing Syria and Iran); threats to Canadian citizens abroad as well as CF members working in observer missions in the Middle East; the Taliban and Haqqani Networks' "threat to the CAF nation building presence there"; the threat of "illegal international activities of the Liberation Tigers of Tamil Eelam (LTTE), (both overseas and within Canada)"; and a list of Asian groups that "challenge democratic national authorities" (DND 2014-1426). In the Americas, Rousseau outlines the threat of FARC and ELN in Colombia, and Shining Path in Peru, cautioning that "terrorism and criminal violence remain a challenge in the Americas, particularly when such activities cross into Canada and the United States" (DND 2014-1426, 7). In pairing "criminal" and "terrorism" threats, Rousseau underlines the point that "Canada continues to work with a variety of partners throughout the Americas to build local counter-terrorism capacity, support criminal justice reform and help tackle the broad security challenges posed by criminal violence and drug trafficking" (DND 2014-1426, 6–7).

In his presentation, Rousseau provides a vivid articulation of the transversal "new global security environment." Underlining an emerging theme of resilience – what scholars have described as an important discursive device in blending security and development (Aradau 2014; Chandler 2012; Duffield 2012) – Rousseau warns that "Canada's success in remaining resilient to the terrorist threat continues to depend on having an approach that is flexible, forward-looking, and adaptable to an evolving *global threat environment*" (DND 2014-1426, 11; emphasis added). Responses to transversal threats in the "new global security environment" have been propelled from countries of the Global North in order to coordinate efforts to govern these insecurities, with a particular focus on those "places of interest" that are deemed to be the most risky. It is precisely in these geographies of (in)security that the above examples of threat translate into aid regimes to develop security, surveillance, policing, and crime control. This chapter presents a concomitant "mapping" by tracing the contours of both the Canadian bureaucracies of "security aid" as well as the "places of interest" in which these bureaucracies and geographies coalesce into security development regimes.

Scholars have noted a growing interest in "mapping as a method" (Loughlan, Olsson, and Schouten 2015), particularly within critical security studies and international political sociology (Bigo 2008; Salter 2010; Shapiro 2007). With an emphasis on the practices of security (i.e., the "practice turn"), scholarship has increasingly focused on mapping security practices as opposed to security discourses (Salter and Mutlu 2012, 85–109; Loughlan, Olsson, and Schouten 2015). As an introductory account of security aid practices, the mapping exercise undertaken in this chapter is exploratory, partial, and evolving. Following Stern and Öjendal's (2010, 8) discussion of mapping the security-development nexus, my efforts are similarly parsimonious, in that "any account of the vast fields that encompass considerations and practices of 'development' and 'security' will undoubtedly be partial." Following other mapping exercises, the exploratory approach that I undertake in this chapter takes shape as a process for critically understanding these opaque, complex social worlds – while also demonstrating the breadth of Canadian contributions to the development of transversal security cooperation.

The chapter proceeds in by three main sections. First, I offer my map of security aid and a discussion of its spheres of practice. Second, I detail the sphere of security aid hubs, exploring each hub's spending and the "places of interest" addressed by its respective practices of security assistance. Third, I examine security innovators by tracing their contributions of security expertise, then again providing an empirical discussion of the "places of interest" where their security innovation is practised. Although many aspects of the security aid regime are detailed in this book – and many others are not – this chapter provides readers with a map of the bureaucracies that feature prominently throughout this study, as well as an overview of the geographies of (in)security in which the practices of security aid are inscribed.

Mapping Security Aid

Figure 2.1 displays how the social field of security aid comprises three spheres. Note that their boundaries are flexible, allowing for travel of actors and information between them spheres while nonetheless retaining distinct forms. The figure provides a basic guide to its topology and some definitions of its composite parts, so that readers can refer back to them (if necessary) during the detailed explorations that follow.

At the centre of the figure are the *security aid hubs*, introduced briefly in the last chapter. Three security aid hubs are managed by GAC – the Global Peace and Security Fund (GPSF), the Anti-Crime Capacity Building Program (ACCBP), and the Counter-Terrorism Capacity Building (CTCB) program – and comprise a major element of Canadian security aid funding. As the primary funding sources, these hubs occupy the

Figure 2.1. Map of Security Aid

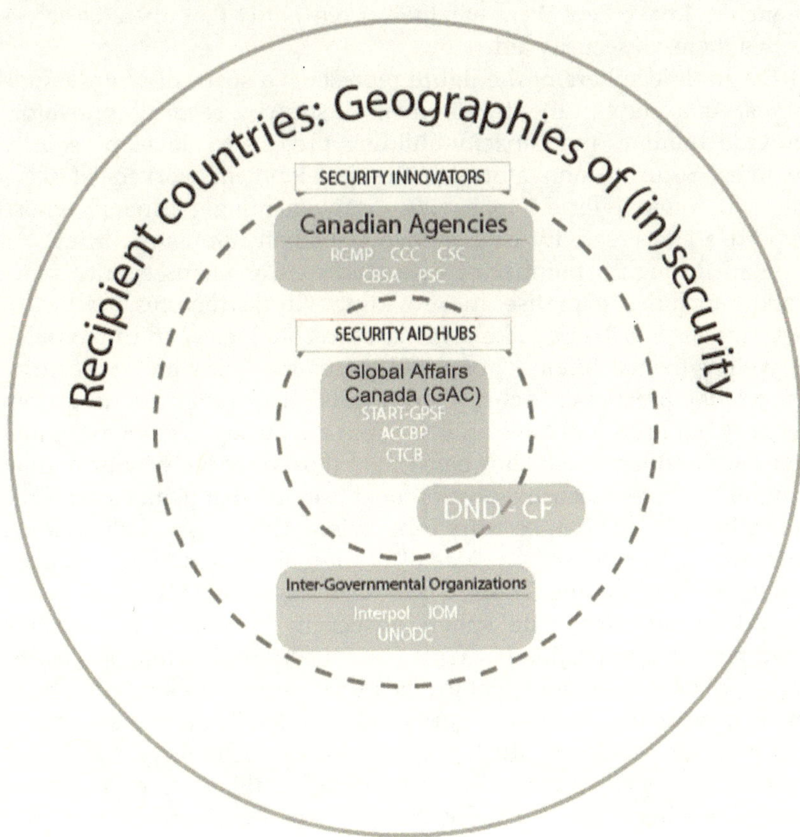

centre of the security aid social universe in that they act as the information and management hubs for Canada's security "assistance" regime. As discussed in the last chapter, these hubs have been created to maximize the strategic impacts of Canadian aid on the "security stage." The principal objective of these hubs is to strategically calibrate the small contributions from Canada into practical and increasingly visible impacts within the transversal security community. The other notable security aid hub is the Department of National Defence (DND), which has numerous elements of funding and a strong political gravitational pull. Yet, unlike the GAC security aid hubs, DND also operated in the field as a security innovator through the Canadian Forces (i.e., military branch). Given the interconnectivity of the funding and implementing branches, I have kept them together as one entity that operates across both spheres of security aid.

The middle sphere of the figure represents a space of *security innovators*. As experts in the development of security, security innovators provide training and capacity-building projects to develop security regimes. Security innovators are the development workers of security aid, often referred to as the "implementing partners" whose expertise and creativity characterize Canadian norm-supporting. As I detail through a number of case studies, Canadian security innovation includes expertise in providing "infrastructures" (which I describe as "hardware"-like enclosures, technologies, and materials), as well as the "techniques" of security (i.e., the "software" of security knowledge-practices). Security innovators receive their funding from security aid hubs and have an interest in advancing their own reputations and influence, which is performed most effectively by providing tangible, concrete security development training that demonstrates the reliability of Canadian security innovation. This is especially evident in norm-supporting the agendas of norm-makers. Prominent security innovators include the RCMP, CBSA, CSC, and Public Safety Canada. An additional actor in the sphere of security innovators is Canadian Commercial Corporation (CCC), a Crown corporation that acts as the monopoly procurement agent for the purchase and "in-kind donation" of "infrastructures" within security aid regimes. They act as a central gateway for involvement of private security technology companies in security development, a process I detail in this chapter and more extensively in chapter 4. Finally, the sphere of security innovators also includes a wide array of non-Canadian entities who act as "implementing partners" of security aid. They can include NGOs who receive security assistance for work in the Global South, but more prominently involve international organizations that are active security innovators within their own mandates. Prominent international security innovators discussed in this book are agencies like the United Nations Office on Drugs and Crime (UNODC), the International Organization for Migration (IOM), and Interpol. While I do not go into great detail on the activities and strategic interests of these security innovators, I do map where they have intersected with Canadian security aid, opening a pathway for further exploration.

The peripheral sphere represents what Major-General Rousseau called the "new global security environment," and what I refer to as the transversal geographies of (in)security. This is the sphere of *recipient countries.* As recipients of assistance, these countries are the sites of security development. In line with development discourses, these countries are sometimes referred to as "partners" or "beneficiaries," although as I detail extensively, these "partners" are viewed as deficient by the donor countries of the Global North. Former UN secretary general Kofi Annan used the term *weak links*[2] to describe how these countries have not fully integrated into global systems of security governance, and Aas (2013) has used the term *deviant states* to underline the reformatory logics through which norm-making countries perceive these "partners."

The purpose of this chapter is to further map out the focus of Canadian security aid; however, it is worth highlighting that this "map" is not a representation of global (in)securities as much as a representation of the spatial focus of Canadian security practices. There are many localities facing tragic violence and insecurity that receive very little funding or attention from security innovators. My point is not to address how or if security assistance would ameliorate these sites of insecurity, or to evaluate places "most in need" of security development. Instead, as I argue throughout the subsequent chapters, the geographies explored represent areas where security development is leveraged by security experts in the hubs to maximize Canadian involvement in supporting the transversal security community.

The spheres outlined above are structures of the security aid regime. Both aspects of the Canadian aid regime – hubs and innovators – share a division of labour and engage in related but separate spheres of practice. However, individual actors often travel between these two spheres. For example, within the security aid hubs are numerous experts who have worked in the field. Likewise, security innovators are often well educated, and are dexterous in the strategic orientations that are managed by the security hubs. Therefore, when referring to individuals or groups I often interchange the terms *experts* and *security innovators* to refer to actors within both spheres of Canadian security aid. As I describe further, the overall character of Canadian security aid itself is produced by the tangible and creative practices of security innovators; therefore the term is applicable to individuals across the spheres

2 Kofi Annan quoted in Patrick (2011, 5): "Our defences are only as strong as their weakest links."

in addition to the particular nodes of expertise that are mobilized in the field for security development.

Security Aid Hubs

Security aid hubs are the funding arm for development assistance; however, it is worth repeating that this funding is not under the category of official development assistance (ODA). These are new hubs, established in the context of the "war on terrorism," operating with the specific objective of managing Canadian contributions to developing global security governance. In doing so, the security aid hubs act as project and information managers for hundreds of projects simultaneously, all of which are developing security in the Global South. As I detail below, the involvement of GAC agencies in security development is often at the bureaucratic level, meaning that security experts within the hubs do not do the on-site training. Instead, they provide assessments, overview, expert opinions, and follow-ups to *all projects* that flow from their funding mechanisms.

For example, a GAC program such as the ACCBP would be asked to design a program if Canada committed $2 million to improve cross-border identity analysis in Jamaica. Employees from the ACCBP would draw up a project proposal, working in conjunction with Canadian security innovators (usually the RCMP or CBSA) as well as representatives of Jamaica or other regional entities. This often involves funding an initial assessment or scoping mission to assess current capabilities and make a plan of development. A proposal would be drafted by experts in the ACCBP, often in consultation with security innovators (other departments) or with private companies regarding technology procurements (biometrics, fingerprints, etc.). Proposals then go upwards within the GAC bureaucracy, which typically entails revisions after consultations with other GAC branches, and strategic considerations from upper echelons of the bureaucracy. After revisions are accepted, the project can be approved by the Minister's Office (a stage of approvals that was recently added by Minister John Baird, discussed below). The security aid hub would arrange the logistics with the implementing partner, who would be responsible for the training and capacity building in the field. In the case of border management in Jamaica, it could involve multiple implementing partners including the RCMP, DND, and CBSA, as well as support for embassy liaisons. This is a demonstration of the whole-of-government approach that maximizes

Canadian expertise in the field of security development, and became a driving rationale behind the creation of the START-GPSF security aid hub.

START-GPSF: Global Peace and Security Fund

Announced in the 2005 as part of the Canada's International Policy Statement, the GPSF was created as the government's lead agency for security aid.[3] Administered by the Stabilization and Reconstruction Task Force (START), the fund was created as an international response to "weak links" in global security. GAC describes the mandate of START-GPSF programming as assisting "fragile states" that "are not properly the responsibility of DND, and are outside the core purposes of Canada's Official Development Assistance (ODA) Program" (GAC 2007, iii). The START-GPSF program was created as a unique global program of security development programming and was used as a model for other rapid-response programming units in Northern counties. Security innovators considered this a major accomplishment and a demonstration of Canadian innovation and leadership. With an annual project fund of $150 million, the START-GPSF has a very large scope of security assistance operations, far exceeding the threshold of "failed states." Notably, almost immediately upon its announcement, a number of NGOs warned that the START-GPSF would lead to a "securitization of development" (CCIC 2005). In many regards this critique is accurate, particularly since START-GPSF quickly became the coordinating agency for security development work in Afghanistan, and the key facilitator of the whole-of-government approach integral to Canada's 3D counter-insurgency strategy (Chin 2009; Klassen 2013).

As a major node of security aid, the START-GFSF has a large bureaucracy to supports its mandate. With a staffing contingent of up to seventy people in five groups of focus (human security; conflict prevention and peace-building; peacebuilding and peace operations; humanitarian affairs; and mine action and small arms), the START-GPSF had a significant influence on the development of Canadian security aid hubs. In addition to the project spending, full costs

3 The program is also commonly referred to as the Global Peace and Security Program (GPSP). Canadian bureaucracies interchange both terms. I have standardized using the acronym GPSF.

associated with running the GPSF security aid hub amounted to over $1.1 billion from 2005 to 2013.[4] With a large supporting cast of experts and managers, START-GPSF had considerable power in framing Canada's security assistance programming. Though initially deeply involved in the less-than-successful "hearts and minds" campaign in Afghanistan,[5] the START-GPSF quickly expanded across a larger field of geographical interest. Because the fund is large, I have not charted it, as I have with the ACCBP below. However, the projects that I detail provide a good illustration of major "places of interest." Outside of Afghanistan, the fund has been very active in Haiti and Palestine, as well as supporting numerous projects in Latin America (particularly Colombia) and Africa. An important aspect of the START-GPSF is that it combines an interest in managing very large security development projects (such as over $100 million in spending in Haiti, mostly on "infrastructures" such as prisons, police stations, and border checkpoints), as well as an array of small projects in diverse locations. It should be noted that, in terms of quantity, the START-GPSF runs hundreds of projects per year that are quite small, and often focused on human security. While these projects represent a large number of the projects, they are typically quite inexpensive and account for only a small proportion of total programming.

As spending indicates (see figure 2.2), the START-GPSF has an annual budget of $150 million; however, beginning in 2011, the significant amounts of assistance funding was allowed to lapse, so was returned to general revenue).[6]

As demonstrated in figure 2.2, the largest funding year for the period under review is 2010–11, with spending of $125.7 million. Spending during the subsequent year (2011–12) dropped to $63.8 million and corresponds with the arrival of Minister Baird (May 2011), as well as the rollback of programs in Afghanistan (see GAC 2012). Spending in 2012–13 demonstrates the funding lapses under the Baird administration, explained below. Planned spending was set at $97.7 million, yet the new system of project approvals caused a slowdown in spending,

4 Figures calculated by the Treasury Board of Canada Secretariat (2015).

5 Although some security innovators continue to promote the Afghan mission as successful, some insiders have been highly critical of the "hearts and minds" campaign (see Levitz 2015; Payton 2015).

6 Figures compiled using the Supplementary Information Tables that are appended to Annual Budget reports for the department; they are available from GAC.

Figure 2.2. START-GPSF Spending, 2009–2014

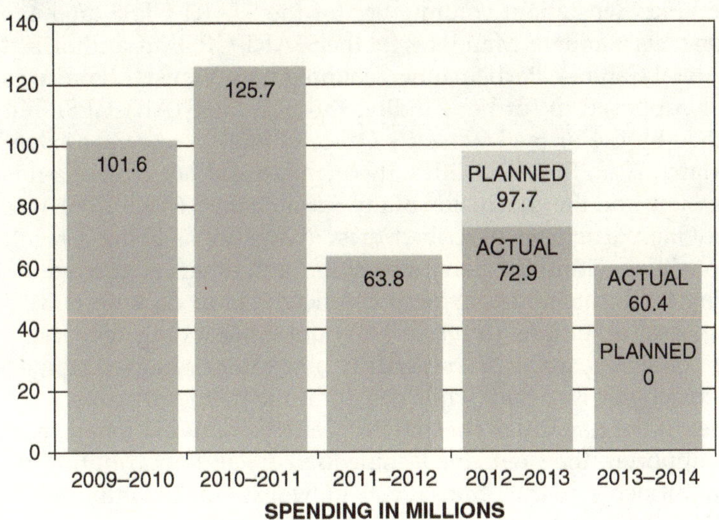

which amounted to $72.9 million. Spending dropped further in 2013–14 to $60.4 million, representing almost exclusively projects with pre-approval before the arrival of Minister Baird.

Under Minister Baird (2011–15), the security aid hubs – and especially the START-GPSF – were subjected to greater interference. Security aid experts have outlined how funding processes of security aid hubs were disrupted, which created inefficiencies in the strategic functioning of the hubs (Monaghan 2015c, 269–331). Two primary interests were behind Minister Baird's activities in reforming security aid funding. First was a pan-governmental effort to reduce budgets, cut costs, and incur lapsed funding through delays. This was not exclusive to the GAC, but an aspect of a political strategy to curb the national deficit before the 2015 election. Second was Minister Baird's personal desire to rebrand the department – long a symbol of small-*l* liberalism – under a more conservative banner, the result of which was to impose more control over funding of projects that accorded with Conservative optics. This included a directive to remove the autonomy of the security aid hubs in spending pre-approved funds, instead requiring all projects to receive ministerial approval. In the attempt to rebrand the GAC bureaucracy for domestic political gains, the START-GPSF did represent a symbolic target that Baird attempted to disband.

A major point of conversation among interview participants was the dramatic unknowns about continuation of the START-GPSF after the expiration of its mandate. Mandates for the START-GPSF are authorized by the federal Cabinet. Participants recounted how Minister Baird was adamantly opposed to further funding through the START-GPSF but was pushed by the Prime Minister's Office to grant a one-year extension in March 2013. By March 2014, the mandate did not receive a further extension, and the conclusion of my research the START-GPSF was in limbo. One participant described these dynamics as being a result of "personalities within the party structure," and others suggested the rebranding (and potential backroom conflicts) had to do with Baird's future political ambitions (Interview 2). Notwithstanding the drama from the politicians, many of the security innovators who participated in my research stressed that, while the domestic politics disrupted the efficiencies of the particular character of Canadian internationalism as a norm-supporter, they remained embedded in, and contributing to, their commitments within transversal networks. Importantly, while the START-GPSF was being undermined by Baird, the other two security aid hubs were being prioritized as mechanisms of strategic security assistance. Coinciding with a move away from mega-projects in Afghanistan, the funding of security aid became more strategic and more practically oriented through the next two hubs discussed: the CTCB and the ACCBP.

Counter-Terrorism Capacity Building Program (CTCB)

Announced following the post-9/11 National Security Strategy (see Canada 2004), the CTCB program is funded from the international assistance envelope with the mandate "to share our expertise" of security and counter-terrorism (GAC 2013c). Providing security assistance through training, equipment, and technical and legal assistance, the CTCB is a funding mechanism intended strictly for countries that meet the eligibility as ODA (though it is not ODA funding). Figure 2.3 demonstrates CTCB spending from 2009 to 2014.[7]

CTCB program funding is not fixed and, as demonstrated by the figure, program spending doubled from 2009–10 to 2010–11 from

7 Figures compiled from the Supplementary Information Tables that are appended to Annual Budget reports for the department; available from GAC.

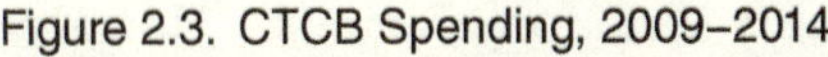

Figure 2.3. CTCB Spending, 2009–2014

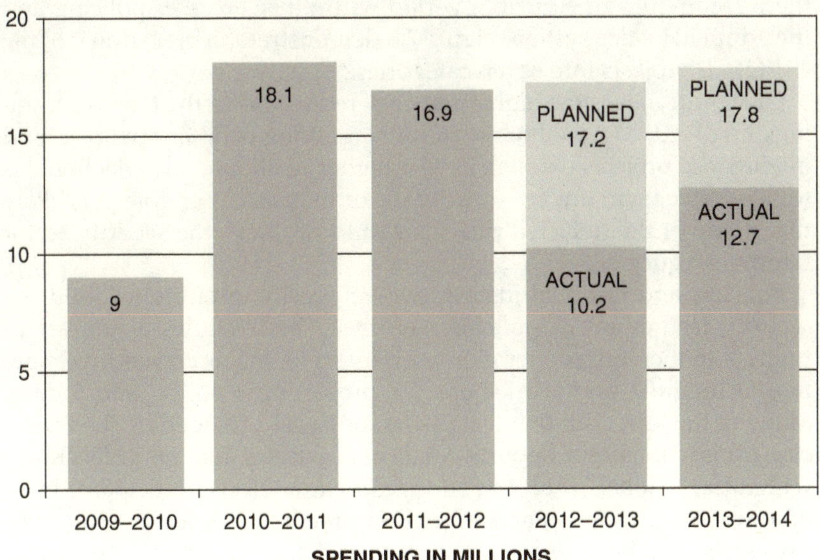

$9 million to $18.1 million. Escaping the purposeful lapsing of funds, spending in 2011–12 was relatively consistent with the year previous ($16.9 million). However, the 2012–13 numbers demonstrate a funding lapse, with $17.2 million in planned spending matched with only $10.2 million in actual spending. A similar lapse in funds has been recorded for 2013–14, with $17.8 million planned, but only $12.7 million in actual spending.

By July 2013, there had been at least 527 CTCB initiatives.[8] Of those initiatives, there were 431 funded projects from the start of the CTCB in 2005 to July 2013. The CTCB has managed projects valued at $149,883,725.58.[9] However, over two dozen projects have redacted spending totals. As a security aid hub with the mandate to develop counter-terrorism capacities, CTCB programming is focused on

8 This is gathered from the numbering of the CTCB projects, which are filed consecutively under year-number.

9 As a result of the accounting practices in the CTCB, the project values include funding figures from other government departments (OGD). I calculate the OGD contribution to this total project value as $15,680,277.72.

surveillance, intelligence, and security sector programming. However, these techniques of security overlap with other areas of policing and the criminal justice system. Figure 2.4 demonstrates a breakdown of the 431 CTCB projects into seven categories.[10]

Of significance is the high number of redactions in the types of trainings involved. My methodology for classifying counter-terrorism and intelligence projects – which have a higher likelihood of redaction – is to categorize them under "security sector reform." Therefore, it is likely that many of the redacted projects would fit under the security sector reform category.

Policing and criminal justice involve specific projects to build the security techniques of policing agencies. This includes a number of projects to increase cooperation with Interpol, major crimes investigative techniques, and workshops for prosecutors, police, and judges. Many of the terrorism financing workshops are provided by the Financial Transactions and Reports Analysis Centre of Canada (FINTRAC) within the "Global" category, and include numerous participants in an effort to integrate and standardize best practices. Border security comprises a combination of airport security and port security trainings and, like FINTRAC and policing projects, displays an overarching objective of integration and coordination. I detail aspects of these security techniques in chapter 5, yet it is worth noting that Canadian security innovation is highly advanced in developing these aspects of the transversal security community.

A breakdown of the regional focus of the fund reveals "places of interest" that are high priorities for CTCB security development projects. The 431 projects can be divided into seven "regions" and an eighth category for redacted locations (see figure 2.5).

As the region with the highest representation of projects, Asia is focused almost exclusively on Indonesia and Southeast Asia. As I discuss below (and in more detail in chapter 5), the arrival of two migrant boats in 2010 sparked a frenzied "anti-human smuggling agenda" that shifted SEA capacity-building responsibilities to the ACCBP. Before the

10 Although project objectives overlap, each project has been categorized according to one "main focus." For example, legislative reforms against terrorism are classified as policing/criminal justice (security sector reform); DND trainings for naval boarding parties are classified as border security, not security sector reform or policing; and training police on maritime surveillance techniques is classified as border security, not policing.

Figure 2.4. CTCB Projects by Sector

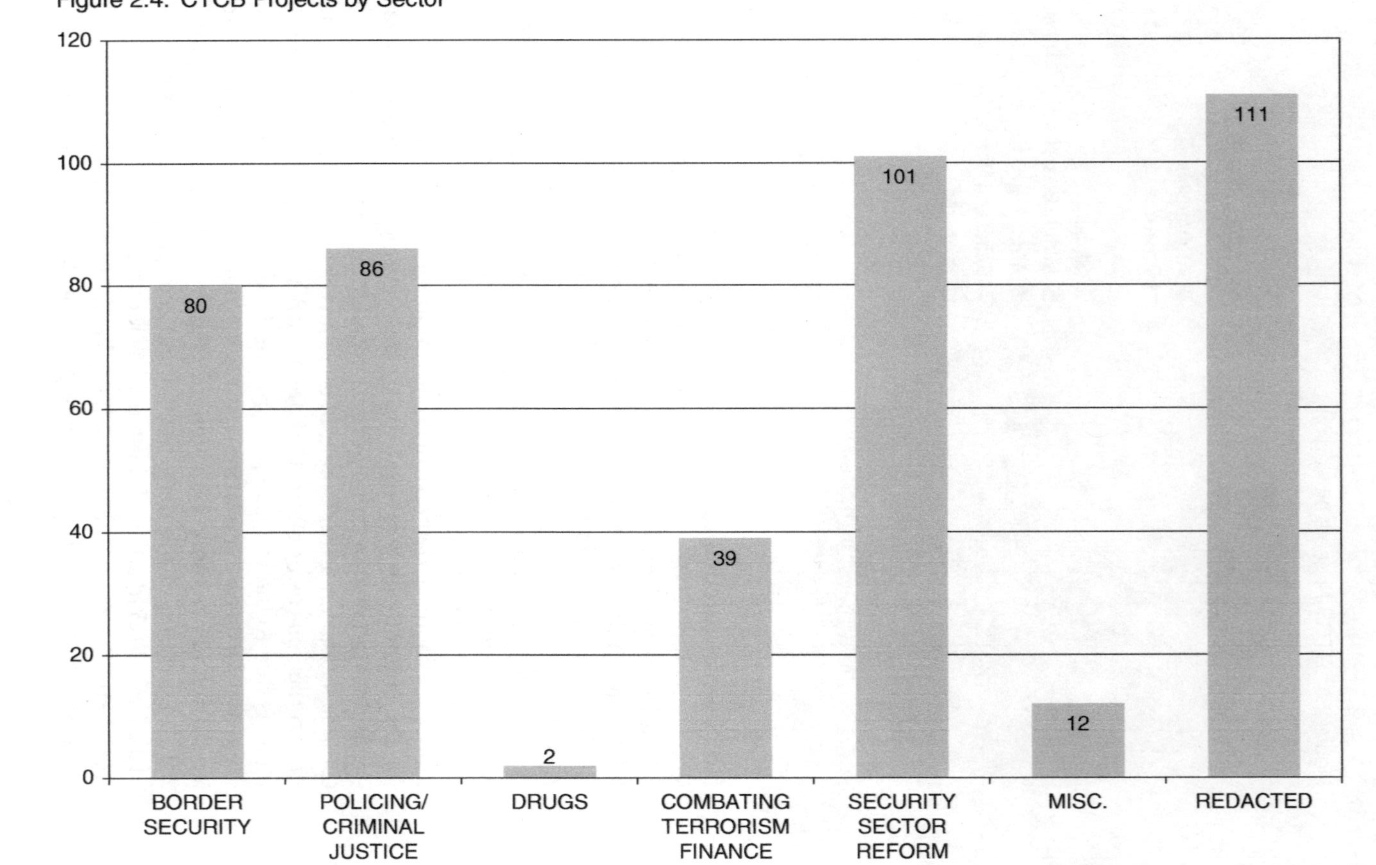

Figure 2.5. CTCB Projects by Region

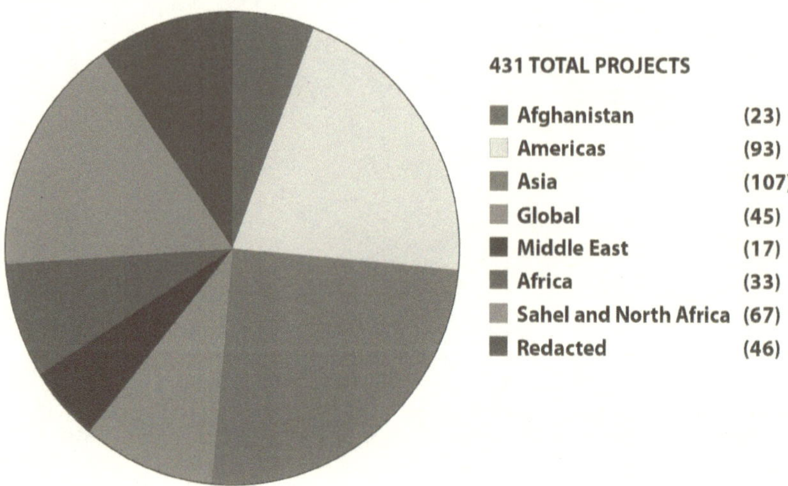

moral panic surrounding what has been framed as "illegal migration" (see Dauvergne 2008), the SEA funding included elements of border/ migration control projects, but had a larger focus on security sector reform and anti-terrorism. After 2010, the focus has been almost exclusively on borders and migration control – and has been directed by the ACCBP.

Of the Afghan projects, only four predate 2010. As the START-GPSF was the primary fund for the "reconstruction" efforts that supported the military counter-insurgency campaign, a shift towards "capacity-building" funding demonstrates an important bureaucratic support for the cut-and-run exit strategy. Corresponding with the exit strategy from Afghanistan and a general broadening of the spatial focus of Canada's "war on terror" agenda, there has been a dramatic reorientation in the "places of interest" of the CTCB. One aspect of this shift in focus is due to the impact of the newer ACCBP fund created with an exclusive focus on Latin America. Of the ninety-three Americas projects listed above, only four were implemented after 2009 (and all in 2010). Likewise, of the forty-five Global category projects, forty took place from 2005 to 2009. Making up for the dramatic fall-off in projects from Latin America and Global, there has been a dramatic increase in programming in the Trans-Sahel region as a "place of interest" where, previous to 2010, there were only two projects.[11] Many of these anti-terrorism projects complement the programming in the "Africa" category, which is focused exclusively on Somalia and the northeastern region.

As one action memorandum written for the minister of foreign affairs in April 2012 opens, "Africa has changed" (GAC 2012-3104, 2). Warning that "links between organized crime and terrorism are growing," the memo details ways in which the "international community is responding to change" (ibid.). In concert with the shift of attention within the "war on terror" towards the Sahel and Sahara regions (see Bachmann 2014; Keenan 2009a, 2009b), Canadian programming has focused almost exclusively on counter-terrorism and counter-insurgency. Spending from these sixty-one CTCB projects has been at least $34,857,127.14, which does not include ten projects that have had their costs redacted.

In 2010–11, the CTCB set up a direct Sahel Fund to support programming in the region. Projects have focused on development of techniques and infrastructures of security. Perhaps the largest investment in security aid has been the CTCB's funding of Canadian Special Forces (CANSOFCOM) participation in a multinational training exercise called Operation Flintlock. Although some additional projects are likely redacted, at least seven projects have gone through DND – at a cost of $5,182,907 – for these Special Forces trainings. Another project worth $2,083,404 can be added to these – though the partner is redacted – which is listed as costs for the purchase of "French Equipment and Training." Likely this relates to Canada paying the French for their participation, a notable case of "aid" being payments to another prosperous country. One other project includes the Canadian Commercial Corporation providing security hardware for a redacted amount.

Operation Flintlock is a major source of Canadian security aid, as it has become an integral training operation for the transversal security community in the Sahel region to coordinate counter-terrorism with "like-minded" African nations. The operation was organized and sponsored primarily by the United States Africa Command (USAFRICOM), whose questionable motives and clandestine violence in the Sahel has been extensively detailed by anthropologist Jeremy Keenan (2009a, 2009b).

11 Within the post-2010 period, I have aggregated a few small projects from the Sahel, Sahara, North Africa region into this category. The Specific breakdown with projects in brackets is Algeria (one), Magreb (three), Mali (four), Niger (five), Nigeria (three), and Sahel (fifty-one).

In addition to U.S. Special Forces, a "secret" briefing note for the minister of defence outlines how the operation incorporates special operations forces of "select international partners," including the United Kingdom, France, Netherlands, and Denmark, as well as "several Western African nations" (DND 2013-486, 2).

Much of Canada's previous funding and capacity building in the Trans-Sahel region targeted enhancement of the security forces in Mali (DND 2013-590, 2012-621, 2012-1962). Through the Military Training Cooperation Program (MTCP) (discussed below), three Canadian Forces trainers were in Mali at the time of the coup, and nine Malian officers were "studying in training establishments across Canada on various courses under MTCP auspices" (DND 2013-590, 43). Following the coup in 2012, Canada suspended programming and military cooperation.[12] Ironically, following the coup, Canada immediately – and secretly – began preparations to send Special Forces to Mali in support of the ousted government (Brewster 2013; DND 2012-1962). In 2013, the CTCB sent $5 million to the Trust Fund in Support of the African-Led International Support Mission in Mali (AFISMA).

Having participated in Operation Flintlock since 2009, Canada is involved in a program that "trains national Counter-Terrorist (CT) and/or Special Operations Forces (SOF) from the Trans-Sahara Counter-Terrorism Partnership (TSCTP) nations" (DND 2013-486, 2). Until 2013, Canada had an extensive trading and aid relationship with Mali (DND 2012-621), but redirected all programming assistance after the 2012 coup towards the international Trust Fund to Support Peace and Security in Mali (GAC 2014-847, 19–39). For the 2013 training program, the minister of national defence signed a "CT partnership" with security forces from Niger. The secret briefing details the Canadian aid as including a Special Operations training team, "a [redacted] from the Canadian Special Operations Regiment," and a "Special Operations Aviation Detachment (SOAD) composed of [redacted] armed CH-146 Griffon helicopters" (DND 2013-486, 3). In addition to the parlaying of counter-terrorism techniques, the documents detail that CTCB also approved the "donation of 150 sets of non-lethal individual soldier

12 From a DND briefing note to the minister of defence: "The coup has damaged Canada's, and DND's, long and productive history of cooperation: aid to the government is suspended and other kinds of assistance are in jeopardy, including military cooperation. Canada wishes to resume productive exchanges once constitutional order is re-established" (DND 2013-590, 43).

equipment for the Niger Army," which consisted of "boots, rucksacks, First Aids kits and other similar items" (ibid.).

As detailed in chapter 3, there has been an increasing role for the military within security aid regimes. Canada's aid programs in the Sahel region demonstrate how these assistance programs fit within a broad scope of Canadian innovation in the transversal security community. As the ACCBP programs in Latin America demonstrate, a major contribution of Canadian security aid projects has been to promote tangible techniques of security governance. Demonstrating how the Trans-Sahel region has become a particular site of intersection for development and counter-terrorism practices (Bachmann 2014; Miles 2012), Flintlock is a key initiative for Canadian security assistance and demonstrates how security aid funds – like the CTCB – promote Canadian security innovation in the broader context of norm-supporting the transversal security community.

ACCBP: Anti-Crime Capacity Building Program

The newest of the security aid hubs, the ACCBP emerged as a crown jewel of the Harper government's foreign affairs strategy. Announced during the North American Leaders' Summit in 2009, the ACCBP was designed as an element of the government's three-pillar "re-engagement strategy" with Latin America.[13] Long an area under the norm-making influence of the United States, the transversal security community has expanded the security and surveillance regimes in Latin America dramatically (Arteaga Botello 2009, 2012; also Guzik 2013; Müller 2012; Swanson 2007), and the ACCBP has positioned Canadian security innovation within this transformation. Given that Canadian foreign policy towards Latin America has been driven by a combination of supporting U.S. policy while advancing Canadian resource extraction interests (Brown 2014; Studnicki-Gizbert and Bazo 2013; Veltmeyer 2013), the "re-engagement strategy" has fused economic interests with humanitarian overtures of democracy and rule of law. As the "master narrative of liberal order building" (Neocleous 2008, 5), security has been centred as the bridge between resource extraction and the rule of law, while

13 The three pillars of Canada's re-engagement strategy are "the promotion and enhancement of prosperity; security; and the fundamental values of freedom, democracy, human rights and the rule of law" (GAC 2010-2423, 1).

Figure 2.6. ACCBP Spending, 2009–2014

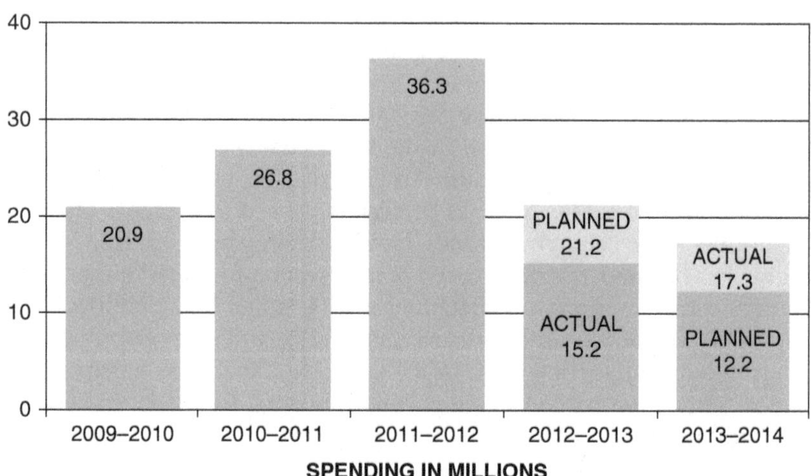

raising the Canadian profile as a reliable and practical norm-supporter of transversal security governance.

Intended as a program to enhance the capacities of "like-minded" countries in criminal justice, security, and the rule of law, the ACCBP was designed to allocate up to $15 million annually. Unlike other security aid hubs, the ACCBP has over-spent in some years. In addition, the AACBP was designed as a lead agency to disperse funds under the Canadian Initiative for Security in Central America (CISCA) funding envelope, which supports crime control projects in Central America. Prime Minister Harper announced the five-year, $25-million funding envelope in April 2012 (Canada 2012). Figure 2.6 represents ACCBP spending from 2009 to 2014.[14]

As demonstrated by figure 2.6, the ACCBP experienced a consistent increase in spending over its first three years of operation: from $20.9 million, to $26.8 million, then $36.3 million by 2011–12. Similar to other hubs, the 2012–13 year illustrates a dramatic cut in planned spending ($21.2 million) as well as significant lapsed funding, having spent only $15.2 million in programming. However, the ACCBP

14 Figures compiled from the Supplementary Information Tables appended to Annual Budget reports for the department; these figures are available from the GAC.

spending figures recovered somewhat in 2013–14, with planned spending set at $12.2 million, but program spending at $17.3 million.

The fund was focused originally on strategic interests in Latin America, but has since broadened the "places of interest" for security assistance, including a considerable focus in Southeast Asia (see chapter 5). Figure 2.7 illustrates the regional division of 225 ACCBP[15] projects from January 2009 to February 2012.

As noted above, the ACCBP was created specifically to advance Canadian strategic interests in Latin America. As figure 2.7 illustrates, a large percentage of ACCBP programming from the 2009–13 period is focused on Latin America, representing approximately 74 per cent of the projects (including Mexico and hemispheric projects).

In addition to security aid, Canada's re-engagement strategy with Latin America has included a range of security commitments. Latin America has emerged as a central "place of interest" within Canadian security aid. To help advance Canadian strategic interests, security aid in Latin America is performed by being a norm-supporter of the U.S.-driven hemispheric security agenda. A briefing note prepared from Minister of State of Foreign Affairs (of the Americas) Diane Ablonczy, written for OAS meetings in 2012, captures this relationship (see figure 2.8).

Demonstrating the centrality of security governance as a vehicle for broader strategic interests, the briefing note demonstrates the weight of U.S. interests on the calculation of Canadian "security assistance." The second bullet regarding Canada's influence as a "driving" force shaping other donors' strategies for security assistance in Latin America is particularly demonstrative of the Canadian character of norm-supporting. Not possible without the norm-making direction of the United States, the second bullet points to the high prioritization of Canadian knowledge practices in providing practical and technically oriented direction in the region.

In terms of security assistance to South America, spending declined from the 2009–2011 period and the 2011–2013 period (see figure 2.7). Despite an overall decline in spending for the region, it is worth highlighting that Colombia, the primary recipient of the aid, has remained stable. In addition to funds from the ACCBP, Colombia received $15 million between 2005 and 2009 from START-GPSF (GAC 2010-0549). GPSF programming for 2010 totalled $5,699,518, and spending in 2011

15 Regional overlaps on many projects have resulted in a total value of 296 for this graph.

Figure 2.7. ACCBP Projects by Region

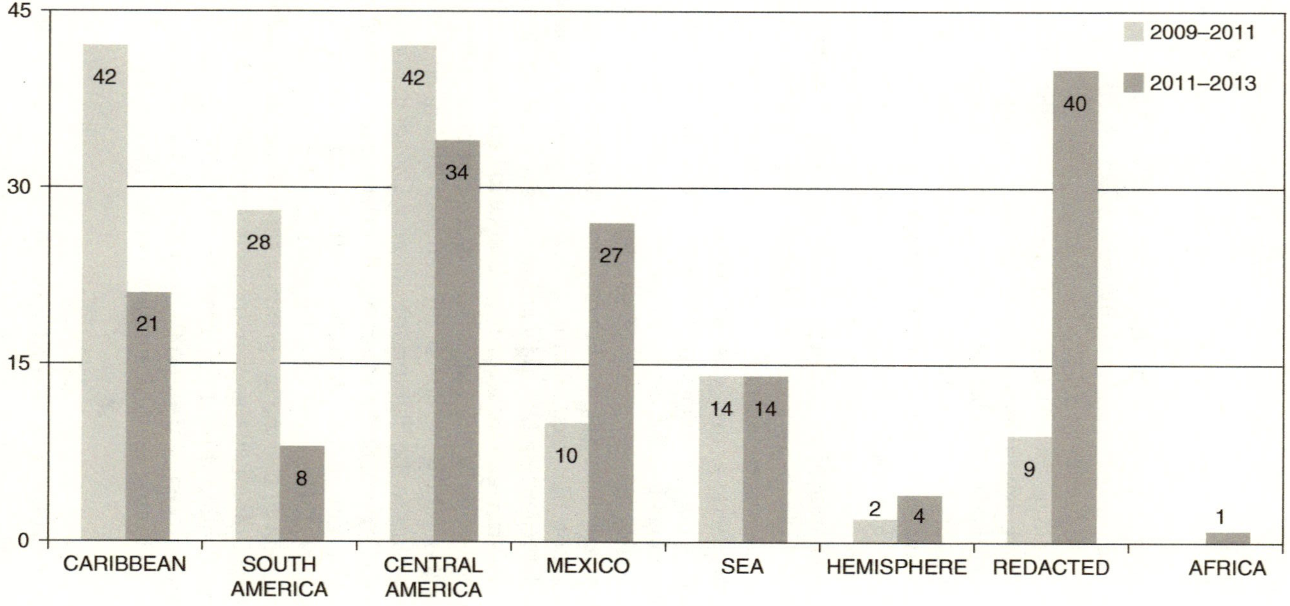

Figure 2.8. Briefing Note for Minister of State of Foreign Affairs (of the Americas), 2012 (GAC 2012-1956, 67–8)

Security Remains a Top Concern

Regional security and stability are fundamental to U.S. interests, particularly in Mexico, Central America and the Caribbean. This is also the most prominent area of Canada-U.S. cooperation in the region.

- Five years into the U.S.-Mexico Mérida Initiative, the two neighbours cooperate intensely, from strengthening Mexican institutions to disrupting transnational crime. The Obama administration is confident that it can work with whomever Mexicans choose as their next president.
- Central America has developed its regional security strategy. Canada and the United States are driving forces shaping donors' response.
- In the Caribbean, a more informal process allows Canada and the United States to coordinate security assistance.

totalled $3,491,266.32.[16] As a result of numerous conjoining interests (in particular the mining and recourses sectors and U.S. relations), the Canadian government has sought to increase relations with Colombia in recent years through the Canada-Colombia Security Consultations (GAC 2010-2427; GAC 2010-2429). Demonstrating the strategic orientation behind such security cooperation, one briefing note from 2010 to the minister of foreign affairs explained, "Colombia is Canada's 6th trading partner in Central and South America and a growing investment destination for Canadian companies, in particular in the extractive sector" (GAC 2010-549; see also GAC 2010-540). Security aid in Colombia is a unique venue for Canada to learn from Colombian "best practices." Most security aid programming flows from North to South, but documents related to capacity building in Colombia underline the mutual benefits that can be accrued through Canadian assistance programming. For example, in the context of Canadian counter-terrorism capacity building provided through the CTCB, discussants at the Canada-Colombia Security Consultations remarked, "Canada underlined the fact that the day's discussions further supported the

16 Funds for 2010 calculated from GAC 2011-1373, and 2011 from GAC 2011-1374. It is worth noting that many of the START-GPSF projects in Colombia are human security projects that aim to provide NGO-directed assistance to specific at-risk groups. These projects do not have the objectives of integrating security governance agencies, yet funds through other hubs have explicitly tried to build collaborative security capacities.

like-mindedness of Canada and Colombia on most matters relating to illicit drugs, organized crime and terrorism and articulated the apparent desire of both countries to learn more from one another's experiences through tangible cooperation by building on areas where we actually work well together already" (GAC 2010-2429, 9).

Reflecting Foucault's (2003,103) notion of the "boomerang effect" – where techniques of security developed and tested abroad travel back to the Global North (see also Graham 2011; Coaffee and Murakami Wood 2006; Shapiro 2007) – Canadian security aid has been used to fund "collaborations" to harness Colombian expertise in military and counter-insurgency techniques. Here aid funds are directed towards "capacity building" in Colombia, and a boomerang effect "brings home" more enhanced and systematized counter-insurgency capacities to Canadian agencies. This relation is made clear in an email from René Gervais, Canada's defence attaché in Colombia, discussing the Canada-Colombia Security Collaborations (see figure 2.9).

Figure 2.9. Email Regarding the Canada-Colombia Security Collaborations (GAC 2010-2427, 101–2)

From: Rene.Gervais@international.gc.ca [mailto:Rene.Gervais@international.gc.ca]
Sent: Wednesday, 1, October, 2008 10:21 AM
To: Henrichon PS@ADM(Pol) DWH Pol@Ottawa-Hull
Subject: RE: CDMA bilaterals: Colombia/Mexico

Hi Patrick,

For ICT's purposes, the text below is OK with changes shown. The underlined portion should be left out as the mix of troops that will eventually be sent [redacted] will include engineers but likely other expertise as well.

There is more to this drug eradication proposal by Colombia than meets the eye. [redacted] The Colombians will bring counter-drug expertise based on 40 years of fighting terrorism, insurgency and drug trafficking in the jungles of Colombia. They have learnt many valuable lessons [redacted] If our aim is to have a bilateral discussion on possible ways ahead in [redacted] as well as possible Canada-Colombia cooperation in specific counter drug efforts there, we will need to be prepared to share experiences and lessons learned from both op environments, and find common ground. [redacted] This implied that we should get together and exchange lessons learned. The security consultations could serve as a bridge to a specific meeting on counter drug ops [redacted]

[redacted] The Colombian approach to counter-narcotics in Colombia has been no-nonsense and quite effective. [redacted] I would recommend that our DND/CF experts in this area participate in this portion of the security consultations with Colombia, and as a minimum sit down with ICT prior to the event to confirm our policy and technical position on crop eradication and counter

06/05/2011

The message concludes that "the Colombian approach to counter-narcotics in Colombia has been no-nonsense and quite effective," and counsels DND-CF to "at a minimum sit down with ICT [GAC] prior to the event to confirm our policy and technical position on crop eradication and counter drug operations" (GAC 2010-2427, 101–2). Although Canada did not engage in crop eradications (unlike the United States) as a counter-insurgency tactic, the important aspect of the message underpins how the knowledge systems of security techniques need to be cultivated and enhanced. Doing so makes them deployable in the future – which is the thrust of Gervais's email – and suggests that the knowledge practices that would "come home" would have practical value far beyond the counter-insurgency in Afghanistan.

Another significant "place of interest" for ACCBP programming has been Central America. Although funding decreased over the period examined above, ACCBP programming in Central America and the Caribbean has, with only a few exceptions, aimed at building capacities in combating drugs. Often cited within Canadian documents as a "transit area," countries have received significant aid funds under the mantle of the drug war. The overarching aim of these programs has been to integrate regional and international systems of intelligence and policing. As a central "security technique" to professionalize policing and surveillance in the Global South (which I detail in chapter 5), the integration approach aims to network these recipient countries into the broader surveillance and policing web. A quick overview of some of the programming demonstrates Canada's approach to this character of the transversal security community:[17]

- In 2011, the RCMP were contracted for $1,209,067.71 to provide regional security system training to ten Eastern Caribbean countries with the aim of "professionalizing law enforcement: training, standardization, etc."
- To develop a Regional Container Control Program for Latin America, UNODC was contracted for $3,590,801 to train Central American countries on using the system.
- Demonstrating a fluidity in the categories of aid "recipients," some security aid recipients also engage in training projects. For example,

17 All examples from project charts contained in GAC 2011-1380.

given its valuable expertise in the drug war and counter-insurgency, Colombia was contracted for $1 million for "strengthening law enforcement systems in Honduras and Guatemala."
- Interpol delivered a capacity-building project for policing organized crime to seven Caribbean countries and Mexico ($1,595,813.98).
- As many as twenty Central and South American countries were provided the UNODC's Global Scientific Forensics Support Program.
- $1,491,293.74 of funding was provided to eight Central American states and the Dominican Republic to support "specialized training for authorities from SICA [Central American Integration System] member states in methods of collecting, analyzing and disseminating crime data, implementing regional assessment tools, and developing expertise in investigating security incidents, crime, and violence."

In addition to efforts to develop integrated surveillance in Central and South America, Mexico occupies a significant "place of interest" for Canadian security aid. As noted in the briefing note for Minister Ablonczy (figure 2.8) that discusses Latin American security interests, the U.S. focus on Mexico – particularly the security aid provided through their Merida Initiative (Arteaga Botello 2009, 2012) – is a major consideration for Canadian security aid. One "Strategic Overview" document provided for the minister of foreign affairs during a diplomatic trip to Mexico in 2013 recounts how "security cooperation has evolved into a central pillar of Canada's engagement with Mexico" (GAC 2012-3329, 28; see also PSC 2014-78). The ACCBP has been described as "the main channel of Canada's enhanced security cooperation with Mexico," contributing over $8 million in security capacity-building programming between 2009 and 2012 (GAC 2012-3329, 17, 40). ACCBP programs have "served to train Mexican law enforcement officials in investigative techniques, intelligence-gathering and the use of new technologies" (GAC 2012-3329, 1).

Although originally focused on Latin America, the ACCBP has been expanded to other "places of interest." In 2009, the ACCBP opened projects in Southeast Asia (SEA) to address human smuggling. While the CTCB has been active in African countries for many years, ACCBP approved its first project in Africa in 2011 that shipped $1 million in unspecified policing goods to Benin (through the Canadian Commercial

Corporation) also to address human smuggling. A key unknown variable in the data analysed above is the large increase in redacted projects from 2009–11 (nine) to 2011–13 (forty), which corresponds to the expansion of the ACCBP mandate from Latin America to broader spheres of interest.

In addition to exploring where the ACCBP is active, I have examined what forms of security development are promoted by this security aid fund. While programming can be categorized under five themes – crime control, illicit drugs, security sector reform, and migration/border control – the funding goes towards a wide range of projects that can include, but are not limited to, workshops, needs assessments, document printing, and a host of projects to enhance the technologies and techniques of security. To illustrate areas of focus, figure 2.10 illustrates the division of 225 ACCBP projects into "main sectors" of development from January 2007 to February 2012.

The method for calculating this chart involved counting each project as falling within only one "main sector" despite an obvious reality that programming of the ACCBP most often deals with several agencies. Calculating the "main sector" of security development is subjective, and the representation for the category of policing and criminal justice system is lower than the actual programming involving policing agencies.

Figure 2.10. ACCBP Projects by Sector

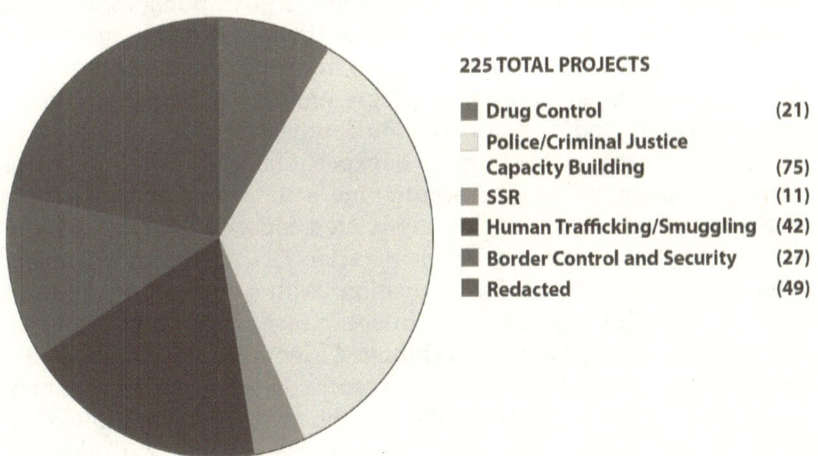

Likewise, the category of "security sector reform" (SSR) could – given its all-encompassing definition– include most of the programming, yet I have limited it to programming that works with security services (as opposed to police). To demonstrate how these projects were classified, consider the following examples: A contract ($511,462) with the UNODC to train over twenty Latin American police agencies on "computer-based NDS by enhancing [their] ability to collect data on domestic and international illicit drug transactions" was classified under drug control, not police capacity building. A contract ($1,595,813.96) with Interpol to "train officers responsible for international police cooperation … to combat transnational organized crime in the Americas" was categorized as policing. A $1,295,267.20 training program with six SEA region law-enforcement agencies (Cambodia, Indonesia, Laos, Thailand, Malaysia, and Vietnam) to "Prevent Human Smuggling through Training & Connectivity to Interpol Systems" was classified as human smuggling, not policing or border security. And a contract with the Organization of American States (OAS) ($1,236,966.25) for a "technical cooperation initiative to assist beneficiary States throughout Americas to comply with international document security standards & other best practices re: travel documents from International Civil Aviation Organization" was categorized as border security.

Despite some limitations, the figure illustrates major priorities of security development and has served as guide for my explorations of security aid practices. Moreover, I would stress that programming areas correspond with the threats from "places of interest." For example, the centrality of the drug war in the security strategies for Latin America has meant that programming in the region has been focused almost exclusively on policing, drug enforcement, and border security. Likewise, the human trafficking programming has been tied almost completely to Canadian security aid in Southeast Asia.

Figure 2.10 represents key areas of expertise and the focal points for the development of Canadian security innovation. In chapter 5, I argue that as the high priority of policing-related capacity building demonstrates, the mobilization of "policing sciences" has become a major avenue of Canadian security innovation. With significant overlaps in drug and mobility controls, a major component of the argument that I develop regarding "security techniques" demonstrates that policing-related capacity-building projects are central to the *integration* norm of the transversal security community. Aiming to integrate multiple countries into surveillance and policing webs, this avenue of "aid" has been highly productive in showcasing security innovation and advancing strategic interests, including but not limited to increasing the visibility of Canada as a norm-supporter of the United States (and other norm-makers), improving bilateral relations with recipient states, increasing support for Canadian security industries, raising Canadian visibility as a security innovator, and – perhaps most importantly – improving the reformatory practices to transform "deviant states" of the Global South into frontline police enforcement agencies in the "evolving global threat environment."

As the main hubs for security aid funding, the START-GPSF, CTCB, and ACCBP are bureaucracies of security expertise. As I argue in subsequent chapters, these bureaucracies are central in the management of developing security governance in the Global South. As hubs for information and management, they liaise between the many actors and spheres of security aid, and their expertise is as much in the management of (in)security knowledges as it is in the navigation of strategic interests. These hubs are pivotal for pairing security innovation with strategic interests, thereby making security aid a venue for Canadian positioning as a supporter of transversal security norms. Having mapped out the practices of the security aid funding hubs, now I turn towards the sphere of security innovators.

Security Innovators

I have defined security innovation as the tangible, concrete, and strategic ways in which knowledges of security are mobilized by Canada as a norm-supporter of the transversal security community. While norm-makers are typically characterized by their abilities to shape and control agendas of global government through "hard power" or normative framing of securitizing discourses, Canadian contributions to the normative imperatives of the transversal security community are provided through supportive practices and expertise of security innovators. As a norm-supporter, Canada does not set the agenda of global security, but contributes projects of security development that focus on infrastructures or techniques ("hardware" and "software") of security, as well as security interventions. The defining characteristic of security innovation is practicality. Security innovators support transversal security collaboration and development through practical, operational contributions. Though security hubs are also embedded within the framework of security innovation, I distinguish a separate sphere of practice where security innovators are principally responsible for the operational, practical "development" of security governance. Below, I explore the practices of two principal security innovators: the Department of National Defence and the Canadian Forces and the Canadian Commercial Corporation. I also include a third category that lists other security innovators who appear throughout this study, though in less central roles.

DND and the Canadian Forces

In the map depicting the three spheres of security aid (figure 2.1), the Department of National Defence (DND) and the Canadian Forces (CF) have been hyphenated because they cross the fluid frontier between the spheres of funding hubs and security innovators. While this conjoining of the bureaucracy (DND) and the military (CF) may offend those who invest heavily in the notion that each solitude has distinct chains of command and authorities, my purpose here is to simplify the explanation of how the Canadian military apparatus (DND-CF) makes significant contributions to both spheres of security aid.

Although DND-CF funds significantly more security aid than any other "hub," there are no definitive figures on the DND-CF's overall security aid funding, because there is a plurality of DND-CF security aid funds, documents are difficult to obtain from DND-CF, and there is no sorting category of security aid within Canadian bureaucracies. Though the availability of information on security aid spending has been very difficult to aggregate, I do present spending figures for DND-CF contributions, including a detailed case study with associated costs of the DND-CF human security intervention in Libya (chapter 3); costs associated with the broader DND-CF Middle East operations (chapter 4); costs involved in the DND-CF donations of "surplus gear" as a form of security infrastructures aid (chapter 5); and costs of the sophisticated Military Training and Coordination Program (below and chapter 5).

A principal guiding mechanism for DND-CF's engagement in transversal security governance is a relatively new doctrine known as the Global Engagement Strategy (GES). Formalized in 2011, the GES was developed through a whole-of-government-approach that attempted to harmonize DND-CF operations with other security hubs and innovators (notably GAC, RCMP, and PSC) to maximize the strategic value of security aid resources. An outline of the GES calls this coordination effort a means to provide "strategic-level guidance to defence international relations" (DND 2011-1137, 18). A primary emphasis of the GES is to create "economic opportunities" and expand "the projection of Canadian influence," primarily through partnerships with the United States. As the GES puts it, the framework "will assist in better connecting the strategic 'ends' and 'ways' with the 'means'" (DND 2011-1138, 47). Figure 2.11, from an internal presentation of the finalized GES to military officials, sets out five priority areas to focus "defence diplomacy resources" to support Canadian strategic interests.

The long-standing primary objective of DND-CF has been to further the close alliance with the United States, resulting in significant interoperability and an integrated defence industrial base in North America (Charbonneau and Cox 2008). However, the overall tone of the GES priorities demonstrates a shift to the "emerging global threat environment" that Major-General Rousseau addressed at the outset of this chapter. In many ways, the strategic trajectory of Canadian involvement is under the United States as a norm-maker. While some might characterize Canada's supportive role as strictly that of solidifying American hegemony (Gordon 2010; Klassen 2013), I would stress that the strategy of norm-supporting allows for supporting American normative power,

Figure 2.11. Outline of the Global Engagement Strategy (DND 2011-1137, 3)

GES Priorities

1. Contribute to the defence of Canada and North America with primary emphasis on partnership with the United States
2. Contribute to whole-of-government efforts in international peace and security
3. Privilege and deepen relationships with key allies
4. Establish and enhance developing defence partnerships in the Americas and with emerging powers; focus on operations and developing capabilities
5. Leadership abroad on issues significant to Canadian and international security interests

FOR OFFICIAL USE ONLY 12

as well as pursuing distinct strategic interests in developing bilateral and multilateral relationships between Canadian security agencies and their counterparts in recipient countries. This GES focus on "operations and developing capabilities" in the Global South corresponds to the broader strategic interests of providing direct development assistance to deviant states within the transversal security community.

The GES is supported by the DND-CF "toolbox," which can "involve a broad spectrum of international activities by the Defence Team," including high-level engagement and visits, the creation of formal defence cooperation agreements, international personnel placements, placement of Canadian defence attachés in embassies and other strategic locations, ship and aircraft visits, joint exercises, and capacity-building initiatives (DND 2011-1138, 1). These activities are supported by the military – the largest department of the Canadian government and second-largest employers in the country – and benefit from the formal Canadian diplomatic channels as well as exclusive military networks.

A major security aid component of the GES is the Military Training and Cooperation Program (MTCP), a capacity-building project focused on the Global South. As a program run through DND-CF, the explicit purpose of the MTCP is to provide military training and education programs to "developing," non-NATO member countries. As one briefing note to the minister of national defence outlined, the MTCP "seeks to work with 'like-minded' countries to achieve common objectives and works exclusively with developing countries" (DND 2014-708, 1). With an annual budget of $20 million, the program's objective is to work towards "building governance capacities of member countries" that are "consistent with DND's Global Engagement Strategy" (ibid.). Although originally created in the 1960s, the renewed MTCP program was made official in April 2014 and explicitly situated within the whole-of-government approach (DND 2013-1523). After extensive consultations between DND and GAC, along with CIDA and PSC, the MTCP was reformed to "expand and reinforce Canada's bilateral defence relations with countries around the world and promote Canada's national profile on the world stage" (ibid., 2).

Reforms to program spending included a reorientation of regional priorities and included increased funding to the Pacific region (coming from withdrawn funding from Eastern Europe). The current regional breakdown for MTCP spending has Africa and the Middle East at 25 per cent, the Americas at 30 per cent, Asia-Pacific at 25 per cent, and Europe at 20 per cent. Since the reorientation of the program, the

MTCP has been increasingly focused on "strategic engagements." This includes greater attention and more funding to strategic allies, as well as efforts to have more comprehensive training programs. One note written for the minister of defence outlined that new "activities will shift to a 'train-sustain' model with emphasis on capacity building outside Canada [OUTCAN]. [MTCP] made clear that this will not consist of 'drive-by' capacity building, but long-term embedded OUTCAN activities. DMTC will begin planning for the FY13–14 Tool Box in early 2012" (DND 2014-708, 4). The objective of the strategic reorientation, argues another note, is that "the Program allows for greater interoperability, burden sharing, and access/influence in countries of strategic relevance" (ibid., 1). As a component for integrating "deviant states" in the Global South, the security innovators with DND-CF look towards "strategic" engagements – as opposed to "drive-by" training – as a means to enhance the coordinated efforts of the transversal security community.

Reformed in concert with the guiding principles of the GES, the MTCP has placed an emphasis on the Pacific region. Yet their engagement with Latin America represents a longer-standing "place of interest" for Canada to develop security regimes. In referencing a recent push to develop programs with Guatemala, one document references that "The MTCP remains DND/CAF's primary tool for engagement in Central America" (DND 2013-702, 2). Canada has numerous capacity-building programs with countries in Latin America and the Caribbean including Colombia, Jamaica, Peru, Guatemala, and Belize. A press release prepared for Prime Minister Harper's visit to Peru (Canada 2014) outlines that, since the MTCP's inception in the 1960s, more than 4,400 "candidates" from Latin America and the Caribbean have received training.

While a significant element of the MTCP training portfolio is focused on anti-terrorism training (particularly in Asia), DND-CF programming in Latin America – like the security aid hubs – is focused almost exclusively upon the U.S.-driven "war on drugs." With the "war on drugs" increasingly conflated with the "war on terror," it is an important site to illustrate the collapsing divides between "internal" and "external" threats. Though the "war on drugs" has a long history of military involvement, that involvement has nonetheless been governed through crime control, border management, and criminal law. This mixing of "external" and "internal" is particularly evident in Canada's large contribution to Operation Caribbe.

Operation Caribbe is a multinational counter-drug program in the Gulf of Mexico and the Caribbean in which Canada has been involved since 2005–6 (DND 2013-702, 28). Directed by the U.S.-led Joint Interagency Task Force–South to detect and interdict drug trafficking, Canada has participated in the mission for "both domestic security and foreign policy objectives" (DND 2011-914, 3). As a security innovator, Canada's contribution has been to provide surveillance assistance, which has included "maritime patrol aircraft and maritime surface and sub-surface assets for counter-drug surveillance and support" (DND 2011-914, 4). To give a sense of the scope of the mission, the 2010 deployment featured four navy vessels – HMCS *Algonquin*, HMCS *Protecteur*, HMCS *Toronto*, and HMCS *Vancouver* – that would have involved over 1,000 sailors. As an example of the integrated approach of security governance, Op Caribbe has included a MoU between DND-CF and the U.S. Coast Guard "to permit USCG Law Enforcement Detachments (LEDETs) to operate from CF vessels and aircraft" (ibid.). The MoU allows LEDETS to operate on Canadian vessels and engage in arrests and interdictions over the course of the missions. Like the communications strategies used by DND-CF in Op Artemis (discussed in chapter 3), these operations are frequently used to generate media coverage in Canada promoting DND-CF's contribution to the drug war.

Op Caribbe is one of many programs used by DND-CF security innovators to develop interoperability and cooperation on transversal threats. DND-CF security aid has pursued multiple avenues to enhance hemispheric capacities to monitor movements. For example, DND-CF funded "IT requirements of the US SOUTHCOM-led Operations and Training building project in Belize" (DND 2013-702, 2). For this project, US SOUTHCOM – the principal node for the U.S. drug war – funded the security aid for the physical construction of Joint Operations Centre in Belize, while Canada funded the IT requirements. A parallel security aid funding agreement was made with SOUTHCOM for a Joint Operations Centre in Jamaica in 2011. As intelligence hubs are integrated through the region, a Canadian briefing note emphasized that the "CJOC support to the establishment of Jamaican and Belizean Joint Operation Centres will be an important step in the standardization of regional operation centres" (ibid.). Using security aid, Canada has developed a (relatively) robust "toolbox" to provide innovative and practical improvements towards increasing mobility and surveillance controls in Latin America. Under the trajectory designed by the GES, security aid programs demonstrate Canadian support for a broader normative agenda of "hemispheric" governance, while also adding to the visibility of Canadian security innovators as reliable and creative partners.

A major component of raising the Canadian profile "on the security stage" is promotion of practical security innovation through "defence diplomacy" and bilateral relations. Canada has recently attempted to increase its formal defence agreements by signing MoUs with countries outside NATO, particularly those in Latin America. The underlining rationale for the MoUs is to promote Canadian security innovation through security aid trainings and the provision of security hardware. A recent MoU with Peru details intentions to cooperate "in various areas, including defence policy, research, development and production, search and rescue, and military training" (DND 2013-169, 1). A briefing note to the minister also highlights that "it is anticipated that this MoU will lead to commercial opportunities for Canadian industry" (ibid.). Likewise, the 2012 MoU with Colombia underlines that "Colombia is an increasingly important economic partner for Canada and has been identified as a priority country in both the Government's Americas Strategy and the DND/CF Global Engagement Strategy" (DND 2013-169, 12). MoUs often complement the security techniques training offered through the MTCP.

Having its own domain of diplomatic activity, DND-CF can host high-level visits to facilitate more intimate partnerships. This is especially evident in Latin America, where Canadian military officials have participated in numerous multilateral initiatives, including recent participation in the U.S.-sponsored Mexico/Guatemala/Belize Cross Border Workshops. According to DND, "These workshops are a means of gaining situational awareness of regional military problems and concerns with the aim of finding *concrete solutions*" (DND 2013-702, 5; emphasis added). Underlining how Canadian security innovation focuses on tangible contributions to transversal policing, notes on Canada COM's second participation in the Mexico/Belize Cross Border Workshop explained that "this iteration of the syndicate based workshop focused on surveillance in the sea, land and air domains" (80).

Key components of Canada's high-level trips are efforts to develop relationships using the MTCP so that Canadian security innovators can establish ties directly. While under the umbrella of U.S.-driven hemispheric processes, security aid can form a gateway for other security innovators to engage with non-U.S. bilateral counterparts. For example, one Canadian Forces document describes how "the CF could play a valuable role as a conduit for connecting Cdn OGDs [other government departments] with MEX, GTM [Guatemala] and BLZ [Belize] militaries and other departments, thereby providing a bridge to Cdn OGDs for their leadership of Cdn engagement in region" (DND 2013-702, 29). The document goes on to detail how the Canadian Forces can work as "a critical enabler for cooperation in the region … [to establish] information sharing agreements and protocols, first between militaries, then among all whole-of-government partners" (30). Here, the embedding of DND-CF within the whole-of-government approach demonstrates how military assets and diplomatic functions are integrated into security governance. Though the military makes up a central role, I would suggest that an understanding of the DND-CF practices as security innovators must foreground the collapsing of an "external" military threat that would reposition the activities of the "military" as themselves aspects of "policing" (Neocleous 2011, 2014).

In exploring a broad spectrum of contributions from DND-CF, I have emphasized their role as security innovators within a transversal theatre of global threats (see also Monaghan 2016). As a "central enabler" within the whole-of-government approach, DND-CF offers an extensive portfolio of assistance programs, all of which illustrate the practical, tangible character of Canadian security innovation. Now, I turn to another prominent security innovator: the Canadian Commercial Corporation.

CCC: Canadian Commercial Corporation

I discuss CCC in further detail in chapter 4, characterizing them as merchants of security. Here, I want to provide a brief introduction to map out CCC's security innovation within the Canadian security aid regime. CCC is a Crown corporation that manages government-to-government security and defence procurements. In the most general sense, CCC is the government agency that facilitates military purchases from foreign government buyers by representing domestic (Canadian) defence and security corporations. Most of its activities (approximately 80–85 per cent) are focused on getting contracts for Canadian companies with the U.S. military.[18] During the 2013–14 fiscal year, CCC

18 Since 1952, arms trading between Canada and the United States has been administered through the Defence Production Sharing Agreement (DPSA), which grants exclusive status to CCC as an intermediary. As an agreement to coordinate a cooperative landscape for the defence industrial sector in North America, the DPSA has been the major factor sustaining arms development in Canada.

facilitated $1.1 billion in commercial transactions (down from $1.8 billion in 2012–13 and $2.2 billion in 2011–12), and claims to support over 18,300 defence-related jobs in Canada (CCC 2014, 22, 4). CCC operates from an annual parliamentary allotment of approximately $15 million, and also charges administrative fees for contracts. Technically a non-profit Crown agency, CCC articulates a strong commitment to market discourses as, ironically, companies wanting to sell to the U.S. military are required to do business through the CCC monopoly. On the global stage, CCC is an unusual entity. As far as I know, Spain is the only other government to have a specialized CCC-like department (called Isdefe).

As a mercantilist entity, CCC acts as a merchant for Canadian security innovation by leveraging government resources to promote the technologies and services of Canadian corporations. In addition to U.S. contracts, CCC facilitates defence and security business across the world. Since the economic downturn, it has made numerous efforts to expand to emerging markets in the Global South. CCC works in approximately sixty to seventy countries (CCC 2012, 2013, 2014) to distribute defence and security products made by several hundred Canadian companies. Countries listed under the sales to "Allies and like-minded Nations" include some NATO countries, but many are global hotspots with even more dubious human rights records than Canada and its "Allies." CCC's list of "like-minded" allies includes Saudi Arabia, Ghana, Colombia, Kenya, Haiti, Ecuador, Peru, and Kyrgyzstan, among others. Most recently, CCC has received critical media attention for their $14 billion contract to export Canadian-made Light Armoured Vehicles (LAV) – produced by General Dynamics Land Systems Canada in London, Ontario – to support the Armoured Brigades Program in Saudi Arabia.[19] Lauding the "largest trade deal in Canadian history," the chair of CCC's Board of Directors commented that the arms deal with Saudi Arabia "was a truly

19 Given the prominent discussions of corporate social responsibility within CCC, it is worth highlighting some of their discussions involving arms sales in the Middle East. The year before the Arab Spring, CCC (2011, 23) reported on business assumptions for the Middle Eastern contracts: "Relative stability within the Middle East and a high demand for security and defence goods and services would lead to a number of high value contracts in the short term." The subsequent year, CCC (19) reported, "CCC's global defence and security sales were significantly impacted by the budget constraints of foreign governments and the lingering effects of the Arab Spring in the Middle East, which have resulted in longer timelines for CCC contracts to materialize in key markets."

extraordinary event for our country and I could not be more proud of the Corporation in this monumental achievement" (CCC 2014, 13). CCC has also facilitated the $65 million sale of twenty-four LAVs to Colombia (CCC 2013, 2). In the 2014 annual report that details the Saudi LAV deal, there is no mention of human rights concerns, related to either Saudi Arabia – accusations of human rights abuses are not hard to find – or any other trading partner. As I discuss in chapter 4, CCC operates in a distinct realm of "security innovation." While the security innovators within security development are completely embedded in an operational environment concerned with (in)security, development, capacity absorptions, and governance indicators, CCC operates under exclusive rationalities of profits and economic wealth. It is worth emphasizing that, as a Crown corporation, CCC makes no "profit." Surpluses accrued from year to year are kept in government coffers, not paid out to investors or owners. Despite its existence as a centrally planned, state-subsidized, government entity, CCC adopts the identity of a free-market, capitalist entity. While the corporation does not make profit, the actors within CCC have interpolated the free market identities of the security corporations in which they serve.

Although the principal business transactions of CCC are traditional arms sales, the corporation provides two important forms of security aid: indirect and direct. The category of indirect security aid refers to the Crown corporation's outreach agenda that includes research, an extensive networking schedule, and a wide range of promotional and marketing techniques to encourage foreign governments to buy Canadian security technologies. To expand beyond the DPSA, CCC has developed "proactive exporter and country strategies and targeted priority markets, such as Colombia, Peru, the Middle East and Ghana where it could be most effective in influencing future export sales for Canadian exporters" (CCC 2012, 23). CCC's indirect subsidization of Canadian security corporations is substantial. As CCC describes it, "[CCC] offers its exporter and foreign government buyer clients a suite of services, including prime contracting, procurement planning and strategy development, solicitation development and bidding, supplier selection, contract negotiations, performance monitoring, right through to project close-out" (CCC 2010, 8). Advantages accrued through such indirect support – much of which parallels the enormous system of corporate welfare that defines the military-industrial complex – similar to what Ball and Snider (2013) detail as the "surveillance industrial complex" – are tremendous.

Through an effective bureaucracy that works through public and private channels, CCC is an important node of security innovation. While its primary influence is in supporting sales to the U.S. military, the Crown corporation is increasingly targeting the Global South to increase Canadian exports. Through its extensive support system, CCC provides assistance to Canadian corporations in procuring contracts, yet these types of direct foreign state contracts are only one element of CCC's contribution to security development. A larger contribution is through *direct* security aid, which became more formalized in 2007 when the CCC signed an MoU with GAC to become a procurement agent for the security aid hubs. Coinciding with CCC's business strategy to expand to developing markets, the MoU has allowed for a significant growth in "procurement services for federal government departments to support their international aid programs" (CCC 2010, 5).

Procurement services of security aid move through several stages: Through consultation, a security-sector issue within a developing country is highlighted as a priority. Canadian agencies (and typically a politician) announce "aid" funding for such-and-such a crime-reduction strategy or reconstruction effort; or support for such-and-such a peacekeeping commitment, or border-enhancement project, or anything presented under the humanitarian sentiments of security, development, and democracy. Then a Canadian security aid hub makes the aid funding available. However, the funding does not go to the developing country. Instead, funds are dispersed to CCC, who then contracts with a corporation (often, though not exclusively, Canadian) to provide the goods to the recipient government. The recipient government gets the security products as "in-kind" donations and, with little fanfare, the corporations that specialize in security and surveillance technologies get the "aid" funding with a "fee" going to CCC for their administration of the development assistance. This is the political economy of security aid, and millions of Canadian "aid" dollars are administered through these steps every year.

Since signing the MoU with GAC in 2007, CCC has facilitated an impressive list of security aid to "places of interest." Documents from the START-GPSF from 2007 to 2011 show at least forty contract payments with CCC totalling at least $83.6 million.[20] Donations were sent

20 Compiled from GAC 2011-1370; GAC 2011-1371; GAC 2011-1372; GAC 2011-1373; GAC 2011-1374.

to Pakistan, Afghanistan, Haiti, Senegal, Uganda, and to Sudan, which received the largest donation, worth $42.7 million for an undisclosed construction project. Though many of the recipients' police and security forces, such as those that I detail in Haiti (chapter 4), have been documented as frequent human rights violators, one would never get the impression from CCC reports that the in-kind donation of security commodities would damage human rights practices. Unlike reporting requirements in other security aid-providing jurisdictions – such as the United Kingdom and the United States – Canadian companies and their government representatives at CCC have no reporting or monitoring oversights built into these donated security and military products. Despite having no bearing on the post-contract use of the goods, CCC nonetheless presents itself as a noble model of corporate social responsibility (CSR) (see, for example, CCC 2009, 7). Notwithstanding CCC's repetitive claims about its CSR practices, the nature of its services within the defence and security industries – combined with its non-existent monitoring of human rights practices associated with the millions of dollars of security materials – gives ample weight to Banerjee's (2008, 52) claim that despite the "emancipatory rhetoric, discourses of corporate citizenship, social responsibility ... are defined by narrow business interests and serve to curtail interests of external stakeholders." In providing direct security aid, CCC plays a crucial role in building security infrastructures that are effective and tangible. In addition to advancing private economic interests, this form of security innovation contributes to broader strategies of Canadian norm-supporting by raising the profile of Canadian know-how as well as the reputation of Canadian security aid bureaucracies in providing reliable and concrete support for global security development. Given trends in transversal security governance, the role of providing Canadian technologies and hardware through "aid" funds will likely increase. I provide further analysis of these trends, in particular CCC's "market focus" in the Global South (chapter 4), yet this field remains in need of far more exploratory research and critical attention.

Other Canadian Security Innovators (RCMP, CSC, CBSA, PSC)

Other security innovators contribute to Canadian support for development of transversal security governance. Many are discussed in this book, most notably the RCMP, CSC, and the CBSA, all of which have – as I quoted in the last chapter – become "contractors" to the security aid hubs.

Perhaps the most prominent contractor is Canada's federal police force, the RCMP. Though the RCMP do not have a formal budget line for security "assistance," they receive significant funding from the security aid hubs to develop security techniques in "recipient" countries. Like other security innovators, the funding for security aid is not, in fact, transferred to "recipient" countries but transferred to the budgets of Canadian security agencies. These agencies then provide in-kind services to develop the security governance capacities of the recipient countries, with the broader objective of integration and coordination on transversal security collaborations. To describe the practices of the RCMP's security innovation, we can divide between two general approaches to their development of security techniques. The most comprehensive approach stems from long-term commitments to specific international deployments; the other provides immediate training or expertise for short-term projects funded by the security aid hubs.

As security innovators under the rubric of international deployments, RCMP officers are embedded within multinational forces to provide stabilization support, civil policing functions, and training programs in hotspots. The RCMP's International Peace Operations (IPO) bureau commits officers through a Canadian Police Arrangement (CPA), which acts as a partnership between GAC, Public Safety Canada, and the RCMP. CPAs also allow for regional and municipal forces to contribute members to peace operations, as demonstrated by several forces – such as Toronto Police, Durham Police, Montreal Police, and the Ontario Provincial Police – sending officers to Afghanistan.[21] Since the inception of the CPA program in 1989, over 3,000 Canadian police have served on close to sixty peace operations around the world.[22] As of January 2014, there were seven CPA missions – Afghanistan, Côte d'Ivoire (UNOCI), Democratic Republic of the Congo (MONUSCO), Haiti (MINUSTAH), South Sudan, Sudan (UNAMID), and the West Bank (EUPOL COPPS) – comprising approximately 150 officers.

In addition to long-term contributions to international deployments, the RCMP make a wide range of short-term contributions to programs funded by the security aid hubs. Along with training, the

21 For example, see Durham Police FOI 2011-331; Toronto Police FOI; RCMP 2011-2021; OPP CSCS-2011-1447; and Montreal Police FOI 11-570.

22 RCMP IPO maintain a tally of their international deployments online; see "International Peace Operations," http://www.rcmp-grc.gc.ca/po-mp/index-eng.htm.

RCMP regularly contribute their security expertise in conducting "needs assessments" to support the programming of security aid hubs. Needs assessments are small "aid" projects that assess the policing or border capabilities of receiving countries. Assessments can range from small projects, like $16,488.95 for the RCMP to evaluate Guatemalan security sector reform plans, to very comprehensive projects, such as a project authorized between 2009 and 2011 in Turks and Caicos for $352,040. In most cases, needs assessments are the first stage in larger security development projects. For example, the Turks and Caicos project was combined with a subsequent RCMP capacity-building project on security sector reform, valued at an additional $600,000, followed by a Department of Justice project to aimed at "strengthening the justice sector" for $346,027.

As a security innovator within both long-term and short-term frameworks of security development programming, the RCMP are a central agency for developing security techniques to advance the knowledge practices of criminal justice systems and enhance the structures of security-related agencies across the Global South. In particular, RCMP capacity-building programming advances the objectives of the transversal security community to "professionalize" and integrate policing agencies of the Global South into transversal networks of surveillance and security governance. As I present in chapter 5, this is most evident in the detailed case study on security aid to Southeast Asia and the broad scope of training offered by the RCMP.

Several other Canadian departments engage in security development as security innovators. In a role similar to that of the RCMP, these departments and agencies mobilize their expertise to engage in capacity building in the field. In addition to being tasked as security innovators within programming from the security aid hubs, many of these departments have international branches, which regularly coordinate security aid under the whole-of-government approach. In particular, Public Safety Canada participates in dozens of forums, working groups, and networks that share "best practices" with other governments. A prominent example of PSC activity in the transnational field is their role in the Roma-Lyon Group (RLG) (see Scherrer 2009; and also Monaghan 2015a). While Canadian participation is far less influential than that of norm-makers (such as the United States), Canada's contributions to the RLG are a dynamic effort to situate Canada within the G8 security community. Providing a venue for Canadian security experts to engage with Western allies (possibly with the exclusion of Russia), transnational networks like the RLG offer a showcase for the innovative features of the Canadian risk bureaucracy. Borrowing from Beck (1992), Heng and McDonagh (2011, 316–17) have used the term *risk bureaucracies* to depict how governments have directed increasing resources towards "forecasting and developing risk-based guidelines to regulate and manage risks." For scholars of security governance, the analysis of transversal risk bureaucracies can demonstrate how experts aim to enhance their own power and institutional currency by showcasing their knowledge of new threats, as well as their techniques and technologies for combating them (Bigo 2008; Hoijtink 2014). Showcasing security expertise within a transnational framework can build prestige, as well as rationalize security budgets for further work. Given Canada's place as a secondary and often marginal actor within the global arena, the exposure from security innovators – however provisional – within this transnational network serves to showcase a practical, norm-supporting commitment.

In addition to Canadian participation in the RLG, there are other notable security bureaucracies that support the transversal security community. The Canadian Security Intelligence Service (CSIS) – which is also under the ministerial authority of PSC – is a leading actor within international and transnational networks. As Canada's primary human intelligence agency, CSIS has been active in the Global Futures Forum, which is an important venue for norm-makers to advance best practices in security governance (see CSIS 2012-194). Communications Security Establishment Canada (CSEC), Canada's signals intelligence agency overseen by DND, has also been a prominent international actor, particularly as a member of the Five Eyes community. Following a number of Snowden revelations, it has become evident that CSEC supports several of the U.S. National Security Agency's global dataveillance projects.[23]

Canada's border security agency – the CBSA – has an active international department that engages in a wide range of technical assistance projects, which I discuss empirically vis-à-vis Haiti (chapter 4), border-policing capacity building in Southeast Asia (chapter 5), as well as efforts to support the Palestinian Authority border management plan (Monaghan 2016; see CBSA 2010-1481; CBSA 2010-4262). Correctional Services Canada (CSC) and the Department of Justice (DoJ)

23 Leaksource maintains a catalogue of CSEC-related Snowden records at https://leaksource.wordpress.com/category/csec/.

International Legal Programs Section (ILPS) are other active security innovators, which are discussed in this book.

Finally, Canadian security aid is also notable for its funding of transnational security innovators. In the mapping of security aid, I have included both non-governmental organizations (NGOs) and inter-governmental agencies (IGOs) in the sphere of security innovator. Though these agencies are quite different in their objectives and political influences – with international agencies being far more subject to the influence of state actors, and NGOs less so – they are both situated within the sphere of security innovation, since they are prominent implementing partners of security aid. Though my empirical research has focused on the role of public agencies, it is important to include NGOs and IGOs on the map of security aid, as they are prominent implementing partners. Like security innovators from public bureaucracies, these agents can also be characterized by their practical, tangible contributions. Yet they have fundamental distinctions. NGOs, for example, are not fundamentally bound within the state-centrism of entities like the RCMP, CCC, or DND-CF. Though many critics have pointed to the role of NGOs in supporting the broader objectives of states that fund them, my research project has not included an exploration of these entities, though I do agree that this research should be undertaken.

It is, however, worth noting the significance of IGOs in the delivery of security aid, particularly since "recipients" rarely receive funding themselves. Security aid hubs distribute funds to hundreds of third-party recipients and, in a recent trend, even these implementing partners are increasingly "bunkered" away from the populations they intend to assist (Duffield 2012). Though increasingly removed from the local population, these implementing partners are the foreign experts who carry out programs that "assist" recipients under a regime of improvement designed by the donor community. Security aid is structured by the same dynamic. Take, for example, a compilation of 555 projects funded by the CTCB (431 from 2005 to 2013) and the ACCBP (124 from 2009 to 2013).[24] Of these 555 projects, only 3 sent funding to "recipient" governments (a fourth, as noted above, funds Colombia to conduct counter-insurgency training in Central America). Recipient governments do receive assistance, but it is almost exclusively in

24 Compiled from GAC 2011-1380.

technologies and techniques that are provided by international organizations, NGOs, or other Canadian departments. By far the largest "recipient" of funds are other Canadian security innovators. For example, an examination of 555 ACCBP and CTCB contracts from 2007 to 2013 reveals that the largest recipient has been the RCMP, with at least 58 projects valued at $13,921,340.36. However, IGOs play a significant role as well. Surpassing any other "recipient" of security aid, for example, is the UNODC, which was funded for 40 projects over that period valued at $30,470,636.18. Another significant IGO security innovator is the International Organization for Migration (IOM), receiving 11 projects valued at $548,156.77. Much of the funding to these organizations is directed to the drug war in Latin America and migration policing in Southeast Asia. The IOM has also received START-GPSF funds for the security aid projects in Haiti (chapter 4). While I map out aspects of the roles played by these IGOs, it remains an under-explored element of my research. Indeed, Pickering and Weber (2013, 94) have argued that intersections of security and development "have created significant opportunities for the expansion of social control by individual agencies." Future work will expand on their place in the security aid apparatus and will benefit from a strong and growing body of critical scholarship on these entities in security development regimes.

Conclusion(s)

Mapping bureaucracies that engage in security aid is an exploratory process. There are numerous barriers for properly illustrating the web of actors involved. Barriers include the difficulty in gaining access to spending figures; navigating myriad projects, programs, or task forces that lack a central registry; and the secrecy protections that are typical of international affairs (and national security in particular). But perhaps the largest barrier is "security aid's" lack of categorical certainty. Security aid is not a fixed or defined entity within policy or governance circles. As a development assistance regime, it has emerged as a set of practices from numerous separate actors and institutions. What I have presented above is only a sketch of these Canadian bureaucracies, though still an expansive mosaic demonstrating the agencies and geographies engaged by security aid practices.

In providing the categories of security aid hubs and security innovators, I trace a division of labour within Canadian expertise in security development. Hubs mobilize strategic knowledge of international relations, diplomacy, risk management, and managerial sciences. They are the information workers of security development, who shepherd the knowledge practices of Canadian security governance into strategic contributions to support the normative, integrationist imperatives of the transversal security community. Working in conjunction with the security aid hubs are the security innovators. As the practitioners of Canadian security innovation, these experts mobilize technical knowledge practices to develop security in recipient countries. These security innovators make the practical contributions of capacity building, training, and enhancing the abilities of "recipient" counties in the Global South.

In examining the practices of security aid, I contribute to security governance studies by suggesting that activities of security bureaucracies – and not the pronouncements of political officials – are important sites for understanding how governance practices "travel" (Melossi, Sozzo, and Sparks 2011; Salter 2010; Scherrer 2009). Acting as "travelling technocrats" (Larner and Laurie 2010), experts in Canada's security aid bureaucracies have practical engagement in the transversal security community. These engagements involve trading in security/insecurity knowledge and providing practical "development" reforms that enhance the coordination of security within deviant states of in the Global South. Having mapped out many of the prominent actors and institutions that narrate the practices of Canadian security aid, I turn to detailed case studies that demonstrate Canadian security aid contributions under the three types of intervention, infrastructures, and techniques.

Chapter Three

Security Interventions: Policing the Transversal

Introducing Security Aid Type 1: Security Interventions

Canada joined the U.S.-led coalition of states in the bombing campaign against ISIL in Iraq and Syria in the summer of 2014. Announced amid growing anxiety and media reports of the potential genocide of the Yazidi peoples in northern Iraq, Canada's decision to join the war effort against ISIL was framed in humanitarian sentiments and received widespread public support. Canada's initial contribution to the war, announced in late August 2014 (Operation Impact), was cautious: Canada would commit only to using Royal Canadian Air Force (RCAF) capacities (one CC-177 Globemaster III strategic airlifter and a CC-130J Hercules transport aircraft) to deliver military equipment – donated by Albania – to unnamed security forces in Iraq. Described as providing "critical aid" for security forces fighting terrorism (see Prime Minister's Office 2014), Canada's initial contribution of security aid was supplemented with a more robust six-month commitment of six RCAF fighter jets and 600 support personnel in October 2014 (Campion-Smith 2015). By 14 January 2015, Royal Canadian Air Force aircraft had flown 335 missions since operations began in late October, including 214 sorties by CF-18s, and the mission was extended for another year in March 2015. The Harper government also announced that it would send sixty-nine Special Forces to "advise and assist" Kurdish security forces in Iraq. And in January 2015, it was learned that those Special Forces had been engaged in front-line firefights in addition to ground-level target spotting for the coalition's aerial campaign against ISIL. In the fall of 2015, after the election into office of the Liberals, who had campaigned on ending the war, the air campaign was terminated but replaced with an increased level of ground-level Special Forces and tactical air support. Though criticisms of the obvious "mission creep" have appeared in the media, the intervention in Iraq continues to draw widespread public support. Moreover, it is rarely described as a war, almost always referred to as humanitarian assistance and providing security against terrorism.[1]

A number of scholars have noted that international military campaigns have increasingly been conceptualized as *policing* practices (Agamben 2000; Bronson 2002; Dean 2006; Dubber 2006; Hardt and Negri 2000; Holmqvist 2014; Neocleous 2011, 2104). Some have developed the notion of "policekeeping" to stress the movement of militaries towards policing functions (Day and Freeman 2003; Dubber 2006). As an expression of the transversal security community, military interventions as policing practices are characterizable through their legitimization as humanitarian governance, a view that the "targets" of the interventions are criminals and thereby conceptualized as crime-control endeavours, not as wars. Nor are the interventions contextualized to geo-political ambitions; they are only immediate "assistance" deployments to protect civilians against security threats (such as potential genocide). In describing the military intervention against ISIL in humanitarian terms, media or government accounts of the interventions are always disconnected from a large context of recent Canadian military activities. In fact, unmentioned in much of the discussion of the ISIL mission is that Iraq is the fifth state in the past ten years in which Canada has engaged in a military intervention on the grounds of providing security aid. In all these cases, the logic of security interventions has been *preventative* and focused on establishing order, as opposed to a traditional military logic of defence and defeat. Given that policing is itself a notion associated with internal (domestic) governance (Dean 2006), *security interventions* illustrate how practices of the transversal security community, grounded in humanitarian reason, seek to intervene from within and reform recalcitrant states of the Global South.

As the first type of security aid, an exploration of security interventions places an emphasis on the role of the military as security innovators. As I detail below, "interventions" are not exclusively bombing

1 Canada's motion in the House of Commons to authorize the mission is an excellent illustration of the twinned invocation of security and humanitarianism. See Canadian Press (2015).

campaigns or occupations, but include a broad field of activities falling under the Department of Defence's Global Engagement Strategy (GES) discussed in chapter 2. Administered under the GES, activities of "military diplomacy" are a series of mechanisms to advance Canadian norm-supporting strategic interests – particularly vis-à-vis working with the United States as the norm-maker – to develop more robust, coordinated, and interoperable policing and surveillance practices. Engaging with debates on security governance and international affairs, the category of security interventions demonstrates how contemporary invocations of "security" and "aid" are channelled as policing operations within the transversal security community.

This chapter analyses how security discourses – particularly human security and the "responsibility to protect" – have become central enablers of interventions throughout broad geographies of (in)security (Morrissey 2011; Rotmann, Kurtz, and Brockmeier 2014). Canada has made a significant contribution to the intellectual project of human security (MacLean, Black, and Shaw 2006) – a testament to Canada's security innovation – and this chapter explores Canadian norm-supporting through a case study of the security intervention in Libya. The security intervention in Libya is particularly illustrative for three reasons. First, the intervention was the first use of R2P as a legal and moral instrument to depose a functioning government, making it an exemplary case for transversal security interventions. Second, the Canadian involvement in Libya illustrates Canada's norm-supporting role – it was a small and technically oriented contribution – and, above all, demonstrates the prioritization of Canadian strategic interests. Third, the security aid regime in Libya shifted quickly into a broader regional commitment of security innovation, specifically through a practical norm-supporting role in the Combined Maritime Forces that police shipping lanes from the Pacific, through the Middle East, to Suez (known as the International Recommended Transit Corridor [IRTC]). In a significant case study of Canadian contributions to the aspirational designs of the transversal security community, I underline how security innovators provided strategic and tangible support in surveillance and maritime policing to enhance cooperative security governance in the region.

The chapter provides an overview of the human security agenda, before detailing Canada's security aid mission in Libya. I use empirical analysis of the Libya intervention to detail its humanitarian rationale and its relation to the practices of the transversal security community. I stress that the type of intervention classified as security aid is also a "gateway" for the two other types of infrastructure and techniques assistance. Detailing how the security intervention in Libya also functions as a gateway for broader practices of the transversal security community – specifically examining Canada's contribution to the Combined Maritime Forces under Operation Artemis – this chapter illustrates the tremendous scope of security aid practices in fulfilling the aspirations of transversal security governance.

The Human Security Agenda and Security Interventions

Debates about "human security" tend to oscillate between "narrow" or "broad" conceptualizations (Burgess and Owen 2004; Chandler 2012; Martin and Owen 2010). Yet most advocates agree that the significant influence in academic and policy areas has arisen from the expansive definition given to "security." Extending beyond boundaries established during the Cold War, advocates of the human security agenda tend to apply its mandate to a wide range of economic, social, civil and political rights (Kaldor 2007). Expressed often as a "value-based approach" to international relations, the agenda's significant contribution has been to foreground the rights-based values of the individual while backgrounding the normative absolutism of state sovereignty. In conjunction with transformations to NATO's "out of area norm" (see Kitchen 2009; 2010a; Koschut 2014), norm-makers of the transversal security community (overlapping with the NATO security community, as well as the more exclusive transatlantic security community) have normalized a conditional and fragmented status of state sovereignty over "security."

Critics of the human security agenda have persistently noted that it represents a "liberal problematic of security," which rationalizes Western intervention under language of state failure, the "responsibility to protect" (R2P), and the protection of civilians (Duffield 2008; Rotmann, Kurtz, and Brockmeier 2014; see also Laffey and Nadarajah 2012; Taylor 2009). While most critics support the underlying calls for human rights and dignity of the populations facing peril, they nonetheless critique the ambiguity and flexibility of the concept (Bellamy and McDonald 2002; Buzan 2004) as well as the motives of Western countries who manage the international interventions under the human security agenda (Chandler 2012). While academic debates have vacillated between more narrow conceptions of human security under the rubric of "freedom from fear" (which often call for immediate coercive actions in the name of global civil society; see Kaldor 2003) to frameworks promoting "freedom from want" (which borrow a broader focus of ensuring material and social resources; see Martin and Owen 2010; Watson 2011), critics have argued that the human security agenda has been constructed and deployed by the Global North in ways that are tied to – and perpetuate – political and economic interests. Martin and Owen (2010, 211) have argued that broad, more holistic conceptions of human security have "all but vanished" in the face of the militarized (i.e., narrow) versions of R2P now dominating the international arena, including within the United Nations.

R2P was first formulated in a 2001 report by the International Commission on Intervention and State Sovereignty (ICISS). Funded by the Canadian government, the ICISS reframed sovereignty as contingent rather than absolute, applying a burden of *responsibility* on both states to protect their populations from mass atrocities, as well as expecting the "international community" (e.g., norm-makers) to protect vulnerable populations when states fail to do so. Spearheaded by what Welsh (2012, 293) refers to as "norm entrepreneurs," the emergence of R2P has "[evolved] to focus on the protection of individual human beings, instead of the sovereign states that might abuse them." Under the ominous shadows of "never again" (Kersavage 2014), human security grants vast privileges for norm-making powers to act against norm-violating states (or non-states in the case of entities like ISIL or Somali "pirates") in the name of protecting vulnerable populations. Although R2P was formalized only in 2001, scholars have placed it within the normative rise of the human security agenda since the collapse of bipolarity (Breslin and Christou 2015). With the accelerations of human security discourses taking shape under the authority of international humanitarian law, the "evolving power of the R2P norm" (Weiss 2012, 324) has enhanced the potential for "humanitarian" interventions under the banner of the UN's Chapter VII, which establishes the faculty for "protection of civilians."

NATO's intervention in Libya has become a focus of recent R2P literature, though it is worth noting that, since the late 1990s, numerous operations have been mandated by the UN under Chapter VII to use "all necessary means" to protect civilians. Interventions in Haiti (MINUSTAH), Burundi (ONUB), Liberia (UNMIL), Sudan (UNMIS, UNAMID), Congo (MONUC/MONUSCO), and Côte d'Ivoire (UNOCI) have explicitly adopted Chapter VII human security discourses. Yet the 2011 mission in Libya presents perhaps the most powerful exercise of force under the rationale of protecting civilians, and the first explicit invocation of the R2P as a legal and moral rationale for security interventions (Kersavage 2014). Moreover, when NATO allies successfully pushed for a UN resolution under Chapter VII to use "all necessary means" to protect civilians in Libya and establish a no-fly zone (Resolution 1973), it was the first time the R2P had authorized an intervention against a functioning government (Bellamy and Williams 2011; Pommier 2011; Weiss 2012). In what represents "a new politics of protection," Bellamy and Williams (2011, 826) have argued that the protection of civilians has now emerged as the dominant norm in which International Humanitarian Law can be mobilized to authorize the use of military force against sovereign states.

As prominent supporters of the R2P have argued, the contemporary management of global (in)securities has propelled the once contested discourses of the R2P from "idea to norm" (Thakur and Weiss 2009; see also Welsh 2013). Placing emphasis on the contested diplomatic and political field surrounding R2P missions, Rotmann, Kurtz, and Brockmeier (2014, 358) have sketched out how R2P is an "evolving norm" shaped by seven "major powers" of Brazil, China, Europe, India, Russia, South Africa, and the United States.[2] While nonetheless contested, the principal norms of R2P involve subordination of sovereignty to human security ideals. As a rationality of humanitarian governance, the R2P doctrine has consolidated a political and civil consensus on extraterritorial responsibility. Weiss (2012, 322) has suggested that the "substantial normative and policy gains of the past decade are here to stay, in spite of the gnashing of Russian, Chinese, and others' diplomatic teeth." Central to the normative power of the R2P is the subordination of a "rogue" or failed state's sovereign authority to the norms of "assistance" and "security" – in other words, to the normative power of security aid.

While territorial integrity is still a prominent rhetorical framework on international relations, NATO's operation in Libya gives empirical weight to claims that sovereignty over life within the geographies of (in)security is now fragmentary and contingent. Security discourses are the means to manage these contingencies and, structured by the power

2 "Major Powers and the Contested Evolution of a Responsibility to Protect," special issue, *Conflict, Security, and Development* 14, no. 4 (2014) includes an article focused on each of these powers.

dynamics of the interlocutors, countries of the Global North are the norm-makers in deeming who and what constitutes a "contingency" within the problematic of (in)security (Dillon 2007; see also Beck 2002; Butler 2004). As the war in Libya demonstrates, the international community no longer requires the nominal consent of state authorities for international policing operations. Instead, interventions can be justified through appeals to norms of civilian protection, humanitarian assistance, and security.

NATO's campaign to provide security aid to Libya began amidst the Arab Spring uprisings of 2011. Following the "days of rage" in towns like Benghazi and Misrata, Libyan President Muammar Gaddafi began a swift and bloody crackdown on protestors. While the crackdown was typical of Gaddafi's long and violent dictatorship, norm-makers of the transversal security community (led by France, the United Kingdom, and – to a lesser extent – the United States) took up an immediate response against Gaddafi. Immediately vilified as an international criminal, Gaddafi was quickly indicted by the International Criminal Court. Despite recent efforts to normalize relations with Gaddafi for almost a decade, which included high-profile visits with Canadian Prime Minister Paul Martin, Canada immediately severed economic and diplomatic relations with Libya. Despite Gaddafi's recent participation in the transversal security community (as a contributor to the "war on terror"), he was quickly rendered into the antagonist of the Arab Spring. Though he was portrayed as a criminal and genocidal villain, Bellamy and Williams (2011, 838) have noted that at the time of the Arab Spring, "none of the world's existing genocide/atrocity risk assessment frameworks identified Libya as being at risk, despite some of those lists extending to 68 countries." Relatedly, a number of authoritarian regimes in the Middle East responded with violence against protests during the Arab Spring – notably Bahrain and Saudi Arabia – though Libya became a global focal point where security aid was mobilized at the juncture of protecting civilians, providing security, and promoting democracy.

In a series of fast-moving events, Gaddafi's forces were perched at the edge of Benghazi and threatening to raze the city. There was little doubt that Gaddafi would make good on his intentions to crush the rebellion and penalize sympathizers or, as he put it, "purify all decisions from these cockroaches … [and] any Libyan who takes arms against Libya will be executed" (quoted in Bellamy and Williams 2011, 838). Facing the imminence of Gaddafi's military offensive, efforts to launch an intervention were led by the United Kingdom, France, and an initially reluctant United States, while supported by what Canadian briefing notes describe as other NATO "a la carte" contributors (GAC 2011-492, 222). Military operations were initially led by the United States along with the United Kingdom and France on 19 March under UN resolution UNSCR 1973, and were subsequently taken over by NATO on 31 March 2011. UNSCR 1973 provides language that NATO forces could use "all necessary measures" to protect civilians and civilian-populated areas from attacks by Gaddafi military forces. Underlining the humanitarian aspects of the mission, Paragraph 6–7 put in place "a ban on all flights in the airspace of the Libyan Arab Jamahiriya in order to help protect civilians," excepting only those necessary to enforce the no-fly zone and those "*whose sole purpose is humanitarian*" (emphasis added).

In the case study below of the security intervention in Libya, I characterize Canada's security aid contributions as flowing from its orientation towards norm-supporting. Emerging and major powers hold a near monopoly on the possibilities to impose non-negotiated solutions backed by the threat of force. Canada's role as a security innovator – particularly in Libya – has been to focus on small and technically oriented contributions to the security intervention campaign, as well as function as a visible and vocal norm-supporter for the moral and legal *responsibility* for norm-makers to take international policing actions in Libya. Typical of all security aid, the case study below demonstrates Canadian practices as a security innovator, while also complicating the narrative of intervention – where "the sole purpose is humanitarian" – to demonstrate that security aid necessitates foregrounding Canadian strategic interests within the transversal security community.

Security Aid in Libya: A Case Study

Given that the UN Resolution did not explicitly endorse a "regime change" in Libya – only a cessation of hostilities and aggression by the country's military forces – the coalition undertaking the security intervention against Gaddafi had a difficult diplomatic issue. Numerous NATO allies, other Western states, and some African Union members objected to NATO's "mission creep," which jumped quickly from a "no-fly zone" into a campaign to depose Gaddafi (Bellamy and Williams 2011; Rotmann, Kurtz, and Brockmeier 2014). During the conflict, some Canadian documents began to refer to the "no-fly zone Plus" as the main component of the mission, though that terminology has no basis in the UN resolutions (see GAC 2011-489, 218). Following the lead of the United Kingdom and United States as norm-makers of the intervention, Canada began to clearly advocate that Gaddafi be removed from power. To augment and justify the rationales for deposing Gaddafi, arguments were put forward to emphasize not only the violence of the Gaddafi regime's crackdown on the Arab Spring, but its failure at governance. Mirroring global aid strategies in general and the human security agenda in particular, the justification for more intensive security interventions rests on the presentation of failed governance practices within recipient regimes. In the case of Libya, norm-makers quickly identified the Gaddafi regime as unfit to govern, which necessitated a change for the protection of the population. A briefing prepared for Foreign Affairs Minister John Baird at the first meetings of the Contact Group for Libya illustrates the representation of governance failure that rationalized the security intervention in Libya: "Canada's analysis is that the unrest in Libya, like other countries in the region, is founded on weak governance structures sustained by abusive security practices resulting in economic disparity. All three – political, security and economic reform – will need to be priorities. We must ensure that we offer coordinated assistance based on consultation with the Libyan people to develop 'sustainable stability'" (GAC 2011-1498, 281).[3]

There is little disputing Gaddafi's authoritarian record. Canada's analysis of the unrest allowed for a reimagination of the Libyan regime as an outlier of "weak" governance and "abusive" security practices. Yet this representation denied that, during the recent period leading up to the conflict, Libya had enjoyed its closest relations with the Global North in a half-century, in large part as the result of Gaddafi's acceptance in – and collaborations with – the transversal security community. Libya's relations with Canada were expanding, particularly through business relationships that I address below. Here, I underline that the reconstitution of Gaddafi as an international criminal with a "weak" commitment to governance was a selective, strategic act of securitization based on the priorities of norm-makers of the transversal security community. In representing him in a rapid discursive shift from ally

3 Baird used similar language in another speech to the Contact Group in May 2011: "We must work together to provide coordinated and value-added assistance. And, finally, we must target 'sustainable stability' – putting in place political, economic and security structures which will work not just in theory but in practice in Libya" (GAC 2011-489, 98–9).

of the security community to villain, norm-makers quickly established the Contact Group to act as a forum to liaise between state actors and the National Transitional Council (NTC). The terminology of "sustainable stability" became a Canadian-driven "buzzword and fuzzword" (Cornwall 2007) to express the desire for a comprehensive program of security development.

The case study below is presented in five subsections, each of which demonstrates a key aspect of Canada's security aid contributions to the intervention in Libya. First, I underline Canada's norm-supporting role and the mobilization of civilian protection and assistance; second, I detail the empirical, practical contributions of Canadian security aid as a form of "intervention"; third, I offer a detailed discussion of the economic strategic interests of Canadian security aid in Libya; fourth (and complementary to economic strategic interests), I detail how security interventions are gateways for further security innovation projects as efforts to build "sustainable stability"; and fifth, I examine declassified military documents that illustrate the expansive function of military operations as policing practices that comprise the transversal security community's reformatory aspirations in the geographies of (in)security.

NATO and the Protection of Civilians

First, it is important to establish Canada's norm-supporting role in the mobilization of the R2P mandate against the Gaddafi regime. As mentioned, a key aspect for rationalizing the security intervention in Libya was the reframing of Gaddafi as a callous dictator, thereby invoking the normative responsibility of protection over the norms of state sovereignty and non-interference. Given Canada has little "hard power," its contribution to casting out Gaddafi had little to do with material contributions to a military intervention. Yet, as a norm-supporter, Canada was especially vocal and visible in articulating the "muscular humanitarianism" (Orford 1999) norms of R2P.

During the diplomatic engagements in the early period of the NATO campaign, a briefing note marked "secret" prepared for Minister Baird's attendance at an emergency NATO meeting had a bullet point as the first entry under "key messages to convey": "Canada welcomed NATO's decision to *accept responsibility* for enforcing the arms embargo, the no-fly zone and most importantly the civilian protection mandate of UN Security Council Resolution 1973" (GAC 2011-1498, 106; emphasis added).

Clearly intended to remind their NATO allies of the humanitarian ethos of the UN Resolution, the Canadian position was at odds with members who were sceptical about the intervention. Further to underlining Canada's diplomatic positioning as a vocal norm-supporter, this statement demonstrates what Bellamy and Williams (2011) refer to as the "politics of protection," by presenting a powerful normative frame in which political opposition or dissention is construed as contesting the moral sentiments of protecting civilians, as opposed to critiques of NATO hypocrisy or international norms of non-interference. Some NATO countries – most notably Germany – presented tepid opposition on technical and operational grounds. But to oppose NATO's "responsibility" for humanitarian policing would risk accusations of moral communion with Gaddafi. In a context where the humanitarian norms of R2P equate with a responsibility to act as global policeman in what Neocleous (2011, 2014) describes as "civilizing offensives," the "key message" demonstrates Canada's normative affinity to this project, as well as a practical norm-supporting role in framing these securitization discourses.

As critics of R2P practices have detailed, a key discursive component for security interventions is through representation of Western militaries as benevolent "external saviours and external judges" (Chandler 2012, 213). Even supporters have called R2P a form of "Empire Lite" (Ignatieff 2003). The humanitarian sentiments that promote the altruism of NATO can be illustrated by Canadian documents that stressed how "Canada is interested in working with allies and partners to help support *a made-in-Libya solution* to the current crisis" (GAC 2011-489, 246; emphasis added). Despite a decade of support for the Gaddafi government and, through Canadian companies, investment in Gaddafi economic projects (which I discuss below), the rapid transformation provided by the Arab Spring realigned Canada's representation of Gaddafi.[4] Canada and NATO allies were careful not to use discourses of "regime change" associated with the 2003 U.S. invasion of Iraq, but instead emphasized the need for "robust civilian protection" (GAC 2011-1498, 295). In media lines prepared to assure the Canadian public

4 In an interesting parallel to the Canadian reimagination of Gaddafi, Canadian documents systematically preferred to use the term *Arab Awakening*, as opposed to the more popular *Arab Spring*, a discursive choice with clearly religious-civilizational overtones.

of the justness of the intervention, Canadian officials twinned *assistance* with the protection of civilians in promoting the value of enforcing the no-fly zone because it "can *assist* in preventing the regime from attacking its own citizens; *assist* in the enforcement of the UN arms embargo and sanctions; and, *assist* in allowing for the safe delivery of humanitarian *assistance*" (GAC 2011-1216, 110; emphasis added). While the intervention may have staved off immediate tragedy, the discursive representations for the security intervention highlight how rationalities of humanitarian governance form the parameters of intelligibility for rationalizing war to the public, as well as providing sufficient legal authorities – what Weizman (2011, 103) calls "lawfare" – for the norm for international juridical authorization. Mobilization of insecurity threats is not intended to promote warfare against a hostile enemy but, instead, to rationalize an intervention that would implement a broad array of assistance projects to reform, manage, control, and govern.

With the case of Libya and the Arab Spring, we can clearly trace how securitizing discourses are strategic games, where the invocations of insecurity correspond to strategic interests of norm-makers. While hypocrisy is nothing new to security development (Egnell 2010), R2P is notable for its "diffuse and discretionary" application (Welsh 2012, 294). Humanitarian norms that apply to Gaddafi's violent suppression of civilians do not apply to Saudi Arabia's, nor do the rhetorical or material expressions of protection and solidarity offered to Libyan people necessarily apply to indigenous people, migrants, or so many groups that have been Othered. Jasbir Puar's work has perfectly articulated the exceptionalism that countries of the Global North grant themselves in disregarding their own moral liabilities, but simultaneously promote an affinity for global altruism (Puar 2007; Puar and Rai 2002). In regards to Canada, scholars like Thobani (2007) have demonstrated how representations of moral evil abroad are twinned with the "exaltation" of a Canadian narrative of moral and normative superiority (see also Bell 2011; Razack 2004). By elevating the former ally Gaddafi to the status of "terror monster,"[5] discourses of assistance enact a performance of

5 While outside of my scope, a primary area of Canadian security aid to Libya was women's rights. The theme of women's rights was central to many of John Baird's announcements, as well as his visits to Libya. As an empirical demonstration, these prominent tropes of saving women support Puar's argument that the gender constructions of Arab and Muslim Others are central tropes for the rationalization of violence – and saviour discourses – of security interventions.

Canada and the Global North as being "responsible" for the protection of civilians – against the barbarism of Gaddafi, thus rationalizing security aid.

Another prominent element of contemporary security interventions has been highlighted by scholars who argue that disorderly governments of the Global South are portrayed not only as threatening their own public, but as citizens of the Global North or global security *in toto* (Duffield 2001, 2007, 2008; see also Amoore 2006; Bell 2013; Bigo 2002, 2014; Hyndman 2009). In underlining how (in)security functions in a system of global governance, Duffield's influential work cautions how security and development are linked through concerns of countries from the Global North about the threats presented by underdeveloped polities. Duffield (2001, 2) argued that "the threat of an excluded South fomenting international instability through conflict, criminal activity and terrorism is now part of a new security framework." Numerous scholars have argued that the "war on terror" – especially its domestic political dimensions – has accelerated the pairing of security with development with the "new" proviso that the insecure spaces of the Third World present immediate security threats to citizens in the North (Chandler 2007; Ericson 2007; Huysmans 2006; Mitchell 2010). Canada's representation of Gaddafi and the civil conflict in Libya mirrored these representations.

In addition to the discursive representation of Gaddafi as a threat to Libyan civilians, John Baird also portrayed Gaddafi as a threat to the Canadian public. In a speech to the House of Commons in the lead up to the war, Baird proclaimed, "The violence in Libya is not a civil war: it is aggression committed against an imprisoned population by a callous dictator. Colonel Qadhafi holds human life cheap, and through his sponsorship of terrorists, such as those behind the Lockerbie bombing, he poses a direct threat to neighboring states as well as to Western democracies, including, let us be clear, to Canada" (GAC 2011-489, 324–5).

Baird's portrayal of Gaddafi as an international threat demonstrates the fluidity of Western narratives regarding Libya and Gaddafi (see Sidaway 2012). The recent friendly relations following Gaddafi's apology for the Lockerbie bombing and valuable work as an intelligence ally in the "war on terror" were instantaneously reversed. Overnight, Gaddafi was recast as a "callous dictator" who "holds life cheap" (which is probably true), playing upon the humanitarian sentiments of Canadians who were called to support a security intervention in

Libya. In his concluding remarks to Parliament, Baird suggested that "the international community and institutions should be ready to assist a new Libya, if asked, and play a positive role in its transition towards a genuine democracy" (GAC 2011-489, 324). Blending the humanitarian sentiments of democratic altruism with the security imperative of protecting civilians, Baird announced that Canada would be providing security aid to the NATO mission in Libya. As a form of security assistance tied to an international policing mission, the security aid package foregrounded the contributions of Canada's navy and air force to the NATO mission, but also made prominent mentions of further security aid funding for "sustainable security" to facilitate Libya's transition to democracy and freedom. Before detailing aspects of the security aid packages to develop infrastructures and techniques of security, I will first examine the "aid" contributions to NATO's security intervention in Libya.

Security Interventions as "Aid"

Given Canada's limited military capabilities, it was only following the leadership of the United States, France, and the United Kingdom that Canadian support for a military role could be undertaken. I have emphasized that the norm-making powers constructed the terrain of political possibilities, and Canada's role as a norm-supporter was to provide visible and vocal moral suasion for the mission. Canada's role as a norm-supporter was particularly relevant, since the NATO mission did not include the full NATO security community, with members like Germany being opposed to security intervention. The NATO "à la carte" composition of the coalition resulted in only seven Allies (including Canada) conducting military operations as part of the "strike group," with the remainder taking symbolic positions. As a demonstration of the fluidity of the transversal security community, the coalition was supplemented by regional non-NATO countries like Jordan, Qatar, and the United Arab Emirates. After the rift within the NATO security community, Canada was granted an excellent opportunity to demonstrate its security innovation and maximize its visibility as a norm-supporter. While the overwhelming majority of the military contribution came from the United States (who adopted a strategic position of "leading from behind," according to one Canadian briefing note) and the United Kingdom, Canada was entrusted with a symbolically visible role for the NATO campaign. Most significantly, Lieutenant-General Charles

Bouchard was named commander of the NATO bombing mission, dubbed Operation Unified Protector (OUP), and another Canadian held the position of tactical air director.

During a press conference to explain Canada's role within the NATO coalition, Canada's Minister of Defence Peter MacKay explained the importance of Canada's norm-supporting role: "We have contributed both to the mission at a practical level with equipment, with personnel but yes we have contributed in Brussels, in the discussions that have taken place there, high level discussions with the Secretary General, with other member nations. We have had other discussions, Ministers Cannon, myself, others, the Prime Minister have been speaking with our international counterparts and so suffice it to say that Canada has played a very prominent place in where we find ourselves today and I hope in the future the success of this particular mission" (GAC 2011-489, 44).

Taking a "very prominent" position as a norm-supporter provided positive optics for NATO in suggesting a larger international coalition-backed military action against Gaddafi, and allowed for Canadian security innovators to be more prominently placed in the pursuit of broader strategic interests. As an important aspect of normative power, the "very prominent" moral sentiments expressed by Minister MacKay, Baird, or Prime Minister Harper on the protection of civilians in Libya can only be norm-supportive of an agenda shaped by norm-makers.

Canada's overall security aid to the intervention phase in Libya included navy and air force components. In air power, Canada contributed seven CF-18 Hornet fighter jets, two CC-177 Globemaster strategic transport aircraft, two CC-130J Hercules tactical transport aircraft, two CC-150 Polaris strategic air-to-air refuellers, and two CP-140 Aurora aircraft. Naval commitments included HMCS *Charlottetown*, which was described favourably as a "flexible and multi-purpose naval asset with 240 sailors and air personnel" (GAC 2011-489, 25). HMCS *Charlottetown* was later replaced by HMCS *Vancouver*, which is a comparable Halifax-class frigate, both of which are outfitted with a CH-124 Sea King helicopter that performs surveillance, search and rescue, and anti-submarine operations. Canada's total commitment to OUP at its height was 655 members, but it is unclear if that number included JTF2 Special Forces who participated in an undisclosed role during the mission.

Though the contribution made by Canada to OUP represented a significant percentage of Canada's overall defence resources, it is important to underline how these naval and air commitments were only a small element of the overall NATO contingent. While NATO flew a reported 26,500 sorties during the operation, Canadian sorties amounted to only 1,539 – barely more than 0.5 per cent of the NATO air missions.[6] Again reinforcing the strategic importance of a norm-supporter, Canada's modest contribution is better measured by its effectiveness in advancing Canadian visibility and responsibility under the leadership of norm-makers. One significant area of contribution, outside the nominal but symbolically important commanding positions, was the role of Canadian security innovators with the Airborne Warning and Control System (AWACS) crew. As highly sophisticated surveillance aircraft, NATO's AWACS fleet is the world's only integrated multinational aerial surveillance unit, employing crew members and technicians from across fifteen NATO nations. Though Canada had decided in the federal budget of 2011 to conclude Canadian participation in AWACS, before the Libya mission (DND 2012-325), Canada contributed a significant twelve members to the AWACS component of the mission.

CP-140 Aurora aircraft also participated in the surveillance deployments of the NATO mission. Appearing at the press conference beside Minister MacKay to announce Canada's participation in OUP, Chief of Defence Staff Tom Lawson described Canada's role in providing security innovation and surveillance expertise to the mission: "The coalition is of course eager to employ [CP140 aircraft] surveillance and reconnaissance capabilities in support of the NATO arms embargo off the coast of Italy, sorry off the coast of Libya" (GAC 2011-489, 40). In addition to providing practical surveillance and target information, Auroras were also used as propaganda tools where they coordinated psyops operations – originally started by the United States – that broadcast radio messages (in English) to Gaddafi forces (Canadian Press 2011).

In summarizing Canada's security aid contribution, Defence Minister MacKay remarked,

> It's another example of how Canada has stepped forward and played a prominent role in times of crisis, when international leadership was required, when assistance was sought. Canadians and I'm very proud to say that many of them in uniform assumed those leadership positions.

6 Statistics from March 2011 to 25 October 2011 show the breakdown for sorties as CF-18 Hornet fighters (946); CC-150 Polaris tankers (250); CP-140 Aurora long-range patrol aircraft (181); CC-130J Hercules airlifters (23); CC-130 Hercules tankers (139).

> We saw it in Haiti. We've seen it here in our own country when severe storm weather hit and we've certainly seen it for many years in Afghanistan and throughout our country's history this puts the shine on our country. It puts the shine on the capabilities and the leadership within the Forces and what they bring to an effort such as this. (GAC 2011-489, 43)

In the security intervention in Libya, security aid contributions blended themes of "assistance" with humanitarian ideals of safety and well-being. MacKay's emphasis on leadership is notable for illustrating how the activities of a vocal and visible small power can be framed as "leadership" within an operational terrain constructed and directed by norm-makers. In addition to illustrating an articulation of norm-supporting characteristics, MacKay's invocation of Canadian folklore associated with Canadian military personnel assisting in snowstorms (filling sandbags during floods is a similar – though not invoked – allegory of the benevolent Canadian soldier), as well as recent security interventions in Afghanistan and Haiti, demonstrates how the governing rationality of security aid relies upon "aid" as an altruistic form of assistance. As I have argued earlier, the folklore of "aid" has a long history in putting "the shine on our country" in aggrandizing myths of Canadian internationalism. Below, I will further underline that security aid, in particular, was not about altruism and principled opposition to the "crisis" of governance under Gaddafi, but an undertaking to promote strategic Canadian interests. Among these strategic interests in Libya were, as I examine below, prominent economic incentives to topple Gaddafi's regime.

Security Innovation: "Assistance" and Economic Interests

During the build-up to the intervention, Canada displayed its prowess as a norm-supporter by taking nominal "leadership" roles, displaying highly visible normative-value sentiments, making small but strategic contributions to the technical aspects of the intervention, and earning accolades for its support for the norm-makers. These contributions fulfilled Canadian strategic interests by highlighting the visibility and innovativeness of Canadian security (and military) establishments. With the case study of security aid in Libya, however, an even more prominent element of Canadian strategic interests is demonstrated by the centrality of economic motives in the effort to depose Gaddafi.

Prior to the Arab Spring, Canadian economic interests in Libya had been accelerating slowly since the 2001 reopening of the Canadian diplomatic office in Tripoli. Previous to the establishment of the trade office, Canada had limited relations with Gaddafi's Libya. After UN sanctions were lifted in 2003, Canada upgraded its trade office to a formal embassy in 2004 and pursued a number of commercial activities. Canadian exports to Libya were on the rise, reaching $246 million in 2010. According to a briefing note on Canada's commercial activity in Libya, Canadian investment and the sale of services "took Canada's economic interests much higher" (GAC 2011-489, 94). In early 2011, it was estimated that approximately twelve Canadian companies were present in the country (GAC 2011-1215, 57), most notably SNC-Lavalin and Suncor Energy. Ingratiating themselves with the Gaddafi family (Cousineau and McArthur 2013; Hamilton and Van Praet 2014), SNC-Lavalin had won several lucrative contracts in Libya. This included building several large components of the multi-billion-dollar Man Made River Project, while also holding large contracts to remediate lakes near Benghazi, design and build a new airport in Benghazi, and design and build the $275 million Guryan prison – also known as the "Guryan Judicial City" (Daly 2012; Waldie 2011) – in Tripoli, which was slated to hold 4,000 prisoners.

Emails between GAC officials trying to write a backgrounder for the minister of foreign affairs underlined the fact that "prior to 2011, Canada had generally maintained good relations with Libya ... Canada had strong commercial relations with Libya due to investments in the Libyan oil sector and the involvement of Canadian engineering companies in Libyan infrastructure projects" (GAC 2011-1216, 71). With the onset of the Arab Spring, many of the foreign contracts in Libya had been frozen, and there was speculation in the media that contracts might be awarded post-Gaddafi on the basis of how states supported the rebels. A combination of the prospect of losing important business contracts and the potential opening of a socialist, centrally controlled economy presented a significant area of interest for Canadian government officials during the crisis.

Commercial opportunities were of central concern to Canadian officials during the effort to depose Gaddafi. Addressing the topic of post-Gaddafi economic opportunities, a 12 September 2011 email from Ambassador Sandra McCardell with the subject line "Commercial ops" was distributed to senior officials (GAC 2011-1216, 69). After attending high-level meetings with NTC officials, McCardell wrote, "Overall, advice from NTC and like-minded was broadly consistent: previously established companies shd get back RIGHT NOW – to secure their assets, seek payments, re-establish business, re-confirm existing contracts … large companies without existing contacts or medium companies shd be at the ready but careful. The NTC is shifting significantly personnel – not clear who will emerge as players. They are extremely busy and have difficult focussing on anything but key priorities (oil production, completing key infrastructure)" (ibid.).

At a time of widespread speculation about rapid potential contracts to be issued after the conflict – somewhat similar to the Baghdad Year Zero approach[7] (see Klein 2004) – the Canadian embassy was working full-time on economic opportunities. Addressing the prospect of immediate options, McCardell added, "There is very little infrastructure damage – NATO really was precise … There is a misperception that after 6 mo[nth]s of bombing, we are looking at a [redacted word]. This is not the case." Four items appeared under a heading of "early sense of key opportunities" (ibid.). After the first two bullets being redacted, McCardell lists oil and gas ("as highest priority"), followed by IT opportunities (as "Libyans seek to connect with the world in a way not previously possible and [redacted sentence]." Under a heading of "long-range options," McCardell lists mining and the airline industry.

Enthusiasm for the economic opportunities post-Gaddafi played a large part in the prominent role taken by John Baird during the intervention. Baird organized two trips to Libya during the conflict, first to Benghazi in June 2011 and then to Tripoli in October 2011 – both of which came before the formal end of the NATO mission. During his trip to Benghazi, Baird proclaimed he was "incredibly, incredibly moved by the courage and determination" of the rebels and, with the help of the Canadian Commercial Corporation (to be discussed next chapter), delivered 355 military-grade medical trauma kits to assist the rebels on the front lines (Scoffield 2011). Baird explained, "We provided hundreds of state-of-the-art trauma kits as a gift from Canada to the Libyan people" (GAC 2011). As an aspect of Baird's visibility strategy, he personally delivered the state-of-the-art medical kits, by way of Canadian

7 The similarities are best described as general and not direct correlations, mostly because the NTC held far more control over domestic resources than what transpired in Iraq in 2003. In this sense, it was not the neoliberal dream of total deregulation, yet there was a wide-spread recognition that the transformation from socialist central planning would allow foreign investment in resources, which were all considered in play.

Forces transport aircraft. The security aid hub START-GPSF was only notified about Baird's request immediately before his departure. START-GPSF staff then made an "urgent request" with CCC for the medical kits on 17 June 2011, originally seeking "a significant number of military grade first aid kits (approx 1000) to ship to Benghazi accompanying MINA on his planned visit Tuesday next week" (CCC 2012-66, 2). Working over the weekend, START-GPSF and CCC eventually finalized a purchase of 355 tactical trauma kits at a cost of $79,732.12. Export and internal procurement requirements were waived by GAC, and one CCC worker recounted by email the "mad dash shipment of medical kits to Libya, this supplier moved heaven and earth to get that done so fast to coincide with Minister Baird in Libya" (CCC 2012-66, 388). In delivering these security aid goods, Baird was the first leader from a Global North country to land in Libya as a demonstration of support for the NTC and, one month later, further explained the gift as an outgrowth of our moral obligation to support these Libyan "freedom fighters" (Taber 2011).

Baird's second visit took place at the conclusion of the intervention, approximately one week before Gaddafi's 20 October 2011 capture by rebels where he was shot, sodomized with a tent spike, and left to bleed out on a street. Baird's second visit to Libya involved an even more elaborate effort to utilize Canadian security aid to advance strategic and economic interests. A "secret" briefing note for Minister Baird underlined that the objective of the visit was to "set the foundation to pursue Canadian interests, in particular commercial interests in the New Libya" (GAC 2011-1215, 54). To maximize Canadian security aid, Baird's briefing note argued, "A high-level visit at this time would cement Canada's role as a key player in Libya going forward based on our role over the past seven months ... A ministerial visit would reinforce in the minds of the Libyans that Canada is among this elite group of New Libya supporters and sets the foundation for the active promotion of Canadian interests going forward" (GAC 2011-1215, 54).

To actively promote Canadian interests going forward in the "New Libya," Baird was accompanied by senior executives from SNC-Lavalin, Suncor, and Pure Technologies. Canada's embassy organized a separate commercial program for the companies "in support of their individual priorities in the context of re-establishing their presence in – or cooperation with – Libya" (GAC 2011-1216, 53). Travelling together in Canadian Forces aircraft under heavy security, corporate executives and the political elite were able to develop close personal and professional ties, illustrative of what O'Reilly (2010) calls a "state-corporate symbiosis." Briefing notes for the minister underlined economic objectives that Baird could pursue during his visit: "Libya requires new investment in many sectors including management, information and telecommunication systems, global connectivity, education, healthcare, sanitation, water, basic infrastructure, governance, and of course, oil" (GAC 2011-1560, 51). To take advantage of the high-profile visit, another set of briefing notes for Baird emphasized, "You will want to highlight Canada's significant contribution in helping Libya to *free itself from tyranny*" (GAC 2011-1560, 12; emphasis added) and, given the "wide support in Canada for our diplomatic, military and humanitarian efforts … Canadians will want to see a return on our engagement and investment" (ibid.).

Written by senior bureaucrats, briefing notes provide strategic advice and practical speaking points for such visits, and they are not known for their rhetorical flair. In underlining Canada's support for freedom against nothing short of *tyranny*, these notes demonstrate a complex wedding of rationalities within security aid, in that the document exalts the normative and moral underpinnings of Canadian involvement in Libya while articulating an expectation on "returns" for these gifts of altruism.

A major component of Minister Baird's visit with leading Canadian corporations was to "cement Canada's role as a key player" and raise Canada's profile among the NTC leadership. In the strategic orientations of being a norm-supporter, such visibility-cultivation was particularly effective to advance strategic interests. Canadian visibility was noteworthy in the Libya mission, despite Canada's limited military contributions. Baird was also the most prominent Western leader to visit and made sure that Canadian corporate elites had privileged positions in the diplomatic manoeuvres for contracts in the "New Libya." To amplify Canada's role as a prominent norm-supporter, Baird expressed his intention to use his public visit to Tripoli to maximize his media visibility, which was capped with a last-minute, PR-orchestrated visit to the Bab al-Aziziya compound.

A sprawling military compound that served as a primary residence for the Gaddafi family, Bab al-Aziziya was notorious for its large, gold-coloured sculpture depicting a left hand crushing a U.S. fighter jet. Commissioned by Gaddafi after the U.S. bombing of the compound in 1986, it was the backdrop of high-profile visits after Libya's détente with the West and entrance into the transversal security community.

During the Arab Spring uprising, Gaddafi stood in the entrance of Bab al-Aziziya to deliver his chilling public address denouncing the rebellion, where he pledged to punish the "rats" and "terrorists," or die as a martyr. With the fall of Tripoli, the capture of Bab al-Aziziya – along with the iron fist sculpture – became a defining moment of the Libyan revolution and, hoping to parlay this revolutionary imagery, Minister Baird asked security innovators to schedule a media availability at Bab al-Aziziya. On arranging the logistics, Ambassador McCardell wrote in an email, "Bab Aziziya: This should be doable with sufficient preparation. Our team is recceing the site now and will provide final word after consultation with NTC security. Note that our visitor would appear to be the first VIP to visit this site. The fist and plane ended up in Misrata (and, although we have asked, the NTC won't bring it back for us ... ;-)" (GAC 2011-1216, 60).

Baird was accompanied by media to Bab al-Aziziya, where he handed out Canadian flag pins to youth in front of the compound, and invoked Canada's contributions to the security intervention by telling reporters, "Obviously we're fighting for Canadian companies to be able to begin their operations as soon as possible. That'll be good for the Canadian economy and good for the future of Libya" (Clark 2011). Highlighting the importance of these visibility strategies of security aid, senior GAC official Barbara Martin, who was making travel arrangements for Minister Baird, wrote in an email, "O/MINA/Day very happy to hear he can take media for 1 hour around Tripoli" (GAC 2011-1216, 59). Other discussions of media optics revolved upon security issues associated with putting up a Canadian flag at the "ceremonial" reopening of the Canadian embassy for "a pan shot," as well as the optics of Baird visiting the compound of the World Islamic Call Society (WICS), where McCardell noted "no activity or signage which would be problematic but we will check location today ourselves."[8]

In addition to promoting economic interests, a key component of Baird's visit to Tripoli was the announcement that Canada would contribute $10 million in security assistance. In a context where countries were

8 GAC officials were particularly worried about Baird's PR move having associations with Gaddafi's WICS. Although Ambassador McConnell understood the PR element of wanting to distance Baird from the WICS, she also defended the work of the WICS. In an email, she wrote, "(Not that we need to get into this level of detail with 0/MINA but in fact WICS did a lot of really good work on inter-faith dialogue in its day)" (GAC 2011-1216,63).

pledging contributions to the NTC or to humanitarian aid in general – and the Canadian government was tallying these announcements in "Donor Tracking Charts" included in Baird's travel documents (see GAC 2011-492, 39–45) – using the backdrop of the Bab al-Aziziya compound made for a splashy security development-funding announcement. While this provided substantial international media coverage – which Canadian officials celebrated – it helped obscure the fact that Canada's contribution of $10 million was small relative to other donors. Moreover, it also hid the fact that Baird had no specific projects for the spending announcement, despite his months of rhetoric about supporting "sustainable stability." Immediately before Baird's visit, on 26 September 2011, Baird had approved a small $170,000 capacity-building package to address "priority needs" (GAC 2014-1571,1) such as the disarmament and reintegration of militia, capacity building in veterans' affairs, and strengthening the rule of law. Yet it was only after Baird's visit that the security aid hubs sprang into action to find areas where Canadian security innovators could make further strategic contributions.

Security Innovators: Interventions as Gateway to Further Security Aid

An important aspect of the security aid type of "interventions" is that these transversal policing operations function as gateways for further security assistance packages aiming to develop the infrastructures and techniques of security and social order. While advancing economic interests is an important aspects of Canada as a norm-supporter, so too is advancing the influence and visibility of security innovators as contributors to the development of transversal security governance practices in Libya.

Canada made its first announcement of security aid equipment during Baird's surprise visit to Benghazi to deliver the military trauma kits. More indirect security aid came with the provision of a drone known as the Aeryon Scout. Facilitated by the Canadian government, the NTC were able to procure Aeryon microdrones that could engage in covert surveillance and assist with ground targeting (Ha 2011). Similarly, an internal discussion on the provision of arms to the rebels seems to have been opposed and not taken up (see GAC 2011-1498, 309–29). While these two examples are worth noting, work to underscore "sustainable stability" began in earnest after the NTC's consolidation of the revolution. Given Canada's prominent posturing as a supporter of the rebels, security development hubs like START-GPSF quickly began work on long-term security aid projects. The initial START-GPSF project for a small $170,000 capacity building was approved by Baird immediately before his second visit to Tripoli. But given how the project was rushed to approval for its announcement at Bab al-Aziziya, it was amended afterwards for the fiscal year 2012–13 to include an additional $850,000, bringing the project cost to $1,020,000. As the first in what was planned to be a flurry of contracts, the goal of the initial START-GPSF capacity-building deployment was to send Canadian security innovators – hired through CANADEM[9] – to provide an in-the-field perspective on strategic contributions for further aid.

Between October 2011 and 31 March 2013, START-GPSF funded the deployment of eleven Canadian experts – most of whom could be characterized as security innovators – on seven missions to Libya. The deployments included one advisor to the Ministry of Justice to assess prison facilities and medical care, two strategic communications experts to the Ministry of Foreign Affairs, four experts to the Ministry of the Interior to advise on police training, one expert to the Ministry of Defence for make recommendation on pensions and decommissioning rebel officers, an expert to assess police facilities for the Ministry of the Interior, and one legal advisor to the NTC for a review of the legal landscape (with emphasis on commercial contracts).

Although the START-GPSF capacity-building program was sizable, it represented only a small amount of the security aid funding announced by Baird, because no other internal projects were ready. In the meantime, Canadian officials began setting up a system to evaluate and approve proposals. One START-GPSF member wrote about the need to fast track programs because "timely approval of [redacted] proposal is encouraged so that it can begin to effectively engage with the pace of developments on the ground in what is becoming a crowded field of intervention" (GAC 2013-1571, 11). Canadian officials also made trilingual (English, French, Arabic) posters for embassy websites in Tripoli (GAC 2013-1571, 45). In a number of communications, Canadian

9 CANADEM is a private, non-profit, leading actor in networking Canadian expertise into the lucrative security development field. The agency hosts a roster of over 20,000 Canadian experts, supplying personnel for thousands of postings in security, policing, and policy. Since its establishment in 1996, CANADEM has provided GAC with over 2,500 experts in more than 100 projects valued at over $65 million, including 21 projects funded from the START-GPSF (GAC 2013-1571, 2).

security innovators stressed the need for (and frustrations about) efficiencies in the crowded field of security development.

Despite measures taken to fund security aid projects in Libya, few projects got off the ground. Those that were approved faced numerous challenges and did not result in the comprehensive long-term capacity-building efforts envisioned by Canadian security innovators. For example, the final report from the CANADEM project reported myriad barriers including the inability of the NTC to clearly articulate its needs; challenges in identifying stakeholders, coordinating meetings, and locating resource documents, statistics, or other data; barriers in obtaining Libya entry visas in a timely manner; and securing quality interpreters and translators (see full list of challenges in report on GAC 2013-1571, 57). At the conclusion of the project, the Canadian expert on pension reforms refused a second contract because arrangements were chaotic and there was lack of progress. Most notably, the expert on prisons submitted a scathing (and uncharacteristic) assessment of the conditions of women in prison (GAC 2013-1571, 78–9). While the capacity mission did make notable contacts, it did not result in substantive programming.

One other significant project that was approved was a $6-million contract signed in March 2012 between GAC's Global Partnership Program and the Organization for the Prohibition of Chemical Weapons (OPCW). The objective of the project was to allow for "the provision of materials and expertise" (DND 2011-1218,17) for the Government of Libya to "assist the Libyan chemical weapons destruction program" (GAC 2013-330, 1). However, it is unclear what contributions the project made since all purchases and final reports – possibly as many as 600 pages of documents on the project – were completely redacted (GAC 2013-330, 4–630).[10] The fulfilment of another project pledging $4 million to remove explosives and secure stockpiles of conventional weapons – especially shoulder-fired man-portable air defence systems (MANPADS) – is also unknown, though there appear to be no available records that demonstrate it was pursued or completed (GAC 2011-1560, 15). Another general pledge of $5 million in "stabilization assistance for

10 In February 2014, John Baird issued a statement to "congratulate" Libyan authorities and the OPCW for completing the destruction of all declared quantities of mustard sulphur. No information on the quantities is provided, nor is there information on other efforts to destroy chemical weapons (GAC 2014a).

public order and the Rule of Law" also has no indication of implementation or completion, only documents that express a general interest in developing "rule of law" capacity (GAC 2011-1560, 42). As with most programming in Libya, the initial rush to democracy building was interrupted by changing circumstances.

Over the course of Canada's post-intervention involvement, documents from security aid hubs reveal that the goal of security development was frustrated by factors over which Canadian security innovators had little to no control. In a summary account of a scoping mission to Tripoli that took place between 29 February and 16 March 2012, officials recounted many of the challenges to finding and developing further security aid projects. In a highly critical review of current possibilities, the report details how most sectors reflect a "pre-occupation" with the upcoming elections that "leaves little capacity available to think and plan strategically towards enacting basic organizational reform" (GAC 2013-1571, 23). As norm-supporters with a focus on practical and tangible contributions, Canadian security innovators were increasingly frustrated by a lack of coherence between the Libyan recipients and Canadian experts in engaging security development.

Repeating the claims raised by CANADEM experts, the report notes the difficulties in finding interlocutors or locating "capable docking points for such assistance that may be envisioned with the demonstrable capacity to coordinate effectively amongst key stakeholders" (GAC 2013-1571, 24). Overall, the assessment notes that delivering further security aid funding is "fraught with risk ... and challenging with the light footprint that Canada currently has on the ground" (ibid.).

Similar to the bleak assessment provided in the scoping mission quoted above, the Canadian embassy began to report on the waning security environment in Libya. Although Canadian officials displayed naive optimism after the first elections in July 2012,[11] internal reports on violence and insecurities accelerated in late 2011. As became evident to the Canadian and international public with the attacks on the U.S. embassy in September 2011, Western governments had pulled a dramatic about-face on the Libyan revolution by the end of 2011. By mid-2013, John Baird was no longer trumpeting the freedom fighters

11 Direct email accounts from the Canadian Embassy in Tripoli to Ottawa reported on the elections and their outcomes (see GAC 2012-1740).

of Libya, but instead issuing press releases with headlines such as "Canada Concerned by Lawlessness in Libya" (GAC 2013a) and then "Canada Condemns Violence in Tripoli" (GAC 2013b). Like much of the media commentary by Western states that isolated "tribal" factionalism or unnamed "armed groups" as the source of disorder, Baird stressed that Canada was "increasingly concerned over the persistent lawlessness in Libya, notably the armed groups that have besieged a number of government offices" (GAC 2013a). Similar to discourses of "pirates" in Somalia or the tribalism of failed states (Oliveira 2013), statements like those in Baird's press releases place any responsibility for the violence in Libya on Libyans, without any acknowledgment of the security interventions that precipitated the "persistent lawlessness."

At the time of my interviews in August 2014, few participants had any positive comments on their work in Libya. One participant noted that Canada seemed to have no functioning security aid programming in Libya by that time (Interview 3). By July 2014, Canada had withdrawn all staff from the Canadian embassy (GAC 2014b). Within a very short time – between Baird's visit to Benghazi in June 2011 and the summer of 2014 – Canada had gone from participating in a significant transversal security intervention to having no security aid programming or formal diplomatic presence. Though Canada was among a vocal group of norm-supporters that rationalized the war to "protect civilians," the ambitions of the transversal security community quickly deteriorated into an abandonment of the country. Much like in security interventions in Iraq and Afghanistan, the civilians of Libya were central to the humanitarian sentiments that animated the missions, yet the abandonment of the mission demonstrates how these same bodies can quickly become disposable and forgotten. Similar to how Bauman (2004) underlined a parallel in Western cultures between the mass disposal of garbage and the abandonment of unwanted people, the very populations in Libya who were vaunted as our responsibility to protect were tragically re-assumed as forgettable "wasted lives."[12] Illustrating many of practical challenges to developing security governance capacities, Canada's engagement in Libya was far more difficult to implement than expected. And, as they were in other interventions, norm-makers were

12 Using a biopolitics framework to address similar conclusions, Duffield has written extensively using the term "uninsured life" (see Duffield 2010; 2008; 2007; 2005).

reduced to virtual paralysis in advancing their ambitions of democracy and economic prosperity. Moreover, the failed security development mission in Libya illustrates the fleeting humanitarian economy of security aid and how, despite Canadian claims of "assistance" and protection, the lives of the Libyan people were secondary and easily forgotten. Yet the mission – despite the abandonment of the Libyan people – was far from a failure. The success of security aid should not be evaluated on its improvements to venerable populations, but on its advancement of Canadian norm-supporting (Monaghan 2016). Though the development of security governance in Libya was unsuccessful, the security intervention opened a more substantive terrain for development of transversal security governance on a regional level writ large. Following the intervention, Canada quickly refocused its resources from Libya to the regional security assemblage known as the Combined Maritime Forces, which opened a new venue for the practical contributions of Canadian norm-supporting. In the following section, I demonstrate how the security invention in Libya quickly moved from a focus on reforming Libya to a more strategic regional level of attention for transversal security governance.

Security Interventions and Beyond: Op Artemis and the Combined Maritime Forces

Though much of the security assistance in Libya can be characterized as a failure, an integral component of the "success" of security aid can be demonstrated by its ability to enhance the reputation and influence of Canadian security innovators. The influence of the security intervention in Libya advanced Canadian strategic interests substantially. As I outline in this section, the most important aspect of the mission was its use as a gateway into a much larger security assistance mission in the Middle East.

Strategic plans to use the security intervention in Libya for broader regional programming were initiated in late October 2011 (after Gaddafi's death), when documents from DND report that the Canadian Forces had been instructed to begin closure of the mission because they had achieved their objectives. However, the instructions indicate that the "CDS intent is to maintain a forward-deployed presence in the region until December 2012" (DND 2012-981, 56–7). In a post-op report called "Op Mobile Closure and Transition," Lieutenant-General Stuart Beare outlines how the Canadian government planned to transition the initial security aid contribution to NATO into a long-term commitment:[13] "We will transition forces to other operational taskings within the MENA region to provide situational awareness and a ready-response capability for future potential military operations. We will engage all stakeholders to cement the legacy of CF actions and achievement in OUP to sustain the CF's credibility and enhance relations with our Allies and partners in order to validate the sacrifice and efforts made by our people and families" (DND 2012-981, 59).

Upon completion of Operation Unified Protector, and as an effort to "cement the legacy of CF actions and achievements," DND ordered that the HMCS *Charlottetown* be re-deployed to the Arabian Sea to conduct routine operations as part of the Combined Task Force 150, also known as CTF-150. CTF-150 is one of the units organized under the umbrella of the Combined Maritime Forces (CMF), a thirty-member naval partnership based at the U.S. Naval Central Command and U.S. Navy Fifth Fleet at Naval Support Activity in Bahrain. Although the CMF is promoted as a "naval partnership," it is directed by the United States (as the norm-maker) and aims at "promoting security, stability and prosperity across approximately 2.5 million miles of international waters in the Arabian Sea region" (DND 2013-1000, 15). It is under the command of a U.S. Navy vice-admiral who serves as commander of the U.S. Fifth Fleet, also based in Bahrain. As the CMF website details, a key component of the CTF-150 mission is the "interdiction" of potentially risky vessels. With photos of small, rickety fishing boats being intercepted by well-armed teams on Zodiacs, one caption claims, "Maritime Security Operations help develop security in the maritime environment, contributing toward stability and prosperity on a regional and global level" (Combined Maritime Forces 2015).

As a prominent example of coordination and interoperability within the transversal security community, the CMF aggregates a broad coalition under the authority and leadership of the U.S. "war on terror'" to police the International Recommended Transit Corridor (IRTC). Cowen (2014, 129–61) has detailed how the IRTC constitutes a "new space" created to police the Gulf of Aden and protect commercial shipping traffic passing through the Suez Canal. To describe how the "space" of the

13 Another "secret" document acknowledges that, on 15 November 2011, the HMCS *Charlottetown* was given a "Prime Ministerial directive ... to maintain a high readiness unit in the Middle East/North Africa (MENA) region" (DND 2013-1000, 2).

IRTC has been constructed, Cowen (130) argues that an "ensemble of legal experiments [are] recasting political space, international law, and imperial violence" under the combined mantle of combating piracy and terrorism (see also Oliveira 2013). Canada's contribution to CTF-150 is an aspect of this project of the transversal security community, and an extension of a larger commitment to policing the IRTC that dates back to early military missions – particularly Operation ALTAIR – as well as Canada's significant aid contributions to developing security in Somalia (see DND 2012-1782; GAC 2011-2465). It is worth noting that, while Canada has a long record of participation in CTF-150 as an active norm-supporter of the transversal security community, no navy ships have been contributed since 2010.[14] It was only following Canada's security intervention in Libya that security innovators redoubled their norm-supporting role within the CMF with a new mission to the CTF-150 called Operation Artemis.

As a major collaboration of the transversal security community, the CMF consists of three task forces that police the IRTC: CTF-150, CTF-151, and CTF-152. As one branch of the CMF, the CTF-150 conducts counter-terrorism and maritime security operations in the Arabian Sea region, including the Gulf of Aden, the Gulf of Oman, the Red Sea, and the northwest quadrant of the Indian Ocean. CTF-151 conducts counter-piracy operations off the coast of Somalia, while CTF-152 is responsible for maritime security in the Persian Gulf. Under the counter-terrorism mission of the CTF-150, Canadian ships share tasks that "include detecting, deterring and protecting against terrorist activity by patrolling [their] area of responsibility and conducting maritime security operations" (DND 2013-1006, 55). A major component of these marine operations is surveillance and interdiction of suspicious vessels. A number of these interdictions have been drug seizures, which the Canadian Forces have aggressively marketed as part of their communications strategy. One document describes the drug interdiction and subsequent Canadian media coverage as having "significant strategic and newsworthy affect" (DND 2013-1006, 91). As a twinning of the "war on drugs" with the "war on terror," the interdiction of drugs

14 From 2004 to 2008, seven Royal Canadian Navy ships served with CTF-150 while deployed on Operation ALTAIR. For an overview of Canadian contributions to the CMF, visit: http://www.forces.gc.ca/en/operations-abroad-current/op-artemis.page (accessed 5 February 2015).

was also described as support for counter-terrorism operations which resulted "in the loss of funding for terrorist organizations throughout the region" (110).

Though Canada's Op Artemis contribution was originally mandated for approximately one year, it has been continually renewed. HMCS *Charlottetown* was relieved by HMCS *Regina* in August 2012, followed by two crew rotations on the HMCS *Toronto* from January 2013 to February 2014, and was then relieved by a second tour of HMCS *Regina*. In early May 2014, HMCS *Regina* left the Arabian Sea to join NATO Standing Maritime Forces in the Mediterranean Sea and, beginning in December 2014, Op Artemis was extended in order to take a land-based command of CTF-150 until April 2015, which was then extended to April 2016 (DND 2013-1006, 55). Although the financial costs of this security aid mission are difficult to account, documents from DND suggest that, for the period between April 2012 and October 2013, the estimated cost for Op Artemis is $86.8 million (DND 2013-1000, 11).

The surveillance capacities of Op Artemis have been a key component of Canadian norm-supporting, making practical contributions to these practices of the transversal security community. Using their helicopter air detachment and an on-board drone, Canadian ships were to build and report "Pattern of Life" (POL) maps of the areas. One report noted how the *Scan Eagle* drone "provided invaluable covert surveillance" in tracking ships and building the POL data (DND 2013-1006, 76). Another document discussed how HMCS *Toronto* "fused ISR [intelligence, surveillance, reconnaissance] and 'Heroin-Hunting' Tactics" and how the ship's "unique combination of air assets and sensors allowed her to maintain a layered ISR when searching for foreign warships and trafficking dhows" (DND 2013-1006, 110).

As self-congratulatory efforts, post-mission reports from Op Artemis revel in the accolades awarded to Canadian security innovators. One report details how "TOR became known for its Ready, Aye, Ready attitude ... whenever assigned any task no matter where in the JOA [Joint Operations Area] it existed" (DND 2013-1006, 97). Another report recalled, "As a result of the historic and uncanny success of TOR in completing interdictions, accolades were received from our allies naval forces in the area, all knew of TOR and what she had accomplished" (91). As an illustration of the strategic value of Canadian security innovators, notes detailing the creation of Op Artemis illustrate the expansionary character of "security aid" as well as the strategic interests animating these missions. As with security aid projects in general, the

Op Artemis mission especially demonstrates the role played by Canadian security innovators – with their ready, aye, ready attitudes – in supporting the norm-makers of the transversal security community.

Originally under the banner of protecting civilians, Canada's security intervention in Libya transformed into a tangible and concrete role in the transversal policing of the IRTC. Examples of drug intercepts demonstrate how these "counter-terrorism" practices are in fact crime control and regulatory practices of transversal policing. Moreover, Canada's norm-supporting role created strategic opportunities to advance the visibility and notoriety of Canadian security innovators. A "secret" memorandum authorizing Op Artemis from the Chief of Defence Staff (May 2012) offers a wide-ranging account of the priorities and objectives of the engagement, which included contributions to the "war on terror," global economic health, and U.S. strategic interests, all while enhancing transversal security governance. The memo summarizes these strategic objectives succinctly, describing how the commitment would "support Canada's strategic goals in the region, provide visibility, and maximize regional engagement with Allies and strategic partners in the region in accordance with the Global Engagement Strategy" (DND 2014-715, 10–11). Underlining the intersection of broad strategic interests associated with norm-supporting (particularly vis-à-vis the United States as the norm-maker of transversal policing) and protecting the health of global commerce, Canada's contribution to Op Artemis demonstrates how military resources function as security aid. While many documents from DND underline the contribution to fighting terrorism, one briefing note put the objective of the mission more bluntly: "Op ARTEMIS continues to contribute to international peace and security by helping to keep some of the world's most important waterways safe for global commerce" (DND 2013-1000, 11). Notably, documents are careful to continuously repeat how one-third of the global oil trade travels through the area of the IRTC patrolled by the transversal security community of CTF-150. Following Morrissey (2011), we can use the case study of the security intervention in Libya to illustrate U.S.-driven strategy to secure "military-economic security interests" in the Middle East, with a focus on naval control of the IRTC (see also Cowen 2014).

The contribution of security aid to the CMF mission is a particularly salient example of the norm-supporting role played by Canada in the transversal security community. Contributing in a practical way to the coordinated security governance norms within insecure geographies,

Canadian security innovators made small but concrete contributions to the surveillance and policing of the IRTC. With an emphasis on technical expertise in surveillance and management positions within the integrated military chain of command, a number of strategic functions were accomplished through Canadian security innovation. The case studies in this chapter demonstrate how security aid to Libya, grounded in the humanitarian sentiments to protect civilians, can intensify into a long-term transversal policing commitment, and point towards future trajectories of Canadian norm-supporting.

Conclusions: Security Interventions and the Military-Security Nexus

A detailed post-mission report written by J.R. Boyd, commanding officer of HMCS *Regina* during its Op Artemis mission, offered an assessment of Canada's contribution: "REG has engaged HQs and other CMF units, maintained combat readiness and proven her ability to integrate with allied battle groups. Likewise, we have been able to continue building the notion of Canadian units as a preferred strategic partner to allied nations. We have proven the possibility of replenishment by launch and barge and the efficacy of our onboard [redacted] capabilities. We will depart the JOA having left behind the POL information required to effectively conduct MSO within the most significant areas of the CMF AO" (DND 2012-1828, 8). Boyd's assessment is an excellent representation of the strategic value – the "Canada value added" – of security aid. He underlines the influence of Canada security innovators: Op Artemis demonstrated the reliability of Canadian security actors, and their adept use of surveillance and control technologies. The sophisticated surveillance knowledge involving "pattern of life" maps created by Canadian security innovators were to be shared with partners. Most importantly, Boyd emphasized that Canadian security innovators had been highly visible, resulting in the perception of Canada as a "preferred strategic partner" for security governance work and a reliable norm-supporter of the transversal security community.

In detailing Canada's participation in the intervention in Libya, this chapter demonstrates how strategic interests of commercial opportunities and security innovators are driving rationalities of security aid. We can see how security aid interventions progress from the initial category of humanitarian support, then act as "gateways" for two other types of security aid: infrastructures and techniques. Subsequently, development of the Op Artemis mission demonstrates how security interventions can act as further gateways into broad attempts to foster transversal policing and surveillance practices within geographies of (in)security.

This chapter demonstrates that the category of security aid "interventions" corresponds with scholarship that critiques the increasing role of militaries in the policing of transversal insecurities. Scholars have detailed the increasing role of military involvement in transversal policing, particularly given the significant capacities of violence controlled by military security innovators (Bachmann 2014; Huysmans 2002; Hyndman 2015). Within Canada's contribution to the transversal security community, there are clear indications that the DND-CF are taking more active and prominent roles in security aid. This is particularly evident in the Global Engagement Strategy. Though the secretive character of the military establishment makes it difficult to catalogue their efforts to assist and develop security forces of the Global South, other major security interventions have transpired in recent years. These include a contribution known as Operation Caribbe (which involves deep integration with U.S. military and security forces in policing the drug war throughout the Americas); Operation Flintlock, which is directed by the U.S. Africa command as an extensive training mission to capacity-building African security forces; clandestine counter-terrorism operations in the Sahel region discussed in chapter 2; as well as a network of "defence cooperation" agreements that allow for military assistance. In addition to these consistent operations, there are also the case study of Haiti (next chapter), where the DND-CF participated in the removal of Jean-Bertrand Aristide under the banner of humanitarian action. These missions demonstrate that "interventions" do not rely solely on the R2P and the human security agenda to engage in security interventions, but involve activities to "assist" and "develop" security across broad geographies of potential threat.

Underlining the suggestion that R2P is the "new norm," the security intervention in Libya – and subsequent commitments through Op Artemis – demonstrates Canada's role as a norm-supporter in the transversal security community. Rotmann, Kurtz, and Brockmeier (2014, 357–8) have observed that, while R2P is complex, "non-linear, fluid and seemingly contradictory," it sheds light on "conflicts about power, inequality and legitimacy that are fundamental to the changing global order as a whole." Given Canada's recent involvement in the war against ISIL, we can see that the R2P is an "unfinished journey" (Serrano and Weiss

2013) that has cemented extraterritorial norms of the transversal security community to engage in interventions around the world. Exemplifying the humanitarian and securitarian norms of the transversal, R2P reinforces what Mack (2002, 3, quoted in Duffield and Waddell 2004) has argued, in that human security "is less an analytical concept than a signifier of shared political and moral values."

As Kitchen (2010a) and others (Hallams 2010; Huysmans 2002) have noted, the collapsing binary of the Cold War – particularly after the 1999 war in Kosovo – has allowed for a reimagination of NATO's mandate and the shared "security values" of the Global North. As an extension of the transversal security community, the increasing conditionality of sovereignty points towards an accelerated interventionist agenda on humanitarian grounds. For Canada, as a norm-supporter of these transversal dynamics, there is a strong likelihood that "security interventions" will comprise a larger and more powerful influence on its security aid practices. One participant in the study placed special emphasis on the effects of military-oriented objectives on security aid practices:

> It gets very very fuzzy. And you can understand the logic of it: if I wanted to patrol some area and I don't have an aircraft, well the military happens to have those aircraft. But you don't know what they do with that information. And so, you know, the dual use is one thing. Yes they'll tell the civilian body that all is quiet on the border, but what happens with the rest of the information? I don't know. I'm just concerned that the militarization of border security. And I'm not a pacifist, don't get me wrong here, but the balance here is tipping and the reasons for it are … well, they claim financial, but I think there's something lurking in the background with this. Whether the so-called military-industrial complex wants to sell drones all over the place … and here I'm blue skying … you're not going to be able to sit down with those folks at the table and have a discussion on broad policy issues, like mobility rights. They will look at it strictly as a policing issue or a military issue … Now you have a different perception than someone who is a generation back from me and says the military is good because they can support us with their equipment. Except their motivation might be different. (Interview 7)

Stressing that there are "dark skies on the horizon," the participant echoed a common sentiment within literature on the "militarization of aid" that, on a fundamental level, the elevation of military command within aid regimes threatens cultivation of the rule of law. As an important component of how security aid becomes an articulation of politics – in other words, how Canada's practices of security aid make us think about our "place in the world" – the increasing reliance on security interventions and the dominance of the R2P in framing security aid commitments is illustrated by the dramatic celebration of the Libya mission held on Parliament Hill. Canada was the only member of the "alliance" to host a victory celebration (Mcleod 2012), which featured flyovers from the air force jets involved in the mission. At a cost of over $850,000, it speaks to a political opportunism of security aid where the humanitarian sentiments of "aid" are filtered through a romanticization of military culture. Yet the case study of security aid in Libya demonstrates how quickly these animating logics of humanitarian reason can be abandoned. What is left from the security aid to Libya are the strategic advancements of Canadian norm-supporting, while the long-term fallout from the security interventions that afflict the Libyan people is ignored.

Chapter Four

Security Infrastructures: "Hardware" of Transversal Security

Introducing Security Aid Type 2: Security Infrastructures

As a contribution to understanding how states within the transversal security community participate in the globalization of security governance, this chapter explores how Canadian aid provides "security infrastructures" to the Global South. By focusing on the material and physical efforts of security development, I examine how Canadian foreign assistance funds prisons, border stations, and police academies, as well as providing a wide range of equipment – munitions, vehicles, fingerprinting and database technologies, etc. – in an effort to enhance material "hardware" of security agencies in the deviant states of the Global South.

Within literature on the security-development nexus, the theme of material development – i.e., the actual construction or provision of buildings, supplies, and materials – is rarely isolated as a separate stream of foreign assistance programming. Often themes of "reconstruction," infrastructure development, or material supplies are subordinated to the much more dominant themes of governance, democracy building, rule of law, and myriad trainings and capacity buildings – which all aim to enhance the "techniques" – e.g., software – of security governance. While I address these techniques of security governance in the next chapter, this chapter highlights the category of "security infrastructures," which speaks specifically to funds and programs providing the materials needed to govern transversal (in)security.

Distinguishing between infrastructures and techniques is important for demonstrating the scope of security aid programming. While the development of security infrastructures is an under-explored theme in security-development scholarship, attention has been directed towards these assistance regimes as an aspect of "military aid" – particularly from U.S. scholars (Blanton 1999; Craft and Smaldone 2002; de Mesquita and Smith 2007; Derouen and Heo 2004; Gill 2004; Krause 2004; Sullivan, Tessman, and Li 2011). My contention here is that, unlike military aid that is focused on preparing defences to combat external threats, security aid is characterized by the collapsed internal/external binaries of the transversal security community. Instead of conceptualizing violence as stemming from external enemies to be destroyed, security aid is directed towards insecurities and contingencies that need to be managed collaboratively and in a coordinated fashion. To produce "international stability," a significant proportion of security aid funding is directed to infrastructures that do the practical work of security governance. While recipients can include militaries, more often infrastructure aid is focused on "civilian" agencies of border control, policing, and prisons. While the types of security aid are often complementary, this chapter focuses on Canadian security aid funding directed towards civilian security agencies in an effort to develop transversal capacities to manage insecurities.

As a contribution to understanding how security infrastructures fit into the transversal security community, this chapter offers two detailed case studies of Canada's role as a security innovator within developing security infrastructures. First, I examine a central mechanism in the political economy of security aid, and the Canadian Commercial Corporation (CCC). As previously discussed, the CCC is a Crown corporation that exists solely to advance Canadian business interests – particularly the innovators in security-related businesses. A second case study examines Canada's role in building the security apparatus in Haiti. As a country with a long history of subjection to foreign interventions and interference (Caple James 2010; Girard 2010), Haiti has been under a decade-long UN occupation that goes under the acronym MINUSTAH. Since contributing to the forced removal of Jean-Bertrand Aristide in 2004 (Engler and Fenton 2005; Podur 2012), Canada has been an active norm-supporter in Haiti, in a role that included dubious efforts to violently dismantle Aristide's political party and exclude it from elections.[1] Canada's role in Haiti is an ideal case study to demonstrate

1 Regardless of opinions regarding Aristide's legacy (see Dupuy [2007] for a critical account of the Aristide regime, within a context of continuous foreign interventions), MINUSTAH and the security regime have engaged in widespread political repression of the Farmi Lavalas party; see HealthRoots (2011); Institute for Justice and Democracy in Haiti (2014); Johnston and Weisbrot (2011); Podur (2012).

the norm-supporting function of security infrastructure aid, since this funding is central to developing the governance capacities of an illegitimate government. Since backing the intervention in Haiti, Canada has been an unequivocal supporter of MINUSTAH, despite the UN mission's significant crisis of legitimacy. Though the mission continues to receive extensions, Haitian President Michel Martelly has stated that the UN has committed "unacceptable errors" (Trenton 2011) and has pushed very hard – against the objections of Canada and others – for the creation of a Haitian Army to replace the MINUSTAH mission.[2] The Haitian Army proposal has broad public support, given that MINUSTAH is viewed by many Haitians as an occupying force, and considering the significant public controversies involving MINUSTAH troops.[3] Most notably, MINUSTAH has direct responsibility for the cholera outbreak that has killed over 7,500 people (and infecting another 590,000), as well as a minimum of eighty-one reported cases against MINUSTAH officials alleging sexual abuse, gang rapes, and pedophilia (Amnesty International 2011; d'Adesky 2012; Human Rights Watch 2014, 259). These concerns are in addition to criticism of the massacres in poor neighbourhoods, shootings of women and children, and numerous accounts of political violence, extrajudicial killings, and exceptional violence (Alternative Chance 2014; Amnesty International 2014; Caple James 2010; Snyder 2010). One case in point is a 2011 video of MINUSTAH troops beating and gang-raping a detained eighteen-year-old boy (to a chorus of laughter) (Weisbrot 2012; see also Edwards 2012). Even some elements of the UN have acknowledged the widespread

2 A number of briefing notes for the minister of foreign affairs detail Canada's opposition to Martelly's army proposal. In what gives some insight into the long-term expectations of security aid, the notes stress how Canada is more interested in "ongoing development of the Haitian National Police (currently the sole security institutions in the country), in which the Canadian government has heavily invested" (GAC 2012-49, 185). Other briefing notes indicate that Canada directed a vocal backroom lobbying campaign against Martelly's proposal with the U.S. and OAS officials (see GAC 2012-49, 238). An understanding of Canada's strategic interests in opposing the Army proposal is an important consideration, unlike Baranyi's (2014, 167) facile claim that "if the UN and Western powers had wanted to 'militarize' Haiti, as suggested by some post-colonial analysts, surely they would have supported Martelly's vision."

3 Former Haitian president Réne Préval made a similar comment similar to Martelly's when, in April 2011, he criticized the UN continued presence "in a country that has no war" (Charbonneau 2011).

demonstrations against – and resentment towards – MINUSTAH and called for more accountability from the mission's leadership. Yet there is no public record of Canada criticizing any of these activities. Moreover, as this chapter details, Canadian security aid has played a central role in fortifying the capacities of the security state to enable such violence.

The post-intervention regime has been driven by the United States and, to a lesser extent, Brazil.[4] Though Brazil has been the norm-maker for managing the MINUSTAH forces, the central role of the United States has been documented extensively, in particular through diplomatic cables made available by WikiLeaks that outlined the U.S. lead in steering MINUSTAH and the role played by the UN in advancing U.S. policy interests in Haiti (see Beeton 2012; Ives 2011). What I detail in Canada's involvement reflects its character as a norm-supporter. In a comprehensive multinational effort to support the new government, norm-makers directed significant investment and aggressive strategy towards "security promotion, stabilization, recovery and reconstruction" (Muggah 2010, S446).[5] This chapter demonstrates how, in supporting a security governance regime driven by the norm-makers, Canada has taken important functional roles in developing the security capacities of the police, border, and prison agencies of the Haitian state. Focusing on the "security infrastructure" projects, I detail how these "assistance" projects follow the logic of security aid in that they advance Canadian strategic interests – particularly economic interests and the reputations and visibility of Canadian security innovators – while allowing Canada to perform as a reliable norm-supporter in a hemispheric component of the transversal security community.

This chapter has three sections and a conclusion. The first provides a conceptual orientation for this type of security aid. After giving an overview of literature on material assistance programs, I offer three empirical subsections of Canadian security infrastructure assistance, beginning with the case study of CCC. Subsequently, I provide an exploratory catalogue of assistance programs offered by security aid hubs and DND-CF. It gives a vivid picture of Canada's efforts to

4 For an analysis of Brazil's role as a regional norm-maker in advancing a "sub-imperialist" agenda in South America, particularly through a dramatic rise in security and military practices, see Zibechi (2014).

5 While his conclusions are contradicted by most independent sources on the post-coup environment, Dorn (2009) provides an insider perspective on the MINUSTAH security strategy.

enhance what Bigo (2008) refers to as the "archipelago of policing," an assemblage that works towards an aggregation of transversal security governance institutions. The second section of the chapter is a case study of security aid in Haiti. It is subdivided by the areas of development: police, borders, and prisons. The third section places security aid to Haiti within a broader context of developing transversal security governance. In this discussion, I draw particular attention to the norm-supporting role of Canadian security aid. The chapter concludes with comments on security infrastructures as a type of security aid.

Security Infrastructures Aid: An Exploration

While research on military aid has a footprint in foreign policy literature, the notion of "security assistance" is relatively new. An important corollary of military and security aid is that they have a heavy emphasis on providing materials to establish and maintain social control, yet as scholarship on the collapse of internal/external security demonstrates, security governance has replaced "national security" as a principal organizing rationality, giving rise to transversal threats and risks to be governed (Bigo 2008; Duffield 2005; Muller 2010; Valverde 2011). Given that the threat spectrum has assumed its globalized and universal character, the practices of "security assistance" are rationalized by humanitarian sentiments that aim to support and enhance security, economic development, and international stability. Unlike military aid – which, of course, is still prominent – efforts to develop security are directed at the civilian institutions that comprise the assemblages of security governance. In this chapter, I highlight policing, prisons, and border agencies, yet the enhancement of security governance is embedded broadly across institutions of governance, from food safety, to transportation, climate change, and education policies.

Literature on security development has described the efforts of prosperous donor countries to enhance the internal capacities of the Global South. Yet, unlike military aid research, the scholarship on security development has not made significant efforts to detail the material components of "assistance" packages. As Bachmann and Hönke (2010, 100) have argued, the "hearts and minds" campaigns in Afghanistan and Iraq have shown that traditional military-security supplies have regressed as a priority, in contrast to "new security technologies of governing through empowerment, participation, and a new care for those parts of the population who are perceived by many donors to be susceptible to harbouring or recruiting terrorists." While I do not want to draw away from the techniques of security development – which I detail in the next chapter – here I explore how Canadian security aid does exhibit elements of the "old" assistance regimes that are focused on building infrastructure and providing materials of security.

Though a large element of the literature – particularly from a biopolitical framework – emphasizes the "new" modalities of techniques, several scholars do underline how contemporary security development has a concern for building the infrastructures of security. Examining the security rhetoric that led up to the 2003 invasion of Iraq, Sovacool and Halfon (2007, 224) have argued that the "intervention in Iraq is not simply a military conquest, but also remains a significant *development* project" (emphasis in original). In their article, they demonstrate that intervention in Iraq relies "on a convergence of economic, social, and political justifications that expand beyond the confines of conventional notions of security" (ibid.). They highlight how the emerging discourse of "reconstruction" – promoted by experts and bureaucrats, more than politicians and generals – demonstrates a powerful way in which security and development merge to build up the physical infrastructures of security.

Particularly in conflict and post-conflict states, "reconstruction" has become a prominent discursive device to signal a need for foreign aid. These appeals are focused on the "hard" security needed to complement training, capacity building, and governance. While this can include items associated with traditional military aid – like ammunition, arms, and combat zone vehicles – it also includes an array of materials for civilian institutions such as border services, policing agencies, and prisons. Therefore, components of the "infrastructure aid" can range from more traditional items like trucks and riot gear to more sophisticated products like GPS systems or forensics technologies. As I detail, it also includes the construction of buildings like prisons and border stations.

It is difficult to catalogue security infrastructure aid, particularly government funding to corporate third parties or other governments. Many project records obtained through the ATIA are redacted, particularly more sensitive projects associated with providing arms or significant security equipment that would call attention to potential human rights violations or instances of "blowback" (where weapons fall into the hands of non-ally forces). Other records indicate project funding, but provide few details about the materials provided. It can take years before there are responses to further ATIA requests on these files. In publicly available records, rarely are such types of funding arrangements communicated by government departments, with the exception of donations of surplus military equipment (which I address separately below). In security aid funding from security hubs, there are few public records. However, by surveying aspects of spending from security aid hubs we can map out many of the security infrastructure projects funded by Canadian aid.

In the following sections, I outline how Canadian security aid has developed security infrastructure projects abroad. I begin by exploring the role of the CCC, which is a major procurement arm for purchasing and distributing the materials resources funded by security aid. In detailing how CCC functions in the political economy of security aid, I explain how Canadian funding for security commodities operates on "indirect" and "direct" models of assistance. After examining CCC's role, I offer an overview of the GAC security aid hubs funding of security infrastructures. Subsequently, I detail DND's practice of aid donations as "surplus equipment" to countries of the Global South, before moving into the case study of how security innovators of Canadian security aid come together to build a security state in Haiti.

Canadian Commercial Corporation: The Merchant of Security

Unlike security experts, CCC does not deal with contingency or insecurity. Its annual reports, communications efforts, and internal documents are almost exclusively framed in the language of commerce and profits. Rarely does CCC discuss global security challenges, only economic challenges. Never are there concerns about the nexus between security and development. Instead, its concerns are margins, insurance coverage, competitive rates, and the "value proposition" that CCC as a "government-to-government" entity can provide. Never do readers of CCC reports hear about people living in poverty, tragedies caused by disasters, or the violence of civil unrest. For CCC, these concerns are trivial. Readers of CCC documents will hear only about stakeholders, foreign government buyers, Canadian suppliers, and jobs. Finally, readers will also have these lexicons of investment packaged, appropriately, in the language of corporate social responsibility.

Created by statutory authority of the 1946 Canadian Commercial Corporation Act, CCC was intended to support military exports to the United States as an aspect of "the integrated defence industrial base." Until its recent efforts to expand beyond the U.S. market, the primary business of CCC was to integrate Canadian companies into U.S. military procurement systems through the 1956 Canada-U.S. Defence Production Sharing Arrangement (DPSA), which governs all Canadian arms sales to the United States. As a procurement agreement, the DPSA provides special access for Canadian companies to U.S. aerospace and defence markets. Under the DPSA, Canadian exporters are treated as domestic suppliers by the U.S. Department of Defence (DoD), which now includes an amnesty from Buy America provisions. The DPSA has been highly advantageous to Canadian arms companies, who have accrued over $30 billion in sales to the DoD over the past fifty-five years. As critics of Canadian militarism have pointed out, this industrial partnership demonstrates the contributions of Canadian workers to American wars.[6]

Sales to the United States are wide-ranging and a powerful illustration of the security innovation in technologies developed by Canadian private industry. CCC claims to work with over 100 different Canadian companies to sell defence and security technologies and services, including munitions, drones, telecommunications products, avionics, heavy machinery, landing gear maintenance, and fleets of LAVs to the U.S. military.

Despite the lucrative comfort of U.S. arms sales, CCC has been promoting diversification since the late 2000s. In line with the Harper government's trade agenda, CCC has stated that its strategy is "closely aligned with the Government's Global Markets Action Plan, Canada's Strategy for Engagement in the Americas, and the Defence Procurement Strategy" (CCC 2014, 2).[7] As demonstrated in figure 4.1, CCC has a "market focus" far beyond its traditional market of the United States.

Why these countries have been selected as a "market focus" is not detailed, though the political economic interests of selling security products to insecure (and militaristic) areas correspond with Canadian foreign policy interests. Rationales for market targeting discussed in other CCC reports highlight a desire to take advantage of the spending fluidity of emerging economies, as well as wanting to build upon established relations. A mix of rationalities can explain the prioritized markets, and, in recent years, CCC has taken a marked role in supporting

---

6 See the research page maintained by the Coalition to Oppose the Arms Trade, http://coat.ncf.ca/.

7 CCC has claimed to influence development of the Global Markets Action Plan. For example, its 2014 annual report (CCC 2014, 73) describes how "CCC was particularly active in providing input into this Plan, highlighting how its activities in increasing access to foreign markets for Canadian exporters directly support the Government's pro-trade agenda."

Figure 4.1. CCC "Market Focus" (CCC 2014-146, 63)

CCC Market Focus

CCC

North America	Central America & Caribbean	South America	Africa	Middle East	Europe & Eurasia	Asia Pacific
United States	Barbados	Argentina	Ghana	Bahrain	Serbia	Philippines
	Dominican Republic	Colombia	Kenya	Kuwait	Turkey	Thailand
	Honduras	Chile	South Africa	Oman		Vietnam
	Nicaragua	Ecuador	Tanzania	Qatar		
	Trinidad &Tobago	Peru		Saudi Arabia		

Canada

the export of Canadian security industries to the Global South. As I detail below, CCC plays two important functions as an innovator within the security aid regime: "indirect" and "direct" security aid.

Indirect Security Aid

Indirect security aid comprises forms of "assistance" that CCC provides as an agent of the Crown in promoting and enhancing transversal security infrastructures. CCC has an impressive track record in exporting military and security materials, and its 2014 annual report features brief highlights:

- Signed a contract with the Philippines Department of National Defence for eight helicopters that will be manufactured by Bell Helicopter Textron Canada Ltd of Mirabel, QC.

- Awarded a contract with the Mexican Ministry of Defence for the maintenance, repair, and overhaul services on two Mexican Air Force C-130K Hercules aircraft, through Cascade Aerospace of Abbotsford, BC.
- As per the CCC contract with Colombian Ministry of Defence, four Bell 407 helicopters were delivered to the National Police, and two Bell 412 helicopters were delivered to the Naval Aviation Group. The aircraft were manufactured by Bell Helicopter Textron Canada Ltd of Mirabel, QC.
- In accordance with a contract between CCC and the Argentinean Ministry of Defence, an upgraded and modified Lear Jet was delivered to the air force. The aircraft upgrade was completed by Field Aviation of Mississauga, ON.
- New Twin Otter aircraft were delivered to the Peruvian Air Force, manufactured by Viking Air Ltd of Sidney, BC.
- In the largest military sale in Canadian history, CCC brokered a $15-billion contract between General Dynamics Land Systems Canada in London, Ontario, and the Kingdom of Saudi Arabia to provide LAVIIIs to the Saudi Armoured Brigades Program.

Though it was not highlighted in its 2014 annual report, CCC also appears to have signed a $66-million LAV contract with the Peru Navy (CCC 2014-146). In describing the Saudi LAV contract, CCC Chair Ray Castelli celebrated the success of the corporation, given "continued economic uncertainty and rising global competition," proclaiming that "CCC stands out as a successful example of resilience and innovation" (13). The "assistance" provided by CCC innovation is focused solely on how the corporation can accrue financial benefits. The category of "indirect security aid" emphasizes how CCC enhances the export sales (not "aid" donations) of security infrastructures to the Global South. For CCC, "assistance" is only a term to refer to assisting Canadian industry, and it makes no pretence of wanting to "assist" anyone else.

In its provision of indirect security assistance, CCC offers innovative services to export Canadian security infrastructures. In particular, CCC promotes a suite of services to assist Canadian companies in emerging markets. Underlining that economies of the Global South "involve greater risk than developed markets ... CCC adds value by filling the needs of foreign governments to establish robust procurement practices" (CCC 2012, 19). To assist with security exports in risky environments, CCC offers services for government buyers as well as Canadian suppliers.

For Canadian suppliers, CCC provides a mitigation of virtually any financial risk, since the Crown is acting as the prime contractor. Contracts through CCC also reduce or eliminate requirements for commercial bonding, a source of significant cost for businesses. Other financial assistance is provided in concert with Export Development Canada, which can include forms of insurance, guarantees, and lines of credit. As opposed to a form of crony capitalism portrayed as business-government corruption (Kang 2002), the institutionalization of these mercantilist relations demonstrates crony capitalism where business subsidization and support are legitimate forms of assistance (i.e., not illegal). Leveraging the diplomatic channels of the Canadian foreign affairs establishment through close collaboration with embassies, trade commissioners' offices, and defence attachés, CCC also works to avoid risky and costly competition by advocating for sole-source contracts. This is facilitated through a push to sign MoUs on defence procurement with interested countries.

To support the sales pitch, CCC and government agencies offer benefits to foreign government buyers who agree to the sole sourcing of Canadian goods through the CCC. Dealing through the CCC allows the Canada to guarantee the contract terms and conditions, eliminating risk for purchasing governments. CCC also certifies its industry suppliers and negotiates for specific systems, products, and services at a buyer's request. For technical issues, buyers can contact suppliers directly or request CCC assistance. In addition to the contract negotiations, CCC provides contract administration and oversight over the course of the projects and requires that Canadian suppliers demonstrate completion of the project before they are paid.

As one actor within Canada's network of export-supporting bureaucracies, CCC also participates in trade missions and military trade shows. CCC representatives have accompanied the minister of international trade to Libya, Peru, Russia, Ghana, Nigeria, and other locations to export Canadian security and military materials. During an August 2014 trade mission to Peru and Colombia, CCC President Marty Zablocki accompanied International Trade Minister Ed Fast, along with thirty-six Canadian companies (eighteen security and defence companies, eleven oil and gas, and seven mining) (see CCC 2014-146). Talking points provided for Zablocki for his meeting with a senior Peruvian military leader (name redacted) summarize CCC services: "We offer a government-to-government directed contracting channel as an alternative to an open tender process. This mechanism offers the advantages of a rapid negotiating and contracting process, a GoC guarantee regarding the performance of Canadian supplier, and the opportunity to contract with a Canadian supplier already identified" (CCC 2014-146, 29).

Clearly signalling the anti-free-market goals of CCC, these notes demonstrate the mercantilist logic for security infrastructure export regimes. In providing a host of state resources to facilitate advancement of private firms, the notes also demonstrate how the resources of the Crown can be mobilized for expedient tendering. Avoiding lengthy binding processes, CCC assistance programming provides a competitive advantage to Canadian security firms to facilitate exports to the Global South. In a summary for its 2011 annual report, CCC highlights the expediency provided by its services: "Through CCC, foreign governments can significantly reduce procurement time and costs while gaining access to world-class Canadian goods and services. This ultimately leads to increased revenues for Canadian companies, which improves the Canadian economy and creates jobs for Canadians" (CCC 2011, 18).

Rationalized as providing jobs for Canadians and "assistance" to Canadian suppliers, indirect security aid is provided by harnessing an array of state resources to export security materials abroad. As an expression of security innovation, CCC is interested exclusively in maximizing the fortunes of Canadian security industries. It has no regard for the well-being of populations outside Canada. However, unlike "indirect" security aid, "direct security aid" from CCC is an aspect of Canada's larger "aid" contributions to developing the security governance systems of the Global South. As I detail below, when developing security infrastructures, CCC plays an important part in delivery of security aid projects.

Direct Security Aid

Direct security aid is "assistance" funding that is applied specifically to purchasing security infrastructures for the Global South. Structured through CCC, these "aid" provisions are considered in-kind donations (see figure 4.2) in the standard line from many CCC contracts for direct security aid.

Figure 4.2 is extracted from a CCC contract with a Haitian company called Perfecta to provide motorcycles and motorcycle parts to the

Figure 4.2. Contract for In-Kind Aid Donations of Security Hardware (CCC 2014-127, 12)

34. IN-KIND CONTRIBUTION

34.1 The Parties acknowledge and agree that this Agreement constitutes an element of an in-kind contribution to a foreign recipient and is governmental assistance.

Haitian National Police. In providing direct security aid, CCC functions as a logistics manager for Canada's security aid bureaucracies. Much of the direct security aid is provided by START-GPSF, ACCBP, and the CTCB programs, and in 2007, CCC signed an MoU with GAC (then DFAIT) to become a procurement agent for its international procurement efforts.

As discussed with the Global Markets Action Plan, an explicit intent of the plan has been to align trade interests with foreign assistance. Canadian policy has aimed to create a tied-aid formula that rewards trading partners with "aid" while simultaneously translating "aid" funding into trade revenues. As the procurement arm of this "aid" economy, CCC directs "aid" funding to Canadian corporations, although it is important to stress that the role of CCC in supplying direct security aid is not linked exclusively to Canadian companies. In fact, many CCC efforts to provide direct security aid come through non-Canadian companies. This characteristic is important in highlighting how CCC assists in development of security infrastructures, as the Crown is side-stepping its statutory authority to facilitate trade for Canadian companies selling security commodities or Canadian buyers of security commodities. In effect, CCC is acting only for foreign buyers and Canadian security bureaucracies (who are acting as Canadian "sellers"). This expansion of the CCC mandate allows it to act as a middle-manager between government security aid hubs and recipient countries. However, in this arrangement, CCC is not furthering any Canadian jobs except its own, through the "fees" and performance bonuses its claims on transactions.

Though CCC's mandate is to assist Canadian companies, its participation in direct security aid is strictly about advancing the strategic interests of Canadian security aid. As the primary procurement agent for Canada's security aid hubs, CCC will contract any security commodities companies to support programming objectives of security innovators within the Canadian bureaucracy. The result is "aid" donations funded by Canada that proliferate security infrastructures around the world. According to the most recent figures, CCC signed 109 contracts and amendments in 2013–14 for $15.75 million (CCC 2014, 74). Given the non-public disclosures of CCC and the security aid bureaucracies, none of these contracts have been itemized. Yet a number of CCC contracts for security infrastructures have been made available through the ATIA, which gives a sense of what constitutes the direct security aid managed by the security aid hubs.

Security Infrastructure Aid from the START-GPSF, ACCBP, and CTCB

Since signing the MoU with DFAIT in 2007, CCC has facilitated an impressive list of security development projects. It has assisted the Jamaica Defence Force Counter-Terrorism Operations Group with training, equipment, and technical expertise (CCC 2011, 2012). It provided millions of dollars in pickup trucks and parts to Sierra Leone Police Headquarters (CCC 2011), the Rwandan National Police, and the Haitian national police force. Immediately after the Libyan Revolution broke out, CCC facilitated the parachuting of medical trauma kits to Benghazi, as discussed the the last chapter (CCC 2012). Contracts with Canada-based Forensic Technologies Ltd have provided regionally integrated ballistics identification networks in Barbados, Trinidad and Tobago, and Jamaica ($791,556), and a similar regional network for Belize and Costa Rica ($2,084,044). Other efforts to develop transversal policing hardware included $3,160,500 in "investigative equipment" for Guatemala, Honduras, and El Salvador. Similar to systems delivered to Latin America and the Caribbean, CCC facilitated the donation of an Integrated Ballistic Identification System to the Malaysian Ministry of Home Affairs (CCC 2011) and enabled the procurement of audit services and financial mentoring, satellite services, medical equipment, and boats for use in Southern Sudan (CCC 2011). In Costa Rica, CCC procured approximately $1.7 million in security products, which included "state-of-the-art handheld radios, global positioning systems, bullet proof clothing, and a fleet of vehicles" (CCC 2013, 15).

Another notable CCC initiative for developing transversal policing and surveillance capacities was focused on the Pakistan-Afghanistan border. Through START-GPSF, CCC provided up to $4 million to Pakistan security forces for mobile scanners and pickup trucks to monitor the sensitive Federally Administered Tribal Areas (FATA) borderland region.[8] Reports from the project note that the "intent of this in-kind assistance is to provide the Government of Pakistan with the capability to more effectively manage, control and secure its border with Afghanistan ... [using] a 'beyond the border' approach" (GAC 2008-274, 113–14). The "donation" also included having "16-pre screened qualified individuals ... [trained] for operation of the [redacted] Mobile Scanner Units" (GAC 2008-274, 122). As a demonstration of how security aid funding can be tied explicitly to counter-insurgency operations, the proposal for the funding notes, "The porous international border between Afghanistan and Pakistan facilitates ease of movement for insurgents, weapons, and narcotics" (GAC 2008-275, 4). The proposal author adds, "An effectively managed border between Pakistan and Afghanistan is necessary for the stability and security of Afghanistan and for the success of the NATO International Security Assistance Force (ISAF) mission in Afghanistan" (GAC 2008-275, 95). In a rare inclusion of restrictions on the limits of security aid supplies, GAC officials write, "Pakistan will own the scanners" and "use them only for specified activities in accordance with the [redacted] ... and to exercise due diligence as required by Canadian legislation ... and policies" (GAC 2008-274, 101). The inclusion of such language is little more than a rhetorical device. A reality of security development is that, despite the best intentions of the security development workers or policymakers, there are few means to monitor the use of security aid donations.

With the protracted conflict in Syria, security infrastructures aid has been channelled to regional allies like Jordan under the banner of humanitarian assistance. For example, in 2014, the Canadian government announced $9.5 million to "aid refugees in Syria" (GAC 2014-778). Administered through CCC, the aid package – part of a much larger envelope to Syria – was sent directly to the Jordanian Armed Forces for cargo trucks, pickup trucks, buses, water trucks, etc. The package was a complement to another aid project that provided $2 million of equipment to the Jordanian Gendarmerie Force and Public

8 Pakistan security forces have been implicated in widespread human rights violations in the FATA. As a primary site for counter-insurgency operations, the FATA has been the subject of significant debate within security journals because of the common conclusion that it is a site for radicalization and has been a target for many U.S. drone strikes.

Security Directorate for security in and around the Za'atari refugee camp. Although one very candid field report detailed the "far from perfect" (GAC 2014-778, 60) coordination from the Jordanian security/military forces, the Project Closure report details some "successes" of the aid. Mostly related to JAF appreciation for the aid, the note states, "This project has served to strengthen Canada's bilateral relations with Jordan, especially in the sphere of defence cooperation. According to Canada's Assistant Defence Attaché for Jordan at the time, 'Canada has gone from being a Country with no defence-related engagement in Jordan to being regularly featured in updates to the Jordanian Chairman of the Joint Chiefs of Staff'" (GAC 2014-778, 100).

Like many of the security infrastructure packages, these aid donations combine strategic interests of advancing the reputation of Canadian security aid agencies with coordinated responses to govern global contingencies. Many of the projects in Africa have included funds for vehicles to assist with humanitarian missions, particularly in policing refugee camps. CCC has purchased heavily fortified IVEMA Gila vehicles for the South Africa Peace Mission Training Centre, as well as vehicles (also IVEMA Gilas) and "outfitting" the Formed Police Units (FPUs) of Senegal, Burkina Faso, and Uganda for the United Nations Mission in Sudan (UNMIS) (CCC 2009, 2010). Through the START-GPSF, CCC has also provided Zodiac boats for Lebanon (CCC 2009). In supporting international interventions, CCC ensured that Canadian corporations provide policing equipment to Afghanistan (ibid.) and a host of materials (discussed at length in the subsequent case study) to Haiti, including boats, border security equipment, police vehicles, portable police stations, riot control gear, and the construction of a $50-million police headquarters, along with a number of prisons.

Perhaps one of the most comprehensive programs of security infrastructure development has been Canada's aid to the Palestinian Authority (Monaghan 2016). Under the strategic direction of the United States and Israel, Canada emerged as a major contributor, pledging $300 million over five years to "support Palestinian efforts to increase security, strengthen governance and promote prosperity" (CIDA 2010-330, 330; see also CIDA 2012-338). Projects have included $50 million for courthouse facilities in Hebron and Tulkarem, as well as a courts complex in Ramallah, courthouses in Hebron and Tulkarern, and upgrades to courthouses in the West Bank (CIDA 2012-532, 83). Canada has also funded $1.29 million in prison construction, including a prison in Nablus (RCMP 2011-805). Funding from the international community as part of the Palestinian Reform and Development Plan (PRDP) has included money for fifty-two new prisons and eight new security compounds throughout the West Bank (Byrne 2011; also Leech 2015). Unlike the United States or United Kingdom, Canada has no post-sourcing requirements for external investigations on uses of security aid equipment. No documents made available by Canada have expressed reservations about human rights issues, or what Leech (2015, 1012) has detailed as the "shift towards greater authoritarianism" that is condoned by a desire to integrate "the PA as an agent on the US side of the so-called War on Terror" (see also Amnesty International 2013; Youngs and Michou 2011). Similar to what Bayley (2005) has detailed with U.S. police-capacity assistance, projects are frequently framed as building democracy and promoting rule of law. Yet, upon delivery, the vast majority of the trainings are technical and operational, with only vague overtures to human rights. In contrast to a critique of the PA's authoritarianism, Canadian aid documents recount improved security conditions – thanks largely to the policing and security aid.[9]

Aid money for policing and security services in the Occupied Territories has been substantial, including $1.5 million for the Joint-Operating Centres (JOC) – similar to those established in the Caribbean, discussed in chapter 2 – which aim to fuse operational capabilities within the West Bank and improve liaison with Israeli Security Services, the United States, Jordan, and other transversal actors (CIDA 2012-532, 327). The main focus of the Joint Operating Centres is to integrate elements of the Palestinian Authority Security Forces into Israeli command (GAC 2011-2067; GAC 2011-959; DND 2012-866; DND 2013-1963). Canada also funded a $2.9 million small-arms safety-training centre, $3.25 million towards the PA's Ministry of the Interior Logistics Complex, a $1.6 million forensics program, $4.5 million towards police IT infrastructure, $1.3 million to procure and set up two 200-foot communications towers, $2.4 million for the construction and rehabilitation of the Jericho Police Training Facility, and support for development of new training

9 For example, as outlined in one briefing note to the minister of foreign affairs, "Thanks to Canada's assistance, tangible results on the ground can be seen in the security and judicial sectors. Such improvements contribute to the security of Israel and help increase Israel's confidence in the Palestinian Authority's ability to maintain calm and rule of law in the areas of the West Bank under its control" (GAC 2011-2068, 77; see also CIDA 2012-532,246).

programs that "can respond appropriately and relevantly to the 21st Century environment" (CIDA 2012-532, 328; see also GAC 2014-847; RCMP 2012-3277).

While strategic economic interests in the security aid mission in Palestine are more abstract, the aid program has effectively advanced visibility of Canadian security innovation. According to one study participant, this comprehensive program to the PA was "one of the most successful" missions of Canadian security aid (Interview 2). Another participant described the program having to "be strategic to make small contributions have big impact" (Interview 4). Canada's Department of Justice celebrated an illusion that Canada had become "a major player" in the Middle East peace process (DoJ 2010-1638, 10; see also DoJ 2012-2148). A particularly visible element of Canadian norm-supporting is evident in the pursuit of accolades from the United States Security Coordinator General Keith Dayton (2005–10). CIDA meetings with Dayton from November 2009 contained handwritten notes stressing how Canada was "leading from behind," providing a "catalytic effect," "gathering the stakeholders," and describing Canadian participants as "indispensable, couldn't do it w/o cda" (CIDA 2010-338, 19–24) (see figure 4.3). The summary report further noted that Canada, "through its respective programming channels," had taken "a tangible lead and made an indispensable contribution" (CIDA 2010- 338, 25).

Figure 4.3. Notes from a Meeting between CIDA Minister Oda and General Dayton, November 2009 (CIDA 2010-338, 22)

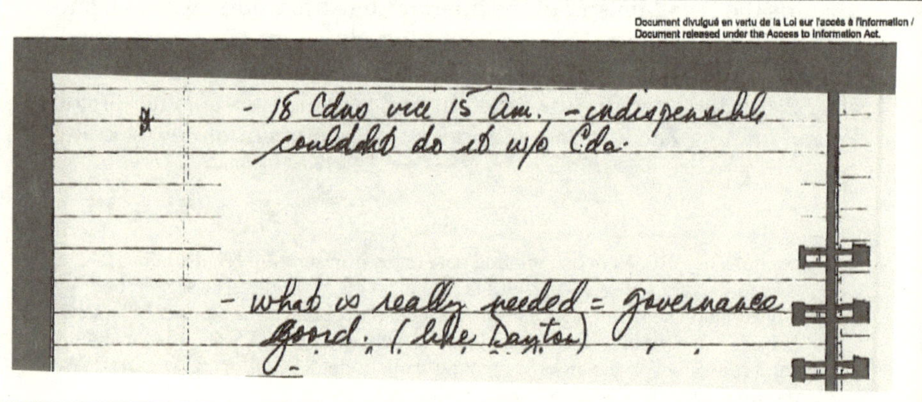

The note in figure 4.3 underlines Canada's significant contribution to the U.S.-directed security development missions known as the USSC. Canada's mission – known as Op Proteus – has made up the largest contingent within the multilateral deployment for several years (more troops than the United States) (see DND 2010-1284; DND 2012-547; DND 2013-1292). Canadian briefing notes regularly recount General Dayton's praises, noting that he had called Canada a "prized" contributor and had been "effusive in his praise for the professionalism and skill of the Canadian contingent" (PCO 2010-558, 1). Though Canada has no influence on the broader Middle East peace process, the security infrastructure aid to the PA demonstrates how security innovation can be leveraged to raise the profile of Canadian norm-supporting.

Although a full catalogue of aid for development of security infrastructures would be very difficult to compile, the listings above demonstrate how Canadian security aid travels to "places of interest." As this examination reveals, the strategic interests fulfilled by these assistance regimes include economic ones, but also broader interests played by Canadian security innovation in supporting development by the transversal security community of security governance in these insecure geographies. As a collection of strategies to develop the infrastructures of security, these aid programs demonstrate how security innovation can be packaged in a range of hardware that develops transversal security capacities in the Global South, as well as advancing the reputation and visibility of Canadian security innovators who can tangibly support the development of security. The projects funded by the security aid hubs are wide-ranging, yet they are not the only sources of aid funding for security infrastructures. As detailed below, DND-CF also provides significant forms of hardware aid.

DND and Surplus Gear

As prominent security innovators, DND-CF provide a distinct role that complements those of the security aid hubs and CCC in the donations of security infrastructures. While DND-CF does not engage in a similar quantity of infrastructures aid as CCC and the security aid hubs, they nonetheless have a unique role that is played through the donation of "surplus gear." Developed in the context of the Global Engagement Strategy (GES), the donation of surplus gear as a strategic component of Canadian foreign policy is a relatively new field, and it is strategically linked to Canadian security innovation in the transversal security community.

A briefing note for the minister of defence explains a new priority under the GES of donating surplus equipment to militaries of the Global South: "As many countries in Central America require basic military clothing and equipment, Canada Command is working with ADM(Mat) staff to identify opportunities where small transfers of surplus assets could achieve significant benefits for partner nations" (DND 2013-701, 65). The note goes on to explain that a Treasury Board directive on disposal of surplus materiel provides the minister with the authority to approve donations "when the donation/gratuitous transfer will serve the public interest more than sale to the public at market value" (ibid.). The "first such opportunity" presented itself in the summer of 2013 with a proposed "gratuitous transfer" of 2,000 tactical load-carrying vests to the Belize Defence Force.

Explaining that the "Tactical Load Bearing Vest is obsolete," the briefing advises the minister that, based on current catalogue price, the overall value of the vests being considered is $380,000. Although they have been "declared surplus by the Canadian Forces, these utility vests have multiple functions and are composed of pockets for arms and additional pockets for alternative use such as small radios and First Aid kits," explains a press release sent out to Canadian media (DND 2013-701, 10). The press release gives a succinct explanation of how surplus donations fulfil an "assistance" provision of security hardware, which in turn supports other security aid efforts to build capacity as well as broader strategic interests: "This donation of equipment is in response to a BDF request for Canadian Forces' assistance with the acquisition of vests, and will support BDF operations and training. These 2,000 load carrying vests represent a surplus to the needs of the Canadian Forces. This support for Belize is a *tangible* example of Canada's implementation of its objective, under the Americas' Strategy, to address insecurity and advance freedom, democracy, human rights and the rule of law through capacity building" (DND 2013-701, 10; emphasis added).

In addition to assisting to build the materiel capabilities of a member of the transversal security community, the CF have emphasized the donation of surplus materiel to enhance their communications and visibility. An email from Lieutenant-Colonel Deane St-Onge outlines the multilayered strategic value of these aid donations and their future use: "As this is but the first in what is expected to be an ongoing string of queries related to the aval of surplus assets for donation/gratuitous under the Department's Global Engagement Strategy, it would be appreciated if you could identify your POC (Maj Guilbault?) for fielding any future queries relating to DSSPM managed assets" (DND 2013-701, 87).

As an element of the GES, the donation of surplus gear has accelerated, although it is unclear to what extent. Most recently, DND-CF has donated surplus gear to Iraq and Ukraine. In late 2014, Ukraine received approximately 30,000 coats, 30,000 pairs of pants, 70,000 pairs of Gore-Tex boots, and 4,500 pairs of gloves (DND 2014). As a contribution to Iraqi security forces, DND announced in January 2015 (DND 2015) that it was donating 6,000 items of winterized and wet weather gear, including 1,000 coats, fleece shirts, and pants for cold weather operations, as well as 1,000 jackets and pants for wet weather.

Though surplus donations are primarily low-tech materials, they are styled as tangible contributions to broader transversal security objectives. Moreover, the circulation of military supplies to transversal policing also demonstrates a "boomerang effect" (Foucault 2003, 102), where military hardware used abroad comes back into domestic policing operations (see also Graham 2011). For example, DND has disclosed that surplus donations to Canadian domestic policing agencies have included night-vision goggles, military apparel, and related field equipment used in Afghanistan (Quan 2014). Other boomeranged goods include the donation of an MCI J4500-model bus to the Winnipeg Police Service, to be retrofitted as a "command vehicle" for major operations (ibid.). Four other police forces – BC RCMP, Edmonton, Windsor, and New Glasgow, Nova Scotia – have received "demilitarized" LAVs that were used by DND-CF in Afghanistan.

As a security assistance practice, the donation of surplus gear is a good representation of the transversal security community and a collapsing of internal/external boundaries. The boomerang effect reflects this blurring, where the technologies from security interventions abroad become normalized in domestic policing. Though the donations of surplus gear are small in quantity, they demonstrate how security assistance is more "successful" when conceptualized as strategically linked to Canadian participation in the transversal security community. Certainly these donations enhance the capacities of surveillance and security forces in the Global South, but a larger influence on the design of these strategies is the desire to increase Canadian visibility and reputation. These donations represent small, practical donations to efforts of the transversal security community and illustrate a humanitarian trope to rationalize Canadian aid.

Highlighting how security aid becomes practised as infrastructure development demonstrates an important aspect of Canadian security innovation. Although the cataloguing of these donations is only partial, the scope of these security aid practices demonstrates how Canadian technologies contribute to transversal governance capabilities, and spotlights the strategic functions of these donations to advancing Canadian visibility as a practical contributor to developing the security infrastructures of the Global South. Contributions from Canada as a norm-supporter of the transversal security community are exemplified by a value-free approach to developing security norms. The centrality of hardware as technical and value-neutral is an important component of Canadian norm-supporting. And it is epitomized by the case study of security aid to Haiti.

Security Aid and the Development of the Haitian Security State

Haiti is an ideal site to examine the category of security infrastructure aid. After the removal of Aristide, the situation in Haiti was declared a threat to international peace and security in the region. Acting under its Chapter VII of the UN Charter authority, the UN Security Council passed Resolution 1542 to establish the United Nations Stabilization Mission in Haiti (MINUSTAH). From the initial resolution 1542 (2004), which legalized an international force to consolidate the coup, a number of other resolutions – 1608 (2005), 1702 (2006), 1743 (2007), 1780 (2007), 1840 (2008), 1892 (2009), 1908 (2010), 1927 (2010), and 1944 (2010) – have augmented the authority of international actors under MINUSTAH to strengthen Haiti's security sector.

In what critics have described as the "UN Occupation" (Podur 2012), MINUSTAH is responsible for an estimated that 80 per cent of security functions in Haiti. With annual budgets in the range of US$650–800 million, MINUSTAH assumes primary responsibility for a wide range of governance reforms, which have a central focus on the criminal justice system. Comprising 6,892 uniformed personnel as of January 2015 (with 4,658 troops, 2,234 police, and additional civilians), MINUSTAH lists contributions from sixty-one countries.[10] MINUSTAH represents itself

10 Military personnel: Argentina, Bolivia, Brazil, Canada, Chile, Ecuador, El Salvador, France, Guatemala, Honduras, Indonesia, Jordan, Nepal, Paraguay, Peru, Philippines, Republic of Korea, Sri Lanka, United States, and Uruguay; police personnel: Argentina, Bangladesh, Benin, Brazil, Burkina Faso, Burundi, Cameroon, Canada, Chad, Chile, Colombia, Côte d'Ivoire, Croatia, Egypt, France, Grenada, Guinea, India, Jamaica, Jordan, Kyrgyzstan, Lithuania, Madagascar, Mali, Nepal, Niger, Nigeria, Norway, Pakistan, Paraguay, Philippines, Portugal, Romania, Russian Federation, Rwanda, Senegal, Serbia, Spain, Sri Lanka, Thailand, Tunisia, Turkey, United Kingdom, United States, Uruguay, Vanuatu, and Yemen. See UN (2015).

as a coalition of international collaboration, and it is influenced largely by norm-makers such as Brazil (Kenkel 2010) and primarily the United States (U.S. leadership was exposed with leaked cables in early 2011; see WikiLeaks 2011; also Ives 2011). Focused on stabilizing the political regime implanted by the United States, following the removal of Aristide, MINUSTAH implemented aggressive policing described as an anti-gang pacification strategy (Cockayne 2014; Dorn 2009). Yet clearly the strategy was deployed to target political opponents of the new government (Caple James 2010; Hallward 2007). MINUSTAH's aggressive policing campaign was accompanied by comprehensive efforts to build new security infrastructures. Canada has been central as an operator in the latter and a more passive norm-supporter of the former.

Carlos Alberto dos Santos Cruz of Brazil, force commander of MINUSTAH, described the efforts to make security an a priori function for economic development, saying that "stabilization and development are two sides of the same coin" (quoted in Muggah 2010, 445). On the security side of the coin, Canada became heavily invested in building the state capacity of police, prisons, and borders. Yet, on the development side of the coin, scholars have detailed how the international community – led by norm-makers – have promoted the extreme privatization of services, largely to international NGOs (Edmonds 2013; Schuller 2010, 2012). L. Zanotti (2010) has detailed how international strategies have promoted NGOs as substitutes for the social welfare state, and Schuller (2012, 7) has provided a vivid ethnographic exploration of NGOs in Haiti acting as "the glue of globalization" – effectively covering up the violence from a failed system of international aid while becoming instrumentalized for ends other than humanitarianism. Barry-Shaw and Oja Jay (2012) have extended this analysis to demonstrate how Canadian NGOs have profited greatly from the "aid" money spent in Haiti, demonstrating what Caple James (2004) calls "compassion economies" in which professional humanitarian agencies make suffering economically productive. And while development is privatized to the humanitarian market or domestic economic elite (Girard 2010), the construction of a "security state" necessitates a reaffirmation of the state's monopoly of force. As Chandler (2006) has detailed, the Global North has used the creation of "phantom states" to hollow out the economies and social services of "aid" recipients in the Global South (see also Duffield 2007; Hoogvelt 1997). However, this is parallel to an enhancement of abilities of the state's security apparatus to govern potential insecurities (Taylor 2009). Canadian aid has been central to this security side of development, with an emphasis on constructing the material infrastructure to enforce order.

Numerous participants in this study brought up Haiti as an example when discussing security aid projects. None of the references were positive. Haiti has been presented as having a fluid and unprofessional bureaucracy, "freelancing" in negotiations to receive more funding, having a deficient political culture, and being a recalcitrant aid recipient that has insufficiently "bought in" to an agenda of security and development. While supporters of the Canadian whole-of-government assistance program (Baranyi 2014) acclaim "successes" from these aid practices, very few successes are evident. As I discuss below, even Canadian officials have acknowledged that, by most measures, Haiti is no better off than before the removal of Aristide, despite receiving over a billion dollars in foreign aid. Moreover, many critics demonstrate that things are worse. What I account for below is how "security infrastructures" have been a major component of Canada's contribution to the interventions in Haiti – a component that has delivered "successes" for Canadian strategic interests, but few benefits for the Haitian people.

Overview of Security Aid in Haiti

Canada has funded thirty-two separate security projects in Haiti. Although several departments have managed these projects, the START-GPSF has been the most prominent, committing more than $100 million in security aid to Haiti from 2006 to 2014 (GAC 2012-49, 189). Most of these funds are officially directed to security system reform, where, according to GAC briefing notes, "Canada is a key donor in the security sector in Haiti, along with the United States" (GAC 2012-49, 185). After the coup to remove Aristide, a minimum annual START-GPSF allocation of $15 million was increased to nearly $25 million since fiscal year 2010–11 to respond to immediate post-earthquake stabilization (CIDA 2011-177). The majority of START-GPSF projects consist of construction and renovation of infrastructure and equipment for the Haitian police, prisons, and "une approche integrée" for border security (CIDA 2011-177, 86). START-GPSF projects have also included the placement of experts, including at least twenty-fvie individuals from CSC and up to 150 RCMP as part of MINUSTAH.

Projects to enhance security infrastructure range from very small prison refurbishment contracts ($89,000 to Prison Cap-Haitian phase 1), or building perimeter fences at police stations ($513,259.67 for the Lower

Delmas station), to large contributions such as the construction and equipment for major prisons, police stations, and border crossings. Following the earthquake, Canada quickly positioned itself to coordinate further security sector reforms. Not representative of any form of shift, projects announced post-quake have been a continuation of security aid policies that existed before the quake. I have previously detailed the 2005–9 security aid spending in Haiti (Walby and Monaghan 2011), and the discussion below highlights how the post-earthquake assistance is a continuation (if not an intensification) of Canada's earlier strategy. In keeping with the tenets of security development, the rationale behind this assistance rests on the notion that security presents a precondition to development. To advance development aspirations, Canada's aid to Haiti's security sector has centred on three areas: policing, prisons, and borders. I address these areas of security infrastructures aid in order.

Security Aid to the Haitian National Police

Haiti's national police force is called the Haitian National Police (HNP). Under the leadership of the United States and Brazil, reforming the HNP has been a multinational effort that has included France, Spain, European Union, UNDP, and MINUSTAH (RCMP 2009-5894, 115). Despite Canada's small number of participants in a very large coalition (150 members of a total exceeding 6,000), the RCMP has recounted the influence of Canadian security innovators: "Canada has become the lead contributor to MINUSTAH's mandate to reform and professionalize the HNP" through deployment of Canadian police officers and provision of infrastructure support (114). In addition to the contribution of personnel from the RCMP, Canada's commitment to enhancing the policing infrastructure has included substantial aid funding.

As the lead procurement body for START-GPSF, CCC has also been active in the enhancement of security infrastructure for the HNP. One element of these efforts has been to supply the HNP with operational vehicles. Through a CCC contract with Hinoto in Port-au-Prince, CCC spent US$2,619,137 to purchase 4x4 double-cab pickups for the HNP. Delivered in the fall of 2010, the pickups were to "assist them [HNP] in delivering their mandate by allowing for officers to carry out patrols, arrest criminals, document crimes and respond to emergencies" (CCC 2012-55, 302). From Perfecta, a company based in Port-au-Prince, CCC purchased a fleet of Black Honda NX4 Falcon motorcycles (US$337,111) and motorcycle equipment (US$300,400) (see CCC 2014-127). Also in

2012, CCC procured Toyota Land Cruisers (US$105,584), tow trucks (US$405,480), and a forklift (US$96,175) for the HNP (ibid.). CCC also handled two contracts for vehicle repairs: a $757,145 contract with a Thailand-based company to train forty HNP mechanics, and a standing order contract of up to $1 million for HNP truck repairs. A third contract worth $176,348.47 was signed with a numbered corporation from New Brunswick (662832 BN Inc.) in April 2012. The contract was to provide "Logistic Management processes to be designed and developed for the fleet of HNP vehicles" (CCC 2014-127, 158).

Canada has undertaken the post-coup building, refurbishment, and equipping of all twenty-one HNP Police Stations. For this project, aid funding has included the purchase of "all necessary office equipment," as well as operational equipment such as "crowd control" and "investigative equipment," helmets, vests, shields, bulletproof vests, batons, handcuffs, cones, traffic vests, fingerprint kits, police line markings, measuring tapes, digital cameras, police blotter, manual typewriters, latex gloves, etc. (RCMP 2009-5894, 110). Canada also funded the installation of an electronic fingerprint database (CIDA 2009-97, 204), the purchase of twenty vehicles and two motorcycles for these HNP stations, and the construction of three Level II Pre-trial Detention Centres.

START-GPSF allocated $2.5 million (through the IOM) to refurbishment of Haitian National Police Academy Training Headquarters. The goal of the project was to enhance facilities at the academy through the "reinforcement of adequate training facility space, including provision of infrastructure and other necessary equipment, in order to strengthen efficiency in delivering professional and specialized training for all profiles of police officers, including border, correctional and special units' police officers" (GAC 2013-1691, 210). The contract included extensive construction of facilities, classrooms, barracks, living quarters, water supplies, cafeterias, an equipped weight-lifting room, dining facilities, a kitchen with appliances, beds, air conditioners, a wide range of office supplies, medical supplies and CPR kits, traffic cones, megaphones, crime scene kits, fingerprint kits, reflective vests, gym mats, portable power washers, construction tools, computers and printers, projectors, and a vehicle for the maintenance team (GAC 2013-1691, 212). CIDA announced and approved funds in 2011 for a new National Police Academy in Ganthier, outside Port-au-Prince (CIDA 2011-191,15). Yet, as of late 2014, the $35-million commitment had had numerous delays and had not passed the proposal stage. In funding temporary facilities, GPSF contracted Alberta's Atco Structures and Logistics Ltd (through

CCC) to provide mobile training classrooms and toilets for the HNP (CCC 2014-127, 105). At a cost of over $77,000 each, Atco provided twelve classrooms in 2011.

Enhancing the training facilities of the HNP has been integral for the plan to build security capacities in Haiti. Canada's security infrastructure aid was supplemented by efforts to train and mentor the HNP, largely through the MINUSTAH mission. Canada has sent numerous groups of policing experts to Haiti through the Canadian Policing Arrangement, as well as while contracted through CANADEM. As one GAC document describes the commitment, "The presence of the Canadian police experts in Haiti is greatly appreciated by the HNP, their colleagues and other countries engaged in Haiti. Canadians are highly sought after in departments where *tangible* results are immediately needed. The expertise and know how of the Canadian officers in Haiti is well known, and the greatest lesson learned has been that in future missions to Haiti, greater numbers of Canadian police experts should be deployed for longer missions" (GAC 2013-1691, 137; emphasis added). Noting Canada's efforts to strategically allocate security innovators, another report on contributions from START-GPSF and the RCMP reads, "Contributeurs [Canadien] adoptent une approche beaucoup plus stratégique ... identifient une niche précise et des poste clés ... [pour] apporter sa contribution afin de mieux faire valoir ses intérêts et ses champs d'expertise ... particulièrement au niveau de la programmation du GTSR [START] en appui à la mise en œuvre de la RSS – police, prisons et frontières" (RCMP 2009-5894, 2).

In order to maximize the humanitarian aid to Haiti for its own strategic ends, Canada focused significant resources on building the security infrastructure of the HNP. Leveraging the aid contributions to the infrastructure of the HNP, the RCMP have highlighted their strategic niches and tangible contributions to the enhancement of the MINUSTAH mission. Using this leverage has allowed Canadian to demonstrate its security innovation and achieve higher visibility. As I discuss below, there is acclaims for Canadian security innovation within documents on Canadian security aid, alongside noticeable absence of comment about the two largest issues facing the Haitian population: human rights and poverty. Although many documents refer to aspirational principles of human rights, few discuss practices of human rights, particularly the extremely poor record of the HNP. Perhaps the most depictive project of the effort to police the extreme poverty in Haiti comes from a START-GPSF-funded effort to create mobile policing outposts.

Through CCC, Canada contracted the IOM in July 2012 to provide "mobile offices" for the HNP. While the contract for the containers described them as "offices," the final report submitted by the IOM described the containers as "Police Commissariat Containers" designed to be deployed in "volatile" and "targeted neighourhoods" (CCC 2014-142, 25). In retrofitting the sea containers into mobile police stations (an innovative feat in itself), the IOM provide pictures in their final report to START that exemplify what Sanyal (2007, 58) has called the postcolonial "wasteland of the dispossessed" and the policing of Haiti's impoverished population (see figure 4.4).

In the final report, IOM note that "an issue beyond IOM and START control was the final destination of the containers once ready for deployment." Indicating that there were subsequent discussions between IOM and START-GPSF with the HNP over the issue of deployment, the subsequent text of the report is redacted. The report notes that at least one location (in the neighbourhood of Delmas 75) was stopped by a community association known as a CASEK (see CCC 2014-142, 26), which provides some insights into the violence and antagonisms in which these stations are embedded.

Notwithstanding the issue of locations – the containers are intended to be mobile – the IOM report details how the containers will function as "fully operational Police Commissariats to be placed in volatile locations identified by the HNP" (CCC 2014-142, 9). According to the report, "[Redacted] out of [redacted] containers were placed in the HNP priority neighbourhoods and other [redacted] remained at the National Police Academy of Port-au-Prince to be deployed around the city" (ibid.). Although redacted in some areas of the document, the report later confirms (as does the original contract) that thirteen containers were provided: "By July 2013, 10 Mobile Commissariats were installed in different locations of Port-Au-Prince and one in the Haiti / Dominican Republic border area of Malpasse." Finally, IOM reported, "The HNP received [number redacted] equipped mobile commissariats, all placed in vulnerable neighbourhoods to ensure a more efficient response to crime through immediate intervention" (26). As in most discussions of "crime fighting" in Haiti, the depiction of the HNP is that of an objective policing force acting to assist "vulnerable" neighbourhoods. This depiction is far from the reality.

Despite the constant refrain from Canadian and international actors to be improving the human rights practices of the HNP, a number of reports have detailed how the HNP have been involved in flagrant

Figure 4.4. HNP Mobile Police Stations for "Targeted Neighbourhoods" (CCC 2014-142, 10–11)

***Photos 1 and 2:** The used sea Container Van being retrofitted to become as an HNP Mobile Commissariat (left); heat insulation being installed under the plywood covering for walls, ceiling and flooring are (right);*

***Photos 3 and 4:** Installation of the office/service area partition. The service area hosts an ACU condenser, a 5KW generator and an electrical panel.*

***Photos 9 and 10:** Office area (left); A retrofitted and equipped container van is ready for deployment (right).*

All ■ container vans were retrofitted in the HNP Academy compound to secure materials and contractor 20(1)(c) equipment. Once contractors completed the works, IOM, jointly with HNP and START representatives, conducted a final evaluation of each van to ensure quality output. The keys to each Mobile Police Commissariat were handed over to the HNP upon a positive evaluation of each unit.

human rights abuses (Amnesty International 2011, 2014; HealthRoots 2011; U.S. Department of State 2013). Allegations of widespread corruption and drug trafficking are regular, and local parlance refers to the HNP as "legal bandits" (Papillon 2014). Even some Canadian documents illustrate the precarious "development" of the HNP. One example is the provision of "non-lethal" equipment to the HNP. At the conclusion of a CANADEM mission that facilitated twenty retired Canadian police officers as senior advisors within MINUSTAH, concerns were raised regarding the disposal of weapons purchased for the Canadian officers. After being informed that the risk of storing the firearms and tasers at Canada House was too great, CANADEM was instructed to "have all lethal equipment destroyed and transfer the ownership of the remaining equipment to HNP" (GAC 2013-1691, 120). However, despite being instructed by GAC to give the tasers (and not the firearms) to the HNP, CANADEM provided the following explanation for their actions: "After consultation with Phil MacLellan [policing consultant], donation of the non-lethal equipment directly to the HNP was not recommended. The MINUSTAH vetting process of the HNP is not sufficiently complete to ensure that CANADEM could guarantee that the equipment would be properly used for HNP police activities, and not sold off into black market activities" (ibid.).

After an attempt to transfer the equipment to the Niger component of MINUSTAH failed, it was shipped back to Canada and destroyed. It is notable that, through examination of thousands of documents on security aid to Haiti, this is the only evidence where provision of security infrastructure and materials corresponds with concerns over its implications. Even more notable, the concerns were raised by a contracted third party, not Canadian officials.

Elsewhere, a "secret" document from December 2011, circulated by the director of GAC's Haiti Task Force, Karen Baudson, demonstrates the tenuousness of the HNP as a recipient (see GAC 2012-49, 59–65). In an email to a list of individuals and departments that comprise the whole-of-government approach to security aid in Haiti, Baudson writes in the opening bullet, "Looking to the security situation, the Police National d'Haiti [redacted] to ensure community security throughout the country, but it was clear that international, and specifically Canadian efforts to build their capacity is having a positive impact." Then, two pages later, another section appears under the heading of "human rights" (see figure 4.5):

While mostly redacted – itself likely an attempt to shelter the Canadian government from criticism and embarrassment – the point is

Figure 4.5. Redacted Human Rights Discussion Regarding HNP (GAC 2012-49, 61)

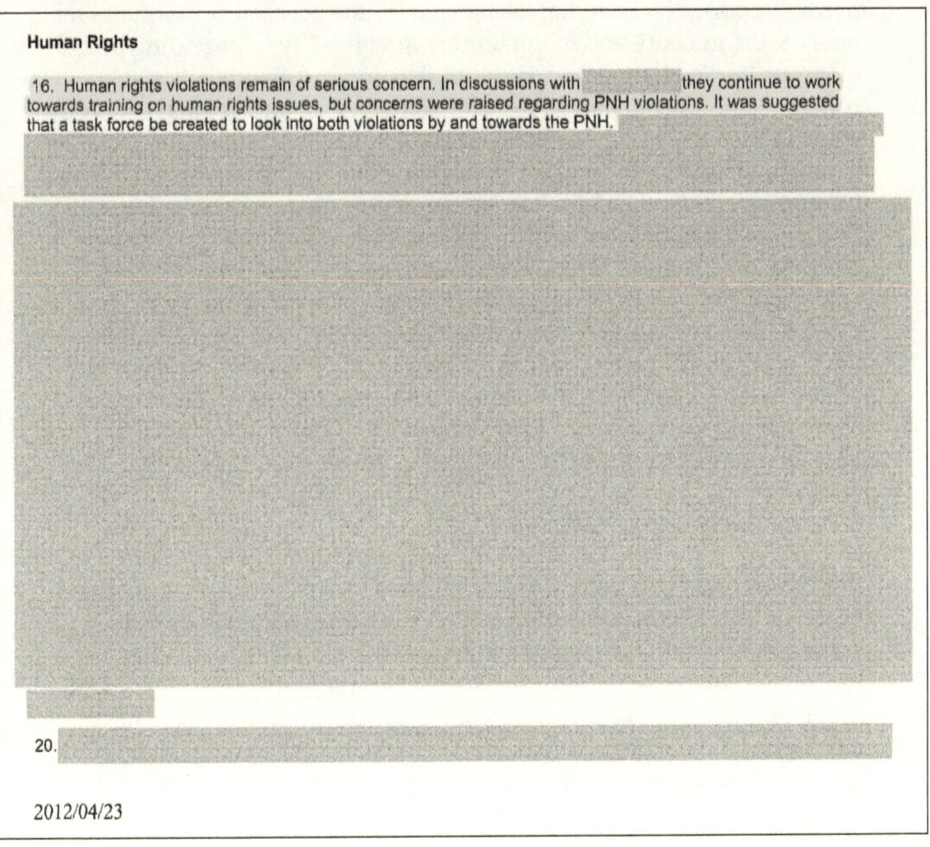
Human Rights

16. Human rights violations remain of serious concern. In discussions with [redacted] they continue to work towards training on human rights issues, but concerns were raised regarding PNH violations. It was suggested that a task force be created to look into both violations by and towards the PNH.

20.

2012/04/23

clear: the HNP are a rogue police force. Baudson expresses this point somewhat cryptically later in her report: "Although training efforts continue, the force remains limited by both the number of officers and an unclear strategy for their development" (GAC 2012-49, 63). Given Canada's "leadership" in developing this strategy over the past decade, the statement would appear to be highly contradictory. Yet, if we understand the constant mention of Canadian "leadership" in norm-supporting, Baudson's statement can be better understood. As a technically oriented contributor, Canada's leadership is in applied expertise, how Canadian security innovators can be seen as reliable and dependable in providing functional support for requirements of the MINUSTAH mission. Canada has limited influence within MINUSTAH, so instead functions as a norm-supporter by showing its backing for the normative rationales for intervening in Haiti, and maintaining high visibility in providing practical security development in Haiti. In that context, Baudson's statement contains no contradiction, because Canada's contributions are from security innovators on a strictly technical plain.

Canada has only technical responsibilities, so the moral responsibilities for human rights violations can be handed to those accountable for the "strategic" goals of the reforms, or simply be regarded as an expression of the lack of "buy-in" from Haitian recipients of aid. Even further, the lack of development with the HNP highlights how human rights abuses provide more rationalization for "development" and "professionalization" of the HNP, thereby calling for further attention to Canada's contribution as a technically focused security innovator. And, though concerns about "professionalization" have been raised, there is no indication of post-aid monitoring or reporting on how these resources are used.

Security Aid to Border Controls

Border security is a second pillar of the security aid regime in Haiti. Much of the Canadian funding is directed through the IOM in order to "strengthen Haiti's capacity to manage regular and irregular migrant flows" (CIDA 2009-97, 202). IOM programming also includes a wide range of capacity building, which corresponds to the third type of security techniques. Much of this work corresponds to integrating Haiti into the transversal security community and "facilitating cross-border cooperation and discussion on matters high on the Caribbean agenda" (ibid.). Canada has also engaged in (very cautious) attempts to integrate Haitian authorities into broader regional efforts at border controls.[11]

Aid to develop the infrastructures of border management has centred on border stations along the Dominican Republic border. Funding to the Pan American Development Foundation (PADF) included a $2.9 million

11 For a funding project that included sending Haitian delegations to cross-border events and trainings, a note appeared within a "risks" matrix: "During the first year of consultations, until momentum and confidence get consolidated, the project team avoided controversial and highly problematic topics (e.g., illegal labour migration) where one particular country would emerge as a source of all troubles in the region" (GAC 2013-1691, 79).

reconstruction of the Belladere crossing. Aiming to "improve security; increase respect for migrant rights; and regularize cross-border flows" (CIDA 2009-97, 205), the new Belladere complex opened in early 2013 and included six buildings for migration, customs, and police. Canadian funding for the rehabilitation of Malpasse border post was coordinated by IOM. As one of four major land crossings, it is estimated that 57 per cent of border traffic between Haiti and the Dominican Republic takes place through the Malpasse crossing (GAC 2013-1691, 225). It is particularly important for migrant workers (many of whom are non-authorized) and market workers. Canada's contribution to developing a border control system is a practical effort to contain these mobilities, which are a preoccupation of the transversal security community that regard the unregulated mobilities at the Haiti-DR border as a source of insecurity.

At a cost of over $4.2 million, the IOM refurbished and upgraded "police infrastructure and supply of necessary equipment at 18 border posts within a 15 kilometer radius of the border" (GAC 2013-1691, 287). In a final report issued in September 2011, the IOM reported that the border refurbishments funded by START-GPSF "to control the 388 kilometer land border with the Dominican Republic as the MINUSTAH mandate and the Haitian government shifted to prioritize the security of border areas" (ibid.). Another project provided over $2.4 million towards refurbishment of border checkpoints at Beliadere, Saint-Marc, Gonaives, Ouanaminthe, Malpasse, Miragoane, Thomassique, Les Cayes Vache, Port-de-Paix, Port-au-Prince Port, and Cap-Haitien (GAC 2013-1691, 70). For these border outposts, aid funding was assigned to cover costs of supplying office and IT equipment, document examination tools, and expert assistance in developing immigration legislation, procedural manuals, and management skills. Funds to the IOM have gone towards purchasing laptops, digital cameras, and GPS units. With START-GPSF funding, IOM coordinated the creation of a Technical Support Unit office, which included refurbished and procured office equipment and furniture. Three new passport offices in Les Cayes, Port-au-Prince, and Cap Haïtian – which were either renovated (Cap Haïtian) or created *ex-novo* (Les Cayes and Port au Prince) – have been installed with new passport-issuing software and materials (GAC 2013-1691, 273).

Refurbishment of the border posts included installation of all electrical equipment, including generators and solar systems, as well as office equipment. IOM also contracted a firm to install IT and VHF radios at the checkpoints. Mobile radio communication equipment was installed in the vehicles at the checkpoints. Also, immigration officers in

Port-au-Prince and at border checkpoints received twenty-five handheld VHF radios as part of an integrated radio communications system. In their contract with START-GPSF, IOM also procured 160 kits and reference manuals for training new border officers in document examination.

These Canadian funds have been directed to build the physical infrastructures of the Haitian border. In addition to the construction and refurbishment of the border, savings from projects were directed towards extra border enhancements. For example, "At the end of the intervention on the 18 police posts, funds were available to rehabilitate an additional 1,44Bm2 of the burned Ouanaminthe Commissariat leaving only one section of the largest commissariat in the country to be rehabilitated" (GAC 2013-1691, 288). As an illustration of Canada's role as a security innovator in the fortification of Haiti's border regime, Japan funded aspects of the Canadian initiative. One report details, "As a result of the lead role the START has played in the initiative to reinforce security along the land border areas, the Government of Japan also agreed to contribute towards the initiative. The Government of Japan's contribution included the supply of vehicles and motorcycles, additional office equipment, and technical and investigative equipment for the 18 border posts. The Government of Japan's contribution totalled 2.3 million dollars" (GAC 2013-1691, 289).

Development of interoperable surveillance systems at the border was addressed by a contract with the IOM ($3.6 million) that "aims to increase the capacity of the immigration service to track migration flows, and improve the service's coordination with other agencies involved in border management, including those tasked with combating human trafficking" (GAC 2013-2554, 8). The project planned to introduce automated Border Management Information Systems at twelve border migration points (GAC 2013-1691, 272). However, the program was fraught with complications, particularly the non-cooperation of Haitian officials.[12] Through a series of setbacks – including two reported

12 One report noted: "It must be however stressed that there exists still a large group of law enforcement officers, some of whom also received the integrated border management team, who is resistant to change and who remains still very much attached to their pre-training working style, as it is unfortunately more lucrative, as connected to corrupt practices" (GAC 2013–1691:242). Though security development workers are quick to point to corruption, Ball (2005) has emphasized that "resistance" is a common organization aspect of security policy transfers. Moreover, from a postcolonial framework, non-compliance is an aspect of the unequal power relations that accompany the "sharing" of security assistance.

instances of deliberate tampering – the plans were downgraded to install twelve VSATs (satellites) at specified posts. However, even those plans faltered, and only three VSAT systems were installed. IOM reported that the remaining nine VSATs had "been donated to the Ministry of the Interior and are stored in a government building" (GAC 2013-1691, 273). In the meantime, IOM also reported that it was quitting the training phase of the project and the VSAT trainings would be led by technicians from the unnamed company.

Complementing security infrastructure aid to bolster land crossings are projects to increase the capacity of water-based migration flows. Funding has been allocated for the Coast Guard (which is run by the HNP) base in the Southern Region in Les Cayes ($7 million) to "help regularize of the flow of people and goods" and "reinforce the presence of the HNP along the southern coast" (CIDA 2009-97, 205). Canada also funded ($3.7 million) the "donation of five vessels to the maritime police unit of the HNP to "complement the construction of a maritime police base in Les Cayes" and "strengthen Canadian leadership in advancing security system reform and stabilization in Haiti" (CIDA 2009-97, 208). Similar to other cases of security aid, "Canadian leadership" is a common label used by security innovators to characterize their strategic, practical contributions to developing security. One document related to construction at the Belladere border crossing reported, "Two billboards have been produced to display, make public and exhibit the design of the border complex in Belladere. Those billboards, which were unveiled during the visit of Minister Maxime Bernier, clearly presented to the public the support and funding of the Canadian Government to the construction" (GAC 2013-1691, 353).

As a norm-supporter, Canada uses the promotion of Canadian "leadership" as a central component for promoting security innovation. Through infrastructure aid to enhance Haitian border controls, Canada has promoted its contributions as a practical support for security development. The governance of mobilities, particularly through trends in "crimmigration" (Aas 2011; Stumpf 2006), is a priority of the transversal security community. As I detail in the next chapter, these efforts are centred on the coordination and interoperability of border surveillance and policing agencies, with recipient countries of the Global South becoming marshalled – or deputized – as frontline managers of unwanted population flows. With a history of poverty and foreign interference, Haiti has long been considered a problematic source of "illegal" migration, and the Canadian security aid to border infrastructures represents a highly strategic and practical contribution to development coordinated by the transversal security community. Complementing the security aid to policing as well as the prison system (as examined in the next subsection), these practices of security innovation have been valuable for enhancing systems of security governance, and even more successful at promoting the visibility of Canada's strategic norm-supporting contributions.

Security Aid to Prisons

A third pillar of the security infrastructure development in Haiti has been prisons, coordinated by Canada's federal prison authority – Correctional Services Canada. CSC was asked to "assist in re-establishing and strengthening the corrections system in Haiti, as a result of the Service's international reputation and correctional expertise" (CSC 2011-172, 1). The reform program has involved extensive prison construction and training programs.

There are seventeen prisons in Haiti and four commissariats (located in police stations). CSC has been working in Haiti since the mid-1990s, with few accomplishments, given the excessively violent and illiberal conditions of the Haitian penal system. In fact, a penal system that was already among the most unjust of the world has perhaps gotten worse. According to the Haitian national police, the number of prisoners in September 2015 was 11,319 – compared with 1,935 in 2004 (Gallón 2016: also Forst 2013). A report jointly report by the UN and a human rights unit within MINUSTAH warned that the prison population continues to increase, "making even more alarming a situation that was already critical, equivalent to cruel, inhuman and degrading treatment" (MINUSTAH and UN 2016, 1). The Port-au-Prince prison is estimated to contain more than 4,000 prisoners, despite being built for a capacity of 750 inmates. Overcrowding in Port-au-Prince mirrors the trend of excessive overcrowding across Haiti where the UN reports an occupancy rate of available space for prisoners in all prisons in the country at 804 per cent while the average space per inmate amounts to 0.55 square metres (ibid.). Remand practices and preventive detention are responsible for much of the overcrowding, with as many as 8,140 prisoners (72 per cent) being held in pretrial detention, including 379 women, 203 boys, and 20 girls, without having yet seen a judge (Gallón 2016, 8; see also Human Rights Watch 2014, 256).

As an effort to assist with the massive overcrowding of non-convicted prisoners, Canadian security aid has funded projects to refurbish and construct more prisons. In particular, Canadian security innovators have focused on building new prisons that could serve as "model" prisons for a major prison expansion. Two prisons in particular are worth noting. CSC has pointed to the Fort Liberté prison as "[un] projet [qui] constitue donc une opportunité pour la DAP de construire pour la première fois une nouvelle prison conformé aux normes internationales, et de ce fait de fournir à la DAP une prison 'modèle' qui pourrait faire l'objet de réplication dans les autres juridictions carcérales du pays" (CIDA 2009-97, 147). Likewise, the Croix des Bouquets prison, described as a flagship initiative located approximately eight miles from Port-au-Prince, was imagined as a prison "[qui] servira de modèle pour d'éventuels échanges d'expériences, de bonnes pratiques et une réplication potentielle dans d'autres juridictions du pays" (RCMP 2009-5894, 1).

Construction costs for Croix des Bouquets were funded by the Canadian government and construction began in May 2009. When the facility opened in 2012, it offered a "bed space" – of 1,024. UN independent expert Michael Forst (2013) noted the facility was far better than current norms in Haiti, but the prison was quickly overcrowded, resulting in a large jailbreak in 2014. Canada has also funded $1.5 million in renovations at the Cap Haïtien civil prison. One report notes that the general capacity of the prison was intended to be 165 people in eleven cellules. Yet at the end of May 2007, the prison was holding 300 people in only seven functional cellules (GAC 2011-1609, 65). The first phase of the repairs focused on opening the four dysfunctional cellules. Subsequently, the PADF had completed additional eight cellules (three for women and five for men), as well as a kitchen and other facilities. Construction was completed by February 2010.

Though Canada has been involved in prison reform since the 1990s, and MINUSTAH has engaged in a variety of efforts since 2004, there are few indicators of improvement. While often noting the objective of human rights, the prisoner abuse is rarely detailed in Canadian documents. For example, nothing appears in Canadian reporting similar to this publicly available U.S. State Department entry from their Haiti Human Rights Report of 2013:

> Following the destruction of numerous correctional facilities in the 2010 earthquake, prison and detention center overcrowding was severe, especially in the National Penitentiary, the Petionville women's prison, the Petit Goave jail, and the prisons in Jeremie, Les Cayes, Port de Paix, and

> Hinche. Only the newly constructed prison in Croix des Bouquets conformed to international norms and was not significantly overcrowded. Others, including the detention facilities in Cap Haitien, Fort Liberte, Gonaives, Petionville, and Port de Paix all held more than four times their maximum number of inmates. In some prisons detainees slept in shifts due to lack of space. Some prisons had no beds for detainees, and some cells had no access to sunlight. In others, cells often were open to the elements and lacked adequate ventilation. Many prison facilities lacked basic services such as plumbing, sanitation, waste disposal, medical services, potable water, electricity, and isolation units for contagious patients. Prisons generally used well water as a source for drinking and bath water. A newly operational sanitation block in the Les Cayes prison contained nine showers and 10 toilets serving a population of 572 inmates. Some prison officials used chlorine to sanitize drinking water, but in general, prisoners did not have access to treated drinking water. (U.S. State Department 2013, 5)

Other organizations have detailed similar abuse, neglect, overcrowding, corruption, and dysfunctional policing and court systems that increase the strains on the prisons (see Alternative Chance 2014). Exasperated with the gross injustice of the Haitian penal system, Forst has recently reported, "On each of his visits, the independent expert spends time in detention facilities, police stations and prisons, but without seeing any real improvement in the situation" (Forst 2013, 8; see also Forst 2012). Forst (2013, 9) concluded that prison conditions in Haiti "amount to cruel, inhuman and degrading treatment within the meaning of the Convention against Torture." Despite the repeated commitment to enhancing the "human rights" capacities within the Haitian prison system, there are few – if any – indicators of improvements. In fact, reporting from Canadian security aid agencies often displays a significant lack of concern about human rights abuses. Nowhere is there language such as that found in the US State Department report or that of the UN independent expert.

While CSC reports mention issues of overcrowding and human rights, rarely do they convey the punitiveness of the Haitian penal regime. Take, for example, one field report after the earthquake notes, "There are no standards associated with staffing complements, in some situations staffing compliments were defined as who could get into work that day, and who stayed at the prison as their house was damaged. During one visit at port au prince I observed [redacted]"

(CSC 2012-450, 5). This is one of the more critical accounts made (or released publicly) regarding the Haitian penal system. Yet not only do Canadian authorities seem to omit the violent realities of systemic human rights abuses in Haitian prisons, numerous documents attempt to portray an alternate reality of progress and development. A good example of this manufactured reality of Haitian prisons can be illustrated by a "Permanent Briefing Book" on the "CSC Contribution to the Federal Government's Role in Haiti" (see CSC 2011-172, 8–12). The four-page document – a briefing book for senior administrators and parliamentarians – from January 2011 provides a background on CSC's contribution to MINUSTAH since 2004, as well as details of the MINUSTAH prison reform program and the training programs provided by Canadian penal experts. Written to impress parliamentarians on how CSC "is playing a key role in Haiti," the document says nothing about the state of the prisons, presenting only a technical view of trainings and Canada's positive contributions.

At a House of Commons committee meeting examining CSC's contributions to Haiti's prison system, CSC spokesperson Marty Maltby was pressed by members of Parliament on the poor conditions of prisons and concerns over the number of individuals in preventative detention. Maltby confirmed that between 2006 and the time of the earthquake the population in preventative detention had at some points reached even more dire levels (CSC 2011-172, 18). Yet the summary of Mr Maltby's presentation to Parliament notes that "CSC's contributions to MINUSTAH have involved improving local prison conditions, recommending and supervising infrastructure projects, and promoting international human rights standards. He highlighted CSC's work in the process of mentoring, training, and providing advice to prison staff at all levels" (CSC 2011–172:17). Pressed by a Conservative MP on whether Canada is leading in Haiti, Maltby detailed how Canadian security innovation was contributing to the MINUSTAH mission. In a summarized version of his response, "[Maltby] referenced CSC's concept of 'dynamic security,' which serves to humanize the prison experience, and has proved beneficial in MINUSTAH's work in Haiti. He made mention of Canada's leadership role in Haiti by means of the leader of the correctional unit being a Canadian correctional officer, the overall expertise of our staff, and the relationship CSC has had with the Haitian correctional system for over a decade" (CSC 2011-172, 19).

In a sanitized version of security innovation, parliamentarians are given the impression that Canadian experts have imparted skills – like "dynamic security" that "humanizes the prison experience" – into Haitian prisons. Though Canadian security innovators have engaged in training, the violent conditions in Haitian prisons are wilfully ignored and suppressed by actors like Maltby. Instead, we see only a portrait of Canadian norm-supporting in the MINUSTAH mission, packaged discursively as humanitarian governance. Like most Canadian documentation of security aid in Haiti, Maltby presents an image of progress and development – regardless of the conditions. However, in some circumstances Canadian reporting has raised significant questions about progress. Though critical accounts are rare, one example is how CSC security innovators warned that the MINUSTAH focus on rapidly building policing capacities would produce a "Haitian paradox" where penal conditions would be worsened (see Walby and Monaghan 2011). In other words, efforts to increase the capacities of security, border, and policing have resulted in an intensification of the very poor penal conditions in Haiti and improvements in one sector means further disorder in another. Though some Canadian efforts have been made to undo this "Haitian paradox" by funding development in the judicial and legal branches, much of the security aid to Haiti's prison system has focused on simply building more prisons.

According to most indicators, few of the security development programs for penal reform have improved conditions for Haitian prisoners. If anything the "Haitian paradox" – produced through foreign design, and not deserving the misnomer "Haitian" – has made conditions worse. Yet some individual efforts have been made by CSC security innovators to advocate on behalf of prisoners in Haiti. Though specifics are rarely detailed, CSC documents reveal frustrations with a lack of movement on aid files. For example, in 2008, a CSC correctional expert reviewed the files of all prisoners housed at the Penitencier National and identified 1,000 of its most vulnerable prisoners (i.e., young, aged, ill, non-violent, etc.) who could be housed at alternative custodial centres. Records indicate that Haitian officials did not respond to the advice. Another report seems to criticize a "cadre of Haitian correctional authorities," but the section is largely redacted (GAC 2013-1691, 157). Other examples indicate advocacy on behalf of specific cases and general concerns over sanitation and human rights, as well as concern about prolonged pretrial detentions.

I highlight these points of advocacy to illustrate that CSC efforts to advance human rights demonstrate an additional component of security innovation. With the enhancement to the security apparatus across

Haiti, prisons have been overcrowding at growing rates and, in their individual capacities, CSC mentors have attempted to alleviate particular problems they encounter. Some of these efforts may have assisted particular people in distress. However, attempts to improve individual conditions, these examples must be contextualized within a situation that is replete with abuse. Moreover, these examples of innovation and advocacy are embedded within Canada's technically focused efforts that are subordinate to a comprehensive security-building project. It is a project in which Canada, as a norm-supporter, is following mandates established by an international regime where these examples of advocacy – while nice – are mere micro-efforts against forces propelled by the macro strategies in which those very same actors are embedded. Regrettably, indicators suggest that building more beds and constructing more prisons will only lead to more overcrowding. As Monture-Angus (2011) has demonstrated in the context of high rates of indigenous incarceration in Canada, the prison system can illustrate "injustice personified." Prisons are the final component of the criminal justice system and, through the people who inhabit them, they "personify" a system that is unjust and discriminatory at every level. In such conditions we can also see the violent and illiberal character that personifies the criminal justice regime. While some Canadian prison experts have been dismayed by the prison conditions in Haiti – and other security innovators have been frustrated by the lack of progress – the general trajectory of security aid in Haiti has been maintained and accelerated, and Canadian security innovation has been integral to this trajectory. And while some individuals have advocated for better conditions within these prisons, other security innovators like Maltby have promoted the work of Canadian security innovators to strategically advance an image of "successful" humanitarian aid.

Discussion and Analysis: Security States, Governance Imbroglios, and Strategic Interests

From the period following the coup to the early post-earthquake period, the security aid regime targeting Haiti has been remarkably consistent. Incorporating humanitarian language of development into its rationale, the transversal security community – with Canada as a norm-supporter – has used tropes of instability to rationalize a comprehensive re-engineering of Haiti's security infrastructure. As an articulation of the security-development nexus, Canadian security agencies have repeatedly rationalized security aid spending to inaugurate a future of economic development. For example, according to one briefing note on aid to Haiti prepared for the minister of international development, "Les reformes du système de sécurité instaurent les conditions *préalable nécessaires* aux efforts de développement à long terme de l'état haïtien et de la communauté internationale" (CIDA 2009-97, 210; emphasis added). Yet, given the levels of poverty in Haiti and, like other phantom states, a continued emphasis on economic neoliberalization is likely to produce future insecurity (Farmer 2011; Fatton 2007; Caple James 2010; Shamsie 2009; L. Zanotti 2008). As with other societies trapped in a security-development nexus, this future of instability will accelerate calls for additional security aid.

This reality is not lost on security aid actors, as demonstrated by a summary of a meeting in Haiti to discuss "the challenges faced and progress being made" by MINUSTAH. The meeting was attended by MINUSTAH Deputy Force Commander Major General Neris Mauro Corbo (Uruguay), Brazilian Battalion Commander Colonel Luiz Guilherme Paul Cruz, Major Bruce Sand (Canada), and other high-level military officials, as well as members of Canada's Department of National Defence, START Director General Robert Deroiun, and Public Safety Assistant Deputy Minister Kristina Namiesniowski. Notes from the meetings indicate that the officials identified three challenges for MINUSTAH: civil unrest, unemployment, and Haitians' high expectations. MINUSTAH officials stated that "maintained pressure on the security front would ensure 'good behaviour' but that the situation as it stood now could not continue indefinitely without an increase in employment opportunities" (RCMP 2009-5894, 99). As a norm-supporter of the transversal security community's efforts to enforce the "good behaviour" of Haitians facing socio-economic injustices, Canada has focused its security aid on the "niche" areas of policing, border, and prisons. In particular, Canada's aid regime to Haiti demonstrates how development of security infrastructures can allow a norm-supporter like Canada to have a "seat at the table" – as one participant put it (Interview 13) – in conversations like those above.

As a program to enforce "good behaviour" of the Haitian population, Canadian security aid to Haiti has focused on building what Hallsworth and Lea (2011) have called the "security state." Emphasizing the role of the state as the central agency of social control, Hallsworth and Lea have explained how security agencies (police, borders, and prisons) and crime-control practices are increasingly mobilized to manage *social fragmentation* (see also Rose 2000). While Hallsworth and Lea (2011) focus largely on the United Kingdom, others have demonstrated how the coercive domains of the "security state" are especially evident in the transversal policing of social fragmentation (Cowen 2014; Hyndman 2009; Nair 2010; Weber and Bowling 2008). Given that market-based economic development models cultivating consumer economies also necessitate a peripheral class of poor and excluded – what Rose (1999) calls the marginalia – security governance practices are needed to manage those populations excluded from consumer capitalism. This is what Weber and Bowling (2008) describe as the "flawed consumers" or "unworthy citizens" within the neoliberal order. As demonstrated by Canadian aid practices, the objective of the transversal security community in offering "stabilization" assistance is to enhance social control capacities, and aid funnelled to security infrastructures represents assistance to developi the physical capacities of surveillance, policing, and border control in the deviant states of the Global South.

In the context of global security governance, the support for "recipient" regimes is significantly different from "aid" clientalism of the Cold War (see Sylvan and Majeski 2009; also Eisenstadt and Lemarchand 1981). While client regimes during the Cold War were outfitted with security and policing materials to ensure political stability, the "aid" regimes of security governance operate in a post-sovereign system of global governance. In a manner that parallels the conditional nature of Libyan sovereignty examined in the previous chapter, assistance to Haiti is twinned with discourses of governance reform. Unlike the silence of Cold War aid clientalism towards the domestic practices of client regimes, security aid funds the infrastructures of the security state while simultaneously demanding a wide range of governance reforms (see Duffield 2005; Eriksen 2011). A central component of security aid are these inducements to reform in the form of constant demands that the Haitian authorities conform to the recommendations of norm-makers and, as one participant put it, "take security seriously" (Interview 10). In parallel with a trend towards the neoliberalization of development practices in Canada (Hyndman 2009), much of the record of Canadian efforts in Haiti details the aim of inducing buy-in from Haitian interlocutors. Like Ilcan and Lacey's (2011) analysis of how aid regimes are promoted to "responsibilize" recipients from deviant states, security aid to Haiti includes demands for neoliberal economic reforms, as well as multilayered approaches to building transversal bureaucracies of security governance.

Calls for governance reform in Haiti have accelerated following the 2010 earthquake. Documents from GAC recount how, in February 2011, Canada and the European Union co-hosted a large conference on Haiti in Brussels. Entitled "Haiti, One Year after the Earthquake," it consisted of two policy discussions: one on the role of governance in reconstruction, the other on coordination of international humanitarian aid. It was an important site for promoting Canadian security innovation and provided an opportunity for meetings with other prominent members of the transversal security community. For example, the evening before the conference, Canada's ambassador to Belgium and Luxembourg, Louis de Lorimier, hosted a reception for participants and key interlocutors – though not including Haitian officials. Following the conference, Canada's ambassador to the EU, Ross Hornby, hosted a closed-door working dinner at which key participants from the day's discussion were able to "engage in more candid discussion on the most sensitive topics of the day" (GAC 2012-49, 8). Excluding Haitians (as well as non-Northern states from MINUSTAH) from these side events illustrates the norm-making power within the transversal security community, as well as Canada's ability to advance its visibility by taking a "leadership" role in advancing the agenda of the United States and other norm-making actors.

Detailing the proceedings of the Brussels conference, the summary provided by GAC's Haiti Task Force begins, "Summary: The elephant in the room has been addressed" (GAC 2012-49, 7). Recounting how the conference "shed light on weak governance" as Haiti's major impediment, participants engaged in "frank discussion held under Chatham House Rule" (ibid.). What becomes clear in the three-page summary of the meetings – which included high-level Haitian participation – was that the "elephant in the room" was Haiti's political leadership and the upper echelons of Haitian bureaucracies. The report underlines that achieving development in Haiti "requires that the Haitian government assume greater responsibility," and that "there was broad agreement on the need to continue to strengthen justice and security systems in Haiti" (ibid.). With a heavy emphasis placed on the failures of Haitian governance being at the root of the problems in Haiti, one paragraph exemplifies the Canadian-supported efforts in Haiti (see figure 4.6).

Canada is not alone in asserting that the problems of Haiti are a result of Haitian mis-governance. Schuller (2012) has detailed how senior U.S. officials, following the earthquake, consistently portrayed similar positions. "We cannot help Haiti. Haiti needs to help itself" was how one official put it (quoted in Schuller 2012, 137). Though debates on

Figure 4.6. Bullet Point on Good Governance Discussions, "Haiti, One Year after the Earthquake" Conference, Brussels, 23 February 2011 (GAC 2012-49, 9)

12. Good governance integral to Haiti's future: The afternoon discussion focused on the role of governance in Haiti's reconstruction, a discussion that in many participants' view was long overdue. There is a growing, collective recognition that despite concerted efforts, eight UN interventions and billions of dollars spent over more than 15 years, the international community has not achieved the results expected and Haiti has not realize its full potential. Much like the humanitarian response challenges discussed in the morning, most of the endemic problems facing Haiti, including political upheaval, widespread poverty, social unrest and a struggling economy, exacerbated by the earthquake, are rooted in democratic deficit and reflect a lack of capacity, and in some cases will, on the part of Haitian authorities and political actors.

post-coup Haiti have solicited polemically opposed positions, I suspect few would disagree with the "problems facing Haiti" listed in the report.[13] Where critics of the UN intervention in Haiti would find significant disagreement is the suggestion that failure of the international communities' efforts are "rooted" in a "democratic deficit" attributable to Haitians. As others have laboriously detailed, Haiti's political history is largely that of foreign interventions and the suppression of authentic Haitian democratic potential (Fatton 2002; Girard 2010; Hallward 2007). A paragraph that speaks of "8 interventions" in a foreign country while simultaneously lamenting a "democratic deficit" is endemic of the normalcy in which the transversal security community regards Haitian sovereignty as conditional and subordinate.

Notwithstanding the negative impacts of the security intervention in Haiti – particularly its most recent iterations – the concluding paragraph of the report signs off with a hopeful tone: "Canada, as a well-respected and revered partner in Haiti has the opportunity to shape discussion and set the agenda on governance in Haiti going forward" (GAC 2012-49, 11). As the subtext to comments such as these, as well as those about the "elephant in the room" and Haiti's "democratic deficit," are the humanitarian sentiments enacted to rationalize security assistance programs. On display is Canada's (and the transversal security communities') altruism

13 The academic journal *Small Axe* solicited four leading analysts on Haiti and the 2004 intervention for a debate in 2009, which is an excellent source for the opposing interpretations of the Aristide regime. Though much of the political disagreements relate to Aristides legacy, the discussants agree on the long legacy of foreign exploitation in Haiti (see Hallward 2009; Kaussen 2009; Nesbitt 2009; Trouillot 2009).

in "assisting" the development of Haiti, despite what is described by donor countries as the recalcitrance of Haitian recipients.

It is important to stress that the success of Canadian aid practices is not to be measured narrowly on the development of security capacities. While the failures of security development are grounds for new practices of reform and intervention, the "success" of security aid is in its strategic promotion of Canadian security innovation. As a norm-supporter, Canada has a strategic interest is mobilizing security aid to increase the visibility and the notoriety of Canadian security experts in their small, though practical contributions to security development in Haiti. When considering the success of promoting Canada as a norm-supporter of security development, the security aid practices in Haiti have been very productive. To illustrate, consider documents from MINUSTAH meetings in Port-au-Prince attended by GAC's Karen Baudson and Rachel Remington from the Privy Council Office. Though Canada is only a minor member of the MINUSTAH forces, the summary from meetings from 28 November to 2 December 2011 describe how efforts to enhance the security state in Haiti have increased Canadian strategic importance in the eyes of norm-makers: "The meetings provided valuable insight into the development of Canada's engagement in Haiti, and in particular the increasing priority on Governance and Rule of Law. The international consensus regarding the lack of governance and rule of law being at the root of Haiti's challenges was underlined, but moreover, it was clear that international partners are looking to Canada to take the lead in moving the rule of law file forward" (GAC 2012-49, 59).

Having developed a record of highly placed senior members within MINUSTAH and a wide range of security infrastructure developments for borders, policing, and prison institutions, security innovators have expanded Canada's reputation as a trusted norm-supporter. In replacing the antagonistic Aristide government, Canadian security aid has focused on operational features that develop immediate capacities to quell unrest and "stabilize" the post-coup political environment. With this practical contribution to the MINUSTAH mission of stabilization and "development," the development of security and governance norms has supported consolidation of new security governance priorities that stress integration with the broader transversal security community. Canada's role as a reliable norm-supporter is particularly valuable, given the widespread criticism of the MINUSTAH mission.

Along with the strategic interests of advancing the influence of Canadian security innovators and the visibility of Canada as a norm-supporter,

Canada's security aid contributions have been described in the context of pursuing Canada's broader regional interests. According to one "secret" briefing note for the minister of foreign affairs, "Haiti is a key platform for bilateral and regional cooperation in support of the Americas Strategy. It notably fosters our engagement with Brazil" (GAC 2012-49, 293). Another briefing note observes, "Canada's engagement in Haiti is a centerpiece of our foreign policy, particularly within the Americas Strategy" (310). As a major component of the Global Market's Action Plan and the America's Strategy, Canada has used security aid to assist norm-makers in their governance reforms in Haiti. This strategy deploys "aid" to advance bilateral and regional relations with prominent norm-makers, particularly with the intention of advancing economic interests. Though economic interests are rarely mentioned in Canadian documents regarding the "aid" mission in Haiti, one leaked document made available on WikiLeaks outlines the centrality of Canada's economic interests. A U.S. diplomatic cable written in April 2008 by U.S. Ambassador to Canada David Wilkens is titled "Haiti: The Centerpiece of Canada's Latin America strategy" (WikiLeaks 2008). The cable reports on Prime Minister Harper's visit to Haiti (2007), as well as the more recent visit by Foreign Affairs Minister Maxime Bernier to announce five major security projects. Commenting on Canadian security innovators' efforts to develop transversal surveillance practices, Wilkens notes, "As in Afghanistan, the border and cross-border cooperation received particular attention in Canada's latest aid programming" (ibid.). Giving details on the transformations to the bureaucracies of security aid hubs, Wilkens quotes from a Canadian source who emphasized that changes to the aid structure will prioritize security aid: "The START team was generally more attuned to security challenges than CIDA's more traditionally-minded development specialists" (ibid.). On the final page of the report, Wilkens outlines Canada's position on economic liberalization in Haiti: "Canada was also looking at further steps to improve the investment climate, such as helping companies with insurance to reduce risk. Canada had been disappointed that the planned and 'much needed' Investment Forum did not come to fruition in November and hopes it will eventually take place; it will have Canada's 'full support.' Canada also plans as the host of the Caribbean Development Bank meeting in Halifax in May to give Haiti prominence on the margins of the meeting … One Canadian NGO – the Foundation for the Americas (FOCAL) – had called for Canada to implement a 'unilateral' free trade agreement with Haiti, but to date the idea seems to have garnered little support" (ibid.).

As Canadian researchers have explored, NGOs like FOCAL have been instrumental as intermediary actors for Canadian government interests in Haiti (see Barry-Shaw and Oja Jay 2012). Advancing a radical project of privatization, these NGOs have hollowed out the Haitian state, making delivery of social welfare services almost impossible (see Edwards 2012; L. Zanotti 2010). Compared to the volume of government documents available regarding Canadian involvement in Haiti, the foregrounding of economic interests in these leaked documents presents a very different representation of priorities. While only a rare glimpse into highly classified discussions, these documents contribute to a broader understanding of the strategic interests pursued through security aid. Combined with research on the role of NGOs in Haiti, these documents also underline a broader characterization of the "capacity building" program in Haiti: privatizing the social welfare functions of the state to non-governmental and market actors, while building the functions of security state to ensure the "good behaviour" of the Haitian population.

As a norm-supporter, Canada has used security aid to make significant contributions to the development of a Haiti security state. Leveraging investments in the development of policing, border, and prison infrastructures has resulted in Canadian visibility and recognition for practical, concrete security innovation. Like most security aid, the rationality of security development does not necessarily translate into practices of security governance. For all the aid to Haiti, most indicators suggest that the security infrastructures developed by Canadian security aid have not translated into smoothly functioning systems of border control, policing, or prisons. Regrettably, the security infrastructure donations have exacerbated illiberal policies of violence and suppression that are endemic to the policing and security forces in Haiti. While corruption is significant, the violence of the Haitian police – as well as MINUSTAH forces – is a result of an enforcement of order put in place by the transversal security community. This conditionality of Haitian sovereignty is at the root of the "democratic deficit," a reality that has been made functional by the practical contributions of Canada's security aid.

Conclusions: Development of Security Infrastructure

As the second type of security aid, "security infrastructure" demonstrates how security assistance programming can focus on the development of physical and material components needed to develop more sophisticated practices of transversal security governance. This chapter details how, through security aid channels, Canadian foreign assistance makes significant contributions to constructing these infrastructures of security in the Global South. With Haiti as an exceptionally clear articulation of the phantom-like conditionality of deviant states, the "aid" regime to Haiti is best described as a security governance paradigm of Redfield's (2005) minimalist bio-politics. Jumping off from what Redfield (2005) describes as the fostering of mere survival through medical humanitarianism, the security aid to Haiti is a set of practices enacted by the transversal security community to contain the insecurities of Haiti to Haiti alone. Developing security practices to maintain "good behaviours" is a survival strategy aimed solely at managing a population by keeping them encamped. Moreover, the abysmal record of governance reforms in Haiti only provide further rationalizations for more interventionary controls and further escalations of security development.

Though security aid is expressed in the language of humanitarian reason, I demonstrate that the practices of security innovation are embedded in a strategic logic to utilize aid to increase the visibility of Canadian contributions to transversal security development. This chapter highlights how these programs of infrastructure development mirror the advancing of the transversal security community's security norms. In sharp contrast to notions of benevolent or altruistic Canadian foreign policy, the case studies of the Canadian Commercial Corporation and the security aid project in Haiti demonstrate how the "success" of security aid is not measured by the (in)securities on the ground, but the achievements of Canadian security innovators at taking "leadership" roles in the norm-making practices of security development. These case studies demonstrate the strategic value of security aid in promoting economic interests in addition to promoting the visibility of Canadian security innovators/innovation. As I explore further in the following chapter on the techniques of security, Canadian norm-supporting practices are tangible and practical efforts to develop interoperability and cooperation in the governance of (in)security. Complementing security aid interventions and techniques, the development of infrastructure illustrates concrete practices that Canada undertakes to develop transversal security governance.

Chapter Five

Security Techniques: "Software" of Transversal Security

Introducing Security Aid Type 3: Security Techniques

Consider the following. Written during a Canadian-funded assessment mission by the UNODC to Palestine in 2008, a report details strategic orientations that should be taken by security aid funding to reform prisons: "It was noted during the mission that funding has been made available to rehabilitate some of the prisons with the future intention to expand this to the rehabilitation of all prisons. However, there is a pressing need for developing the 'software' (staff skills and management systems) of the prison administration" (GAC 2011-1609, 17).

In emphasizing a pressing need for "software," the request represents what I detail as the third type of security aid: techniques. Unlike the "hardware" of security infrastructures, the "software" of security techniques involves knowledge practices aimed at the management of (in)security. Typically, aid in security techniques involves capacity-building assistance, mentoring, and a wide variety of training, within Canada and abroad. The objective of these aid projects is to develop capabilities of recipient countries by enhancing their skills, knowledge, management regimes, training and education systems, technological platforms, information-sharing practices, policy-development frameworks, administrative systems, reporting and assessment mechanisms, etc. – in other words, their "software" of security governance. In the case described above, the Palestine Authority had been assessed as having sufficient prison spaces – unlike the Haitian authorities discussed in the last chapter – yet the UNODC assessors highlighted their lack of capacity in knowledge practices and governance regimes. As an example of an area of security in need of "software" development, this represents one example along a spectrum of programming that encompasses the development of security "techniques."

Detailing a range of security aid projects, this chapter demonstrates the scope of security techniques. Since security techniques can relate to any elements of the security governance spectrum – from borders, to prisons, to human resources management – this chapter is focused on the work of Canadian security innovators in developing areas of policing and border controls. Since policing is central for many of Canada's security development projects, detailing the capacity building of border policing illustrates the scope of "techniques" development, as well as creating an important site to demonstrate Canada's practical norm-supporting of the transversal security community's efforts to manage global mobilities.

The chapter is divided into three main sections. First, I offer a theoretical framework of "techniques" development by situating Canadian security aid practices within a framework of Foucauldian scholarship on the management of circulations. As techniques of security, I underline the scope of Canadian security aid in efforts to manage "good" and "bad" circulations in a context of "governing through risk" (Muller 2010). I offer a broad range of examples to highlight the knowledge practices of security techniques, then explore Canadian efforts to develop transversal policing. In this examination of Canadian security innovation, I further argue that Canadian security aid is focused on two dimensions of techniques development. The first has been highlighted by a robust scholarship on security sector reform, focusing on how to build particular skills and practices in a "sustainable" fashion. A second component builds on key aspects of the transversal security community and advances the need for recipient countries to become integrated into transversal practices of security governance.

The second section of this chapter moves into a detailed case study of Canadian security aid to the Southeast Asia (SEA) region, under the banner of Canada's "anti-human smuggling" agenda. Situated as a contribution to literature on security and mobilities studies, I demonstrate how Canadian security innovators have sought to develop knowledge practices of intelligence-led policing and border management in Thailand, Indonesia, and Cambodia as part of a comprehensive project to stop migrant boats from "reaching Canadian shores." While other norm-makers have long-established border management practices in the region, this detailed case study shows the development of this Canadian security aid project in response to the construction of "illegal migration" and Canada's role as a norm-supporter in the broader project of managing circulations. As a number of scholars in the migration-security nexus have detailed (Aas 2011; Aas and Bosworth 2013; Aas and Gundhus 2015; Guild 2009; Pickering 2014; Pickering and Weber 2006; Walters 2008), transversal efforts to manage migration are rooted in desires to distinguish between problematic mobilities (associated with "illegal migration") and bona fide travellers. As a contribution to literature on "crimmigration control" (Stumpf 2006; see also Aas 2011; Dauvergne 2008), my case study of security aid to SEA demonstrates how Canadian security innovation aims to develop "software" of security as a broader, technical contribution to transversal efforts that "police at a distance" across the Global South (Bigo and Guild 2005b). In seeking to develop the policing techniques to monitor unauthorized movements from its point of departure, the security aid project is aimed to enhance what Aas (2013) has called "deviant states" in the transversal security community. In so doing, the security aid develops capacities to police the borders at a distance, while also serving as a concrete example of how Canadian aid is strategically mobilized to support norm-makers in their efforts to develop transversal security practices.

The final section of this chapter provides a discussion of security aid and its relationship with scholarship on contemporary security governance. In particular, I further my engagement with critical mobility studies that highlight how transversal border policing is a result of managing poverty by underlining how security innovation comprises an important aspect of what Bigo (2008) has introduced as banoptic power. Unlike the indiscriminate targeting of panoptic power, banoptic power is an assemblage of practices to govern flows and circulations of (in)security on a global scale. Yet the concept does not assume a unitary strategy of social control, instead highlighting how plural fields of security innovation operate as the sum of many parts. I further this discussion of discriminatory (in)security by engaging with literature on racial Othering (with a focus in Canada) to explain how exceptional practices are rationalized in the context of the transversal security. Finally, by using the popular concept of "petty sovereigns" introduced by Butler (2004), I close the discussion by illustrating how Canadian security assistance is not animated as much by discourses of neo-Orientalism typical of states of exception, but instead by a humanitarian reason that mobilizes risk knowledges and the discourse of human rights to keep what Canadian officials called "a pool of would-be migrants" inclusively excluded. I highlight how, as a program of "aid," the supportive role of security innovation speaks to Canada's part in assisting the development of transversal security governance.

Security Techniques: An Exploration of the "Software" of Security Development

Aid for the techniques of security appears under a wide range of categories. Assistance projects can be described as capacity building, training and education, train-the-trainer approaches, and a medley of governance "reforms" such as the rule of law. Moving beyond security-infrastructure aid focused on "hardware" of security, the primary objective in developing security techniques is to develop the *practices* of security governance. In using the term *techniques* to describe the "software" of security aid, I borrow from the notion of apparatuses (or dispositif), developed by Foucaudian scholars, which emphasize the technologies of governance (Amoore and de Goede 2008; Aradau and Van Munster 2007, 2008; Bigo 2008; De Larrinaga and Doucet 2010; Muller 2010; Salter 2008). I describe the "techniques" as knowledge practices – often working in tandem with technological hardware – forming systematic approaches for the management of (in)security. Foucault (2007, 45) described this distinctive approach to "security" by contrasting against the disciplinary technologies of prisons: "Discipline is essentially centripetal ... Discipline concentrates, focuses, and encloses. The first action of discipline is in fact to circumscribe a space in which its power and the mechanisms of its power will function fully and without limit ... In contrast, you can see that the apparatuses of security, as I have tried to reconstruct them, have the constant tendency to expand; they are centrifugal ... Security therefore involves organizing, or anyway allowing the development of ever-wider circuits."

For those who have followed Foucault's conceptualization, controlling society is not simply a matter of building the proper enclosure, whether the prison or the hospital, the border or the university. And though security aid is often focused on providing bricks and mortar with barricades, fortresses, border scanners, or more armaments, funds for the development of security techniques aim to advance the knowledge practices of surveillance and enhance the "organizing" structures of security-related agencies to engage in ever-wider circuits of governance. As a form of assistance focused on developing the practices of security, the frequently used term *capacity building* illustrates these aid projects.

Projects under the two "capacity-building" security aid funds (ACCBP and CTCB) offer a wide range of programs to develop security techniques. Spending close to $50 million per year, contracts range in size from a few thousand dollars to several million and demonstrate the scope of Canadian security innovation, including border enhancements, prison management, counter-terrorism, policing sciences, legal and criminal justice reform, and governance and bureaucratic training, as well as the enhancement of information-technology practices.

A sampling of these capacity-building projects demonstrates the scope of techniques as well as their commitment to developing transversal security governance practices. Aid projects have included a 2011–12 CTCB funds of an undisclosed amount for "expanding the use of INTERPOL tools to combat terrorism in Asia and the Horn of Africa." The ACCBP funded two projects with Interpol: one to establish a capacity-building program on transnational organized crime with Mexico, Jamaica, and four other Caribbean countries ($1,595,813.98); and another program, discussed below, with Cambodia, Indonesia, Laos, Thailand, Malaysia, and Vietnam to develop policing training and "connectivity" on human smuggling ($1,295,267.20). In 2012, CTCB funded separate projects: $1,580,000 for "Strengthening the Counter-Terrorism Capacity of Somali Law Enforcement," and $1,527,120 for "Combatting the Financing of Terrorism and Money Laundering in Ethiopia and Uganda." Also in 2012, the World Bank received two contracts of an undisclosed amount: "Anti-Terrorist Financing Capacity Building" in Yemen and the other in Jordan. CTCB has also funded a UNODC project, "Building Legal and Operational Capacities to Financing of Terrorism in the Horn of Africa" ($1,305,356.79), while a 2013–16 project with the IOM ($3,636,780) will provide "enhanced border security for CT [counter-terrorism] in the Horn of Africa."

Canada's elite Financial Transactions and Reports Analysis Centre of Canada (FINTRAC) has been awarded at least eleven projects from the CTCB, for $817,659.94. The capacity-building work of FINTRAC – a world leader in transnational financial analysis and investigations into terrorism financing – has included a "Workshop for Financial Intelligence Units in Select Caribbean States," and an "Information Workshop (Compliance, IT, Legislation, Analysis and Security Training)" in the Middle East. The CTCB funded a three-year (2007–10) capacity-building program for Southeast Asian law enforcement agencies that focused on financial and major crime investigations, and tactical intelligence

($385,340.53), as well as a separate course on RCMP Thailand in-flight security officer training ($184,004.46).

In developing knowledge practices within the criminal justice system, an ACCBP project in Guatemala ($1,196,542) aimed to "strengthen capacity of security systems by coaching prosecutors and police; prosecutor and police collaboration." Another ACCBP project with twelve Caribbean counties ($159,252) sought to "increase capacity of 60 Caribbean Members of Parliament (MPs) to develop and implement anti-money laundering and anti-corruption legislation." A project to provide comprehensive education and justice reform between Canada's Department of Justice and Mexico has provided training to judges ($2,847,715.03) and lawyers ($1,975,356.48), to harmonize criminal legislation and prosecutorial services ($2,653,704.96).

Other professional legal reforms included a contract with the U.K. Crown Prosecutor Service to implement comprehensive justice reform with Trinidad and Tobago ($1,263,511). Some policing projects include RCMP polygraph training to the Jamaican police force ($5,087.95) and $704,900 to the Jamaican Defence Force and Jamaican Constabulary Force for polygraph capacity building and the establishment of a regional centre of excellence. In developing a form of "benevolent watch" (see Moore 2011), Canada has attempted to transfer its model of drug treatment courts (DTCs) to Central America and the Caribbean ($1,719,719.26). Offering a nice empirical demonstration of how the tourism industry has been assimilated in the "war on terror" (see Lisle 2013; Ojeda 2013), ACCBP funded a capacity-building workshop on specialized security training for the tourism industry with Colombia, Guatemala, and Mexico ($1,294,257.39).[1] At the cost of $98,978.73, the RCMP was to provide "behavioural investigative technique" training to Colombia, Costa Rica, and the Bahamas. The ACCBP awarded $1,169,200 to Trade Bites and the CBSA to enhance the capacity of Panama Customs to use modern techniques in detecting illicit goods without disrupting maritime activities.

In addition to the ACCBP and CTCB, DND-CF run the Military Training and Cooperation Program (MTCP), whose explicit purpose is

1 Documents on the Canada-Mexico Security Working Group consultations highlight the importance of promoting the security of Canadian tourists (and the tourism economy). An example is found in a note on police training delivered under ACCBP: "First application of above noted training will be state of Quintana Roo which is principal Canadian tourist region" (RCMP 2011-3711, 57).

to provide security training and education programs to "developing," non-NATO member countries.[2] As one briefing note to the minister of national defence outlined, the MTCP "seeks to work with 'like-minded' countries to achieve common objectives and works exclusively with developing countries" (DND 2014-708, 1). Originally designed to support the military clientalism of the Cold War, the collapsing inside/outside binary created a significant increase in MTCP activity. From 1995 to 1999, the annual budget grew from a traditional baseline of $1.2 million to $12.5 million (Rasiulis 2001, 63). Currently, the MTCP has a budget of $20 million. In establishing its capacity-building curriculums, the MTCP assesses the needs of countries enrolled in the programs, then offers courses for either in-Canada training or more customized sessions abroad. Overall, the MTCP offers training to over 1,000 foreign military officers annually from more than sixty-two member countries (DND 2013-1523). This training includes sessions in a wide range of security techniques, from Canadian Special Operations Forces Command (CANSOFCOM), courses on counter-terrorism, civil-military cooperation for "humanitarian" mission, introduction to psychological operations (Psy Ops), information operations (Info Ops), introductory officer combat training, naval boarding training, and UN military observer courses, among other advanced topics. In addition to tactical courses, the MTCP offers educational programs on topics such as staff and professional development training, English and French language, peacekeeping, junior officer-staff training, and public affairs. While it appears that a large number of tactical courses – particularly from Special Forces training – are conducted during elaborate training exercises abroad, member countries of the program also send upper-echelon military officers for in-depth courses at the Canadian Staff College in Toronto and the Canadian Forces College.

While the these listed projects are only a sample of the thousands of security techniques projects funded over the past decade, they provide a glimpse into the array of security aid projects to develop policing, surveillance, and security techniques in the Global South. Before offering a detailed case study of how these development projects unfold with a case study of border policing in Southeast Asia, I outline a central aspect of security techniques: policing sciences.

2 The criterion for a "developing" country is based on the gross national income (GNI) per capita measure and related categorizations of countries generated by the World Bank. A figure of GNI US$12,275 or less defines a "developing" country.

Policing is an important aspect of security aid because of the wide scope of practices and institutions that implement the techniques of "policing." Canadian policing agencies, as well as retired and contracted police officers, are prominent security innovators within projects funded by Canadian aid programs. The scope of techniques developed through these projects impacts numerous fields including police agencies, border controls, immigration and customs agencies, prisons, security and intelligence agencies, port and transportation agencies, and public security departments. As I detail below, the vast range of techniques assistance programming demonstrates a key area of Canadian security innovation and provides a useful backdrop to discuss Canada's role in norm-supporting transversal processes of border policing.

Policing Sciences: Professionalization and Integration

Consider the following table, which is one page of eleven from the RCMP database on capacity-building training from 2012 to 2013 (see figure 5.1).

On the second-last column to the right is the listed RCMP trainer. Note that the trainings themselves often involve multiple agencies from Canada as well as other agencies representing donor countries of the Global North (Interpol is a frequent partner). As can be seen from the table, the scope of "capacities" to be developed is wide ranging: professionalism in border management, major crime scene management, interviewing techniques, best practices for drug scene investigations, synthetic drug courses, community policing, etc. Emblematic of contemporary policing in the Global North, these projects aim at what has been termed problem-oriented policing (Scott 2000). Often described by its advocates as an offshoot of community policing approaches hoping to address "root causes" of crime, problem-oriented policing is better described as emphasizing "building a knowledge base for police operations" that involves more systematic forms of aggregating and analysing information (Brodeur and Dupont 2006, 16). Ratcliffe (2008, 85) has outlined how elements of the knowledge-based approach contained in problem-oriented policing have evolved into contemporary notions of intelligence-based policing, demonstrating how intelligence-based policing is not simply about "intelligence" work but serves as a business model for police work "in its own right." In his conceptual framework, Ratcliffe (2008, 85) has demonstrated how intelligence-led

Figure 5.1. Excerpt from the International Database That Tracks International Law-Enforcement Training (i.e., Political Sciences Courses) Offered by the RCMP (RCMP 2013-1985, 9–10)

15	2011-09-14 to 2014-02-01	Regional Security System (RSS) Training Institute	G 565-677	St. Vincent & the Grenadines, St. Lucia, St. Kitts & Nevis, Grenada, Dominica, Barbados, Antigua & Barbuda	RSS		St. Vincent & the Grenadines, St. Lucia, St. Kitts & Nevis, Grenada, Dominica, Barbados, Antigua & Barbuda	14	Salary in-kind	DFAIT	English	Godrow	This program proposes, via the creation of a centralized training facility, to prepare Police, Customs, Military, Coastguard and Immigration personnel to perform Staff functions of a general nature that are appropriate to their ranks and to provide the foundation for their subsequent professional development. It is also designed to further develop the management and operational command skills of potential senior security personnel. Specifically, the project's prevention focus would be on addressing gang-related major crime and its potential links to transnational, organized crime and terrorism. The training received by RSS graduates is considered to be integral in the development of senior and middle management members of the security sector.
16	2012-10-08 to 2012-10-19	Royal Thai Police Visit & Workshop	G 565-7	Vancouver, Toronto, Ottawa	RCMP "E", "O","A" & "NHQ	DFAIT,RTP,RCMP	RCMP	6	Salary-in-kind	DFAIT ACCBP	English/Thai	Godrow	This project is related with the Seahorse Project. The LO would like to showcase the RCMP involvement in Seahorse. The RTP will visit MSOC, IBET & NHQ. The RTP will also receive a workshop on Ethics and Major Crime Management
17	09-04-2012 to 2012-09-14	Ship Boarding Training	G-565-20-1	Jakarta and Semerang, Indonesia	Indonesian National Police	DFAIT, INP RCMP	RCMP	12	Salary-in-kind	DFAIT ACCBP	Indonesian	Godrow	This project is related with the Seahorse Project. The INP requires training on ship boarding as an operational requirements. Equipment and training provided under DFAIT MOU.
18	2012-10-29 to 2012-11-02	Regional Security System (RSS) Training Institute SOCO & Train-the-trainer	G 565-677	St. Vincent & the Grenadines, St. Lucia, St. Kitts & Nevis, Grenada, Dominica, Barbados, Antigua & Barbuda	RSS	DFAIT, RCMP	St. Vincent & the Grenadines, St. Lucia, St. Kitts & Nevis, Grenada, Dominica, Barbados, Antigua & Barbuda	12	Salary in-kind	DFAIT	English	Godrow	A workshop to discuss best practices in crime scene management.
19	2013-01-21 to 2013-02-01	Interviewing Techniques Course Activities I and II of III		Morocco	Morocco police	DFAIT, RCMP	Morocco and the Sahel Region	48	Salary in Kind	DFAIT ACCBP	Francais	Villeneuve	Deliver a Interviewing Techniques course to 24 candidates. Once completed indentify 5 candidates to become trainers and have them with our assistance deliver the next course.
20	2013-02-18 to 2013-02-22	Criminal Intelligence Course		Mexico City Mexico	Mexico	DFAIT , RCMP	Mexico	28	salary in kind	DFAIT	Spanish	Godrow	
21	2013-01-21 to 2013-01-25	Investigation Techniques workshop	G 561-21	Santo Domingo, Dominican Republic	Dominican Republic National Drug Control Directorate (DNCD)	DFAIT RCMP	DNCD	24	Salary in Kind	DFAIT	Spanish	Godrow	Investigational Techniques Workshop focusing on best practices in drug crime investigations to assist in future bi-national cases
	2012-10-8 to 2012-10-12	Synthetic Drug Workshop CANCELLED		Dominican Republic	Dominican Republic National Drug Control Directorate (DNCD)	INTERPOL	DNCD	24	Salary in Kind	INTERPOL	Spanish	Villeneuve	A basic Sythethic Drug course and Chemical Diversion workshop

	2012-11-19 to 2012-11-23	Synthetic Drug Workshop **CANCELLED**		El Salvador	El Salvador	INTERPOL	El Salvador Police	24	Salary in Kind	INTERPOL	Spanish	Villeneuve	A basic Sythethic Drug course and Chemical Diversion workshop
	2013-02-18 to 2013-02-22	Synthetic Drug Workshop **CANCELLED**		Guatemala	Guatemala National Police	INTERPOL	Guatemala	24	Salary in Kind	INTERPOL	Spanish	Villeneuve	A basic Sythethic Drug course and Chemical Diversion workshop
22	2012-11-26 to 2012-11-30	Community Policing Workshop	G-565-6-1	San José, Costa Rica	Costa Rican Law Enforcement Community	Fuerza Publica	Costa Rica	19	Salary in-kind	DFAIT CTCB	Spanish	Godrow	A workshop to discuss best practices in community policing strategies. Will encompass drug awareness, gangs, domestic violence and child sexual exploitation.
24	2013-02-18 to 2013-03-01	Ship Boarding Training	G-565-20-1	Jakarta and Semerang, Indonesia	Indonesian National Police	DFAIT RCMP	Indonesia	12	Salary-in kind	DFAIT CTCB	Indonesian	Godrow	This project is related with the Seahorse Project. The LO would like to showcase the RCMP involvement in Seahorse. The RTP will visit MSOC, IBET & NHQ. The RTP will also receive a workshop on Ethics and Major Crime Management
25	2013-02-25 to 2013-03-01	South East Asia Thailand, First Responder		Bangkok, Thailand	Thai Police and Military	DFAIT RCMP	Thailand	24	Salary-in kind	DFAIT CTCB	Thai/English	Villeneuve	
26	2013-03-11 to 2013-03-15	Interviewing Techniques Course	G565-25-1	Niger	Niger Police	DFAIT RCMP	Niger	24	Salary-in Kind	DFAIT CTCB	Francais	Godrow	Deliver a Interviewing Techniques 4 courses to 24 candidates

policing is "a managerial model of evidence-based resource allocation through prioritization ... that places an emphasis on information sharing and collaborative, strategic solutions to crime problems" (ibid.). As a mechanism of (re)organizing police agencies to become more professional (i.e., evidence-based and objective), these training missions aim to develop the capacities of recipient counties to "manage information about threats and risks in order to strategically manage the policing mission" (Sheptycki 2005). In developing these techniques, security aid projects aim to professionalize the recipient countries, modelled on the practices of "policing risk" (Ericson and Haggerty 1997; see also Aradau and Van Munster 2007) from the Global North.

A central actor in the development of security techniques is the Canadian Police College (CPC), based in Ottawa. As a policing educational training centre, the CPC specializes in advanced courses where policing agencies send senior members for skills upgrading. Formed initially by the RCMP as a centre to advance and train Canadian policing agencies, the CPC has expanded its operations to include a capacity-building component for foreign "like-minded-nations." Every year, the CPC hosts hundreds of foreign officers through capacity-building programs.[3] Courses offered by the CPC have a number of objectives, chief among them are increasing bilateral relationships, improving interoperability and cooperation, and "professionalization" of other police forces (particularly the courses funded through security aid).

Training courses are offered on a range of topics on contemporary police sciences. To illustrate, CTCB paid for fifteen Pakistani security and law enforcement personnel to come for courses on drug investigative techniques, strategic intelligence analysis, police explosives technicians and radiography, senior police administration, and major case management team commander training (GAC 2008-274, 198). A separate program funded by CTCB focused on "increased professionalization ... [on] counter-terrorism best-practices," offering courses on forensic identification, major crime investigative techniques, and tactical intelligence analysis. Reports on the program stress that "professionalization will ... assist

3 It should be noted that many of the "developing" countries who receive courses through security aid funding are keen recipients. For example, "Pakistani law enforcement agencies currently face significant resource and expertise scarcity in investigational techniques. Western training opportunities are welcomed. Pakistani security agencies are consistently asking the RCMP liaison officer in Islamabad for training opportunities" (GAC 2008-274, 197).

Pakistan to maintain the rule of law and to address security concerns," in addition to providing "a *tangible* way ... [to address] cross-border movement of insurgents from Pakistan to Afghanistan [which] remains a key priority for the Government of Canada" (GAC 2008-274, 201). As with much of the security aid to Afghanistan and Pakistan, the Canadian interest is in the immediate safeguarding of troops deployed as part of the war in Afghanistan. However, in a broader sense, CPC capacity building comprises an underlying objective of having more "professionalized" policing agencies serving as a front line of security in a "place of interest." In developing these technical projects, Canadian security innovation aims to enhance transversal security governance regimes.

Like the MTCP, Canadian policing entities also provide extensive training abroad. Take, for example, RCMP contributions to the security aid programming in Palestine, to support the "professionalization of the Palestinian Civilian Police (PCP), training crime scene first responders and police investigators in evidence collection, and providing UNODC/Interpol investigation training" (CIDA 2012-532, 328). Of the many funding initiatives to the PCP, $3 million has been allocated for public order policing. In addition to leading the "transformational change" of the organizational structure of training in the PCP, Canadian officers conduct courses on local informant recruitment, advanced investigative interviewing, the use of the fonfa (police baton), and a course on the role of the police during an election (RCMP 2012-3277, 25; RCMP 2011-805, 148).[4] Public order policing, i.e., the training of police to deal with political protests, has been an area of preoccupation for the Canadian RCMP trainers. Canada has also supplied equipment to the PCP public order units and assisted with the training of 1,000 police in public order policing, directly in relation to the January 2009 elections (RCMP 2011-805, 132). Although the presidential elections have yet to take place and the Palestinian Authority has been increasingly criticized for its repression of political opponents (Tartir 2015), the capacity-building mission has been regarded as highly successful by the United States and Israel (Monaghan 2016). Moreover, the PCP has increasingly been tasked by the Israeli Defence Forces as a lead agency to deal with

4 Canadian officers are also engaged in worldly diplomatic activity: "Lastly, this month the writer entered the Guinness Book of World Records. Attending with the Head of Mission, I participated in an event at a small village to eat the world's largest plate of a local Palestinian chicken dish. The Prime Minister of Palestine was on hand, along with many other V.I.P.'s and media to witness the event" (RCMP 2011-805, 162).

public order policing (J. Zanotti 2010), most recently during IDF bombings in Gaza and during Arab Spring demonstrations.

Another notable example of security aid linked directly to broader geopolitical alignments is Canada's contribution to training Iraqi police officers at the Jordan International Police Training Centre (JIPTC) between January 2004 and December 2005.[5] Although Canada did not join the invasion of Iraq, it provided aid to support the logistical training of Iraqi police recruits. With a deployment of twenty police officers, Canada provided the third-largest contingent of police trainers (following the United States and the United Kingdom) "involved in the academic and tactical aspects of the training" (RCMP 2014-99, 90). This included sections for general policing, tactical instruction unit, driving instruction unit, and a defence tactics instruction unit. Canada's largest contribution (seven trainers) was to the Firearms Instruction Unit (including one individual promoted to team leader). During the training program, paramilitary training was added "due to the security situation in Iraq" (12). Illustrating the humanitarian reason of the assistance mission, the emphasis of Canadian programming was on "democratic principles, human rights, prohibition against torture, domestic violence, rights of children and women and other features of community policing" (ibid.). Demonstrating how these policing capacity buildings indicate Canada as a norm-supporter, documents from the Iraq training mission underline that "as is usually the case in missions, the Canadians are slowly being recognized for their contributions and are being advanced to higher levels of responsibility" (156). Another report notes, "Canada immediately committed to be part of the training staff and has been a very active partner and has played a lead role in training the cadets" (331). Highlighting the appointment of Canadian officers promoted to the deputy directorship of the JIPTC, one document underlines that it will "entail a strategic influence on the management of the training center and provided Canada with public visibility" (18).

As two important actors within Canadian policing sciences, the CPC and RCMP have a long history of developing the professionalism of policing in the Global South. With the acceleration of intelligence-led policing as the management framework for policing and security agencies of the Global North – what Ratcliffe (2008, 85) called "a business

5 When the Iraq training program was abruptly terminated in 2007, this training facility then became a primary centre used to train the Palestinian Authority police and security officers.

model and conceptual philosophy for policing" – these organizing principles have also become a major focus of security development. In evaluating the security aid programming in developing techniques of policing, it is useful to highlight how these projects are rationalized on two levels. In line with what has been detailed in literature on security-sector reform, the first dimension is a commitment to impart "best practices" to recipient countries and develop their capacities, skills, and professionalism. As demonstrated by the list of projects managed by the RCMP, as well as the training provided by the CPC and Canadian police officers in Jordan, Canadian security innovators have sought to build the capacity of recipient agencies by imparting specific, tangible trainings and mentoring. This is the common theme within security-sector reform literature and often the primary aim of many of Canada's security assistance projects. The second dimension demonstrates the extent to which the organizing principles of transversal governance are at work in security development. This emerging dynamic relates to efforts that aim to *integrate* policing into broader regional and transversal "webs" of policing (Brodeur 2010). In other words, the aims of developing policing techniques are rarely limited to skill development, but often honed into a more contemporary logic of risk policing, which "places an emphasis on information sharing and collaborative, strategic solutions to crime problems" (Ratcliffe 2008, 85). As a future-looking practice of policing, security aid projects have tried to develop practices of aggregating information that Aradau and Van Munster (2007, 100) describe as "taming the infinities of risk and integrating it within a dispositif of governance." This can be illustrated by the courses listed in the RCMP grid above, which include "regional security" workshops, as well as training involving multiple recipient countries. To further illustrate how security aid techniques operate not only as immediate "skills" to be developed but also intelligence-led practices for "ever wider circuits" of security, consider a list of recent ACCBP-funded projects:[6]

- A project with the UNODC (costs redacted) to develop and disseminate a "Global Scientific Forensics Support Programme" that would standardized forensic training and reference materials for Latin America

---

6 All listed projects gathered from GAC 2011-1380.

- Another UNODC project with redacted costs to "create network of Central American anti-org crime & drug units to strengthen capacity to handle complex, transnational org crime cases. Networks for sharing info & intel on trends, orgs, routes, methods"
- A $511,462 contract to UNODC to train over twenty Latin American countries on the "strengthens [*sic*] [of] computer-based NDS by enhancing its ability to collect data on domestic and international illicit drug transactions"
- $1,595,813.96 funded to the Interpol Capacity Building Program on Organized Crime for the Americas, which aimed to "train officers responsible for international police cooperation," with the goal "to improve performance of and intl cooperation of the national central bureaus and law enforcement agencies to combat transnational organized crime in the Americas"
- An OAS contract ($1,236,966.25) for a "technical cooperation initiative to assist beneficiary States throughout Americas to comply with international document security standards & other best practices re: travel documents from International Civil Aviation Organization"

The examples above are focused on Latin America. However, as I illustrate below in security aid to Southeast Asia, efforts to integrate global policing and surveillance techniques are at the core of the development agenda of the transversal security community. As the examples above demonstrate, "software" of security has extensive and diverse areas of development. Before providing a detailed case study of Canada's elaborate security aid project in the SEA region, I outline the scholarship on migration-security to demonstrate how these areas of Canadian security innovation contribute to managing "good" and "bad" circulations.

Circulations of (In)security, Visions of Control: Transversal Policing of Borders

Unlike a world of fixed borders and the normative superiority of non-intervention and unconditional sovereignty, the transversal security community has solidified the norms of extraterritoriality with fragmented and conditional sovereignties. Most explicitly in border policing practices, countries of the Global North have developed systems of extraterritorial enforcement into geographies of insecurity and, particularly when working with countries of the Global South, created hybrid areas of global border enforcement (Andreas and Nadelmann 2006; Bigo and Guild 2005b). Pickering and Weber (2013, 94) have detailed how policing functions of border mobility have progressed towards a "de-territorialized existence which is unbounded in many respects by temporal or geographic constraints." Although far from a norm-maker in efforts of the transversal security community to globalize border management, Canada (2011) has adopted a strategy to "push the border" that follows the design set by norm-makers such as the EU and the United States. Underlining Foucault's emphasis on the organization of "good" and "bad" flows, scholarship on the policing of mobility demonstrates how security is more about control of circulations, rather than defence of territory. Moreover, the sites of border policing have "pushed out" from the specificities of the borderline into places viewed as the sources of insecurity or potential risk.

In demonstrating how this movement away from immobile border regime corresponds to the blurring of internal and external security functions, Bigo (2014, 211) has identified "three social universes of border control" under the typology of the military-strategic field, the internal security field, and the global cyber-surveillance social universe: "We distinguish a first social universe – characterized in terms of 'patrolling,' intercepting; in terms of 'containment'; as well as in terms of a geopolitics of enmity, of 'walls' and of lines to defend – from a second social universe, which is characterized in terms of 'filtering,' of 'separating legal and illegal travellers,' and of the management of flows of people."

As the third universe, Bigo describes a composition of databanks and analytics, characterized by computers and virtualization where borders are not solid or liquid but gaseous. Although this third universe penetrates and reframes the first two, it does so "without having the capacity to impose itself as predominant" (Bigo 2014, 211). This third social universe influences both of its precursors, particularly through "smart border" designs and a growing concern with "speedy" access for good circulations (Bigo 2011a; see also Côté-Boucher 2008). Critiquing an emphasis on the "militarization" of borders, Bigo underlines the much more pervasive practices of everyday control that comprise the "second universe" of border management. Under the metaphor of liquidity, Lyon (2010) also highlights how security and control logics of border management are sorted through filters and channels (see also Lyon 2006). Under these logics, borders are spaces for sorting and surveillance and, as Bigo (2014, 213) explains, function as places where hybridization is possible: "They are zones that may be composed of mixed flows and may become places of exchange. Borders need to remain open while being kept 'secure.' Security is not about stopping, but about following mobility." Inasmuch as the traversality of border control is about policing "bad" circulations, it has been matched by regulatory complexes to encourage "good" circulations, particularly for finance, trade, exploitable temporary labour, and mass tourism.

Though the effort to "open" borders to commerce while governing unwanted populations is not new, the de-territorialized and universal character of contemporary bordering practices has characteristics distinct from those of previous efforts to control migration. Weber and Bowling (2008) have noted a lineage of historical and structural forces that have resulted in the movements of – and controlled strategies towards – surplus populations. As they have argued, mobile populations have long been interpreted as "problems of order" characterized by vagrancy, idleness, deviance, and moral contagion. In response to these threatening mobilities, they write, "Nation states have adopted a defensive posture against the incursions of surplus populations and have sought to assert and extend their sovereignty through aggressive border control" (369). The defining characteristic of "globalizing neoliberal order" is precisely in the movement from the "first universe" of defensive enclosure to the "second universe" of border liquidity. Globalization itself involves a novel transformation to the pace, forms, and networks of movement – requiring what Weber (2013) calls "policing a world in motion" – and border management is not only unhinged from its territorial anchor but has moved from a logic of enclosure to a logic of immanence.

As a product of the transversal security community, the most pervasive characteristic of global security governance has been the acceleration of preventive and pre-emptive techniques to assess and intercept potential risks (McCulloch and Pickering 2009; Zedner 2007). Policing for good and bad circulations has been an essential element of preventive risk formula, particularly when protecting the Global North from unwanted migration. Following the EU, the Canadian national security strategy (Canada 2004) explicitly links managing border flows with security and prosperity. Demonstrating the unique feature of contemporary efforts to governance of surplus populations, Weber and Bowling (2008) have adapted Bauman's (1998, 77–102) suggestion that neoliberal globalization can be represented by the contrasting images of the "tourist" and the "vagabond," though Weber and Bowling (2008) contend that today's "bad" circulations are best described as "flawed consumers" or "unworthy citizens." In adopting preventive risk practices that "push the border out," extraterritorial border policing seeks out potential threats and "suspicious citizens" (Muller 2010) before these human threats arrive in the Global North.

As scholars examining extraterritorial border policing have detailed, countries of the Global North have emphasized the *legal* regime of migration as a means of curtailing "illegal" migration. In contrast to the legalization of migration as it unfolded in the twentieth century, Dauvergne (2008) has argued that the moral panic around "illegal" migration is a marker of the twenty-first century. Providing a detailed architecture of the legal complexes that "make people illegal" in Canada, Dauvergne (15) outlines how "the 'illegality' of people is a new discursive turn in contemporary migration talk." What have been presented as "problems" of "irregular" migration is a discursive formation produced by an aspirational vision of transversal control (Bigo 2002; Bigo and Guild 2005a; Squire 2010), and the criminological problematization of migration as "illegal" demonstrates a further collapsing of internal/external security universes and the embedding of mobilities controls into the policing of crime. In an emerging domain of what has been termed "crimmigration control" (Stumpf 2006) – a term that conjoins criminal law and administrative laws on migration – prosperous countries of the Global North have accelerated control using internal powers associated with the criminal justice system to curtail and suppress mobile populations seeking entry or transit. Bigo (2014) has remarked that police officers and border guards alike now see border controls as an internal security problem with an external dimension.

Human smuggling has become a leading area of collaboration of global crimmigration control (Mountz 2010; Wong 2005). Aiming to control the flows of "illegal" migration, norm-makers such as the United States, EU, and Australia have taken increasingly sophisticated pre-emptive and extraterritorial steps to intercept migrants before they reach ground (Bigo and Guild 2005b; Mountz 2010; Pickering and Weber 2013). Maritime travel has been an especially highlighted area of "illegal" migration and efforts to crack down on unauthorized travel, particularly refugees. In Australia, Pickering (2014, 189) has detailed how asylum-seekers arriving by boat have been the subject of "unprecedented legislative activity, including the use of offshore detention, the judicial censure of executive power as well as the deployment of almost incalculable material (as well as political) resources to agencies charged with responding to this so-called crisis" (see also Grewcock 2009). Following the arrival of a boat of asylum-seekers in 2001, Dauvergne (2008, 51) has suggested "Australia has been the global leader in the refugee law race to the bottom."

In establishing a transversal border regime, deviant states of the Global South have been incorporated into an enforcement design set by norm-makers. Pickering and Weber (2013, 94; emphasis added) have argued that, while processes of "geographical transversality influence where border control functions are performed," scholars must examine how "changes in governance characteristic of globalizing, neoliberalizing states are bringing about a dispersal of authority across networks or chains of actors which effects *who* performs these state-defining functions." Below, I examine how security aid from Canada has contributed to the *who* of border security practices by developing techniques of surveillance and control in the Global South. Focusing on Canada's security aid project in Southeast Asia, I trace how the threat of migrant boats arriving in Canada has created an immediate response to develop the "software" of border police in Thailand, Cambodia, and Indonesia. Squire (2010, 1) has correctly noted Canada's limited involvement in developing the global border control regime, pointing out that it "would seem to reflect the geographical specificity of Canadian border regions, which lie at a significant physical distance from regions of the global South." Though Canada has been late to integrate into the "global crackdown on migration" (Dauvergne 2008), the security aid program to SEA demonstrates a rapid acceleration of interest in supporting the practices already being developed by norm-making powers of the transversal security community. Consistent with Canada's character as a norm-supporter, the security aid program has privileged Canadian expertise in border "management" and intelligence-led policing, thus allowing strategic contributions from security innovators to development of transversal security governance.

A number of scholars have underlined fundamentally unequal divisions of wealth at the root of the transversal security community's desire for global surveillance and security governance (Aas 2011, 2013; Duffield 2007, 2010; Pickering 2014; Weber and Bowling 2008). Similarly, in a project proposal for security aid to SEA region, Canadian officials pinpoint the divisions of North-South wealth as the root of global migrations and the crimmigration lens through which these travels are interpreted: "The smuggling of migrants continues to pose a threat that challenges the integrity of borders and undermines the rule of law, and in so doing brings attendant security, social, and economic risks. It also creates significant physical risk for the migrants themselves, and many die during the smuggling process. Smuggling of migrants by sea is a global and increasing phenomenon, where wealthy and advanced nations are inevitably targeted by migrants and the criminals who smuggle them ... Relatively large and relatively impoverished populations mean a large pool of would-be migrants attracted by the opportunities offered by countries such as Canada" (GAC 2013-2551, 6).

Given the "large pool of would-be migrants," Canadian authorities determine that the threat posed by unauthorized travel must be stopped at its source. The passage above highlights how prosperous countries are "targeted" by the "global and increasing" threat of illegal migration, as well as how policing and security resources are harnessed to pre-empt these threats. As I detail, Canadian security aid is deployed strategically in support of efforts by norm-markers, giving the security-oriented response a communitarian identity set in what Walters (2004) calls "domopolitics" – a politics of the home. For Walters, domopolitics articulates a reactionary politics that fuses notions of home, racial citizenship, and security. On a transnational level, a shared domopolitics is emerging where prosperous countries of the Global North feel a set of common shared values about how our "homes are at risk" from the "pools" of "would-be" migrants (see also Aas 2013; Fekete 2009). Adding an important humanitarian reason to the security aid funding, Canadian authorities also underline in the passage above how the migrants themselves are potentially victims. As Aas and Gundhus (2015, 12) have demonstrated with their analysis of EU bordering practices, migrants can be viewed with empathy, but "their hardship is as a rule seen as a subset of (organized) crime, rather than an object of knowledge in itself." A key component of the security techniques developed by Canadian aid is to strengthen the circuits of circulation so that "truthful" migration is ensured, while unauthorized migration is suppressed. Though inasmuch as the efforts to develop security techniques in SEA are represented as an effort to protect migrants or the global order, I conclude by highlighting how the project aims to advance practical strategic interests. Or, as the conclusion of the project proposal quoted directly above put it, "Canada and Canadian citizens benefit from this project in a number of ways."

Below, I detail the security aid program to SEA region, the techniques that Canadian security innovators aim to develop, and the "benefits" of the program for Canadian strategic interests. As critical scholarship on crimmigration controls and border policing have noted, threats posed by "illegal" migration are discursively represented as threats to global security. Similarly, the Canadian security aid regime in SEA is rationalized under the same motif, such as when documents repeat claims that migrant smuggling is "a challenge not only to the immediately affected countries, but to the international community in general" (GAC 2013-2551, 93). Yet, as the exploration of this security development project underlines, the layers of Canadian engagement – from the construction of the threat, to the capacity building of SEA border police, to partnerships with other norm-making Global North countries – Canadian security aid is embedded within a trajectory of transversal governance where, as Hills (2009) describes, "security is not for all." Instead, I demonstrate that the "international community," protected by these security aid regimes, are mostly privileged Northern countries whose goal is to manage the repercussions of global wealth disparities by "inclusively excluding" (Agamben 1998) populations of the Global South.

Crimmigration Control and the "Software" of Border Policing: Exploring Canada's Security Aid in Southeast Asia

One study participant, a security innovator with expertise in transnational border development, raised the issue of "migrant smuggling" during a discussion of the strategic interests that are embedded in Canadian security aid programs. Emphasizing how capacity-building projects should have a tangible domestic priority, the participant said, "Especially if you're doing something like border management, if you do something successful capacity building with countries – I mean international border management is everybody, it's not just like the United States – you have all kinds of things you have to discuss with them, and you can help them, for example if you help somebody with migrant smuggling, well that's good for us, because *you don't get so many boats arriving* and things like that" (Interview 6; emphasis added).

Like other Northern and prosperous countries, Canada receives only a small fraction of the world's refugee, asylum, or immigration claimants, or other "things like that." Moreover, although only a small number of these claimants arrive from maritime ports, the Canadian government has made maritime "human smuggling" a major issue of its crime control agenda. This is only a recent development, stemming in general from the rise of crimmigration discourses, and specifically from the maritime arrival of Tamil asylum-seekers.

Below, I address the issue of migration smuggling after its recent emergence in Canada. Since the maritime arrival of Tamil asylum seekers, Canadian security aid has been directed towards building the capacities of intelligence and surveillance in Southeast Asian countries. I explore this security aid project in four sections. First, I detail the securitizing discourses that constructed the threat of "migrant smuggling." Second, I describe the elements of Canadian security development programs, offering an overview of the courses and "techniques" that security innovators have aimed to develop with border policing agencies in the SEA region. Third, I detail a series of documents that discuss border policing development, with emphasis on the barriers and obstacles encountered by security innovators. In particular, I analyse these documents because they illustrate the broader transversal practices of security development and demonstrate how security "aid" to recipient countries comes with a "requirement" to engage in the front-line police enforcement designed by norm-makers. Finally, a fourth section outlines how tangible security-development programming enhances Canadian reputational value as a norm-supporter of the transversal security community's efforts to govern the (in)securities of the Global South.

Constructing the Maritime Migration Threat

The "so many boats" referred to by the participant above relates to only two actual cases of migrant vessels arriving on Canadian shores. Aside from the statement from the participant above, many documents explicitly link the attention to threats of "migrant smuggling" specifically to the arrival of two ships of Tamil refugees, the MV *Ocean Lady* carrying 76 migrants in October 2009 and then the MV *Sun Sea* carrying 492 migrants in August 2010. One other case (MS *Alicia*) has been promoted in the media as an alleged case of eighty-four Tamils trying to reach Canada before being intercepted by Indonesian authorities in June 2011. As one CBSA note describes it, "The heightened engagement was a product of the large migrant smuggling operation based in Bangkok that resulted in 492 Tamil migrants claiming refuge in Canada via the MV *Sun Sea* vessel which arrived on our shores in August 2010.

Because of this incident CBSA established a stronger presence in Bangkok to work on enhancing enforcement, and migrant smuggling writ large became a concrete priority of the Government of Canada" (CBSA 2013-13161, 21).

As a concrete priority, the Canadian government has initiated projects that target potential boat migrants, particularly – though not exclusively – Tamils. Fleeing the conclusions of the civil war in Sri Lanka – along with war crime allegations that Prime Minister Harper has himself criticized (Prime Minister's Office 2013; Bascaramurty and Ibbitson 2013) – the migrants aboard the ships were subjected to securitizing discourses on multiple levels (Moffette and Vadasaria 2016). Sriskandarajah (2014, 912) has noted that the arrival of the MV *Sun Sea* refugees was framed "by pre-existing discourses of Tamils as terrorists, queue jumpers, and illegitimate refugees." In circulating caricatures of Tamils as terrorists and queue jumpers, the Harper government used the maritime arrivals to pass Bill C-31, Protecting Canada's Immigration System Act. As an effort to crack down on "human smugglers [that] are targeting Canada," the Act empowers the minister of public safety to designate the arrival of a group of persons in Canada as an "irregular arrival" (PSC 2012). Once labelled "irregular arrivals," refugees are subject to enhanced powers of detention and investigation, which were rationalized in the Act as a deterrent to future migrations.

As securitizing discourses in border policing are typified by racial imaginations of inclusion and exclusion (Ibrahim 2005; Tsoukala 2008, 61–5), the Canadian government's response to the maritime arrivals conveyed a "closeness" between the foreign "places of insecurity" and Canada's coastline. Together with a rise in racial nationalism centred on public debates of threats presented by "outsiders" (see Park 2013), one aspect of the effort to combat these illegal migrations – in addition to the domestic legal manoeuvres – has been to enhance border policing of countries in Southeast Asia. This included an immediate creation of security aid packages to Thailand, Indonesia, and Cambodia to develop transversally integrated systems of surveillance and interdiction.

It is worth noting that Canadian security aid hubs were active in SEA before the Tamil maritime arrivals. Under the banner of fighting the threat of global terrorism, the CTCB had offered more than $4 million for regional initiatives since 2005. With the construction of "migrant smuggling" threat, in 2012 Canada pledged an additional $12 million (over two years) through the ACCBP. While funding involved security hardware and software, there was emphasis on developing the pre-emptive risk-policing capacities of surveillance and intelligence gathering to enhance the abilities of recipient countries to interdict vessels before they reached open waters. As one document from GAC explained, "Although the circumstances and capacities present in each of the three countries differ greatly, intelligence-led policing is underdeveloped in each" (GAC 2013-2551, 7). To develop these techniques of policing, security innovators from the RCMP and CBSA created programs that would train border officials from Thailand, Indonesia, and Cambodia to act as a first line of defence against the "would-be" migrants leaving for Canada.

To privilege the "legal" means of migration, countries of the North have not only emphasized the need for migrants to abide by the rules of official migration, they have also paired "irregular" migration with criminal activity. A tacit recognition of the security emphasis on migration stems from wealth disparities and the desire of people from the Global South to relocate to the North, yet the security framing of "migration smuggling" resituates mobility within a context of criminality. Aas and Gundhus (2015, 11) have shown how asylum-seekers intercepted during their travels are "clearly framed in the language of state security, and consequently even when addressing migrants' vulnerability, tends to frame it in the language of state security and organized crime." Take an example of asylum-seeking maritime arrivals from Sri Lanka: "Typically irregular migrants are attracted by countries of relative prosperity when compared to their countries of origin and the prospect therefore of economic betterment for themselves and their families. In some cases migrants have been, or intend to be, involved in criminal activity or in other activities which pose a threat to the national security of the destination country … [The vessels] illustrate both the extent to which relatively wealthy countries are seen as destinations of choice for migrants from the developing world, and the complete disregard for human life typical of those engaged in human smuggling" (GAC 2013-2551, 43).

Potential affiliations with the Tamil Tigers and involvement with illegal smuggling have been central points of issue within the legal saga in Canada. For upwards of three years, the asylum-seekers aboard the MV *Sun Sea* and MV *Ocean Lady* were detained, investigated, and scrutinized as potential terrorists or criminals (Canadian Council for Refugees 2013). Canadian authorities challenged most of the refugee claims, "successfully" arguing at the Immigration Refugee Board to have over 100 of the passengers declared illegal and subjected to deportation. In at least two cases, individuals deported have been taken into custody and tortured. One is dead (Quan 2013). Given Canada's blanket refusals, the positioning of a "complete disregard for human life" is particularly notable, given the supposed protections afforded to asylum-seekers under international law. Yet these "irregular migrants" are not discursively recognized as refugees (though many have been legally recognized). Canada's lack of regard for the migrants was further illustrated by CBSA documents acquired from the Canadian Council for Refugees, indicating that the agency had developed plans before the *Sun Sea*'s arrival to detain passengers for as long as possible (Canadian Council for Refugees 2011). The long period of detention included a number of children and involved the intentional protraction of legal proceedings. As van Liempt and Sersli (2013) have commented, such efforts to frame "migrant smuggling" have the effect of casting criminal suspicion over migrants, stripping these individuals of personal agency and silencing their personal decisions to take great risks – at significant costs – in an attempt to start a new life.

Constructing the boat arrivals as security threats plays to a particular xenophobic domopolitics (Walters 2004; also Chandler 2007), but it also opens a platform for humanitarian governance to provide security to the smuggled migrants by enhancing transversal border controls. In the wake of the boat arrivals and securitizing discourses from political figures, Canadian security innovators within security aid hubs designed programs to develop the capacities in Southeast Asian countries. As a strategy of "pushing the border out," aid projects were created to develop abilities of recipient countries to engage in enforcement and interdiction, as opposed to having migrants processed once they arrive to Canada. CBSA explained how security aid could assist with the curtailment of boat migrants: "The most effective way of achieving both of these goals [protecting the 'integrity' of the border, and deterrence of potential 'smugglers'] is through interdiction of vessels prior to departure combined with increased, intelligence-led, investigative efforts that aim at dismantling the criminal networks and prosecuting the key perpetrators that organize and drive such migrant smuggling operations" (GAC 2013-2551, 43).

Focusing on the goal to intercept "prior to departure," a major emphasis was placed on developing the intelligence and pre-emptive capacities of recipient countries. Canada's security aid project commenced soon after the arrival of the migrant ships, and required commitment from SEA countries that they would "buy in" to the project, as well as requiring a whole-of-government approach from the recipient countries and Canadian security innovators.[7] Unlike the characterizations of recalcitrance that typified discourses of security aid in Haiti, the SEA program emphasizes how the phantom states of the region have demonstrated sufficient political will to reform according to the designs of norm-makers of the donor community. One note explains, "As per the World Customs Organization's '3P' approach to capacity building (People, Partnership, and Political will), CBSA recognizes that country-specific buy-in is key to capacity building activities and feels that this buy-in is significant in Thailand and the project will therefore be successful" (CBSA 2013-13161, 23).

Based on the willingness of the SEA recipients to engage in the reformatory practices of norm-makers, documents indicate that a whole-of-government team, composed of members from the RCMP, the CBSA, the Privy Council Office, and GAC conducted a needs assessment mission in Indonesia, Thailand, and Malaysia, from 23 September to 4 October 2011. A major component of the mission was preparation of security aid projects that could be announced during Harper's trip to Indonesia in 2012. One memo written for the president of the CBSA, Luc Portelance, in November 2011 details the assessment mission and the rollout of ACCBP funding as part of Canada's strategy to "provide capacity building to source and transit states in Southeast Asia." It is worth highlighting the discursive use of "source and transit states" in this document, as opposed to the much more common (and value-neutral) "partner" or "recipient" state identifiers in security aid documents. With a label of "source and transit" states, there is a clear identification in the document that Canadian officials see these countries as deficient in border management. In detailing extensive efforts to fortify EU borders, Aas (2013, 30) has used the term *Northern penal states* to categorize norm-makers within the EU that export the best-practice regimes of surveillance and border control to norm-taker counties. Underlining the normative power of the transversal "bordering,"

7 Underlining the interoperable character of the transversal security community, one CBSA proposal document underlines the agency's objective of having Thailand develop a whole-of-government approach: "I believe it is important that they do participate, as TIB branch was/is a major contributor in dealing with the migrant file (detainees still remain in the immigration detention centre). The importance of bringing together all the different departments was an underlined factor in discussion when the assessment team was here ... including demonstrating how Canada operates with a 'whole of government' approach" (CBSA 2013-13161, 9).

Aas differentiates between Northern penal states and "deviant states" by their "capacity to govern crime according to its ability to respond to issues on the international crime control agenda" (ibid.). Under the label "source and transit" countries, SEA recipients are categorized as "deviant states" who are viewed primarily as part of a problem.

Demonstrating the strategic value of security aid in contributing to transversal security governance, documents detail how security aid hubs quickly developed programming in the SEA region. This effort was led by the security aid hubs who aimed to strategically marshal Canadian aid funds. For example, one memo to CBSA President Portelance goes on to explain that *"DFAIT has placed significant pressure on the CBSA* to obtain the necessary in-house approvals to proceed with the Thai project in advance of the Prime Minister's visit to Thailand" (CBSA 2013-13161, 15; emphasis added). Underlining the high-profile status of the "anti-human smuggling" agenda, a GAC note explains that the project is in "direct support of the PCO-OSAHS led initiative that seeks to detect and prevent future human smuggling vessels destined for Canada. The prevention of human smuggling vessels reaching the shores of Canada is a top foreign policy priority for the Government of Canada" (GAC 2013-2551, 14). In addition to the heightened importance of making Canadian security aid visible, an emphasis on stopping the vessels from "reaching the shores of Canada" makes clear the government's strategy to evade legal obligations to refugees who set foot on Canadian soil.

Spotlighting the priority of the issue and its direct support from the Privy Council Office (PCO), the security aid project to SEA countries has been designed to impart an integrated, intelligence-led policing "software" to recipient countries. Given the expertise of the CBSA as security innovators, officials with GAC, PCO, and the Prime Minister's Office emphasized the need to include a tangible and concrete training facet to the security aid project. A document from CBSA underlines that "adoption of CBSA best practices would enhance the capacity of Thai administrations (customs, immigration, police, etc) to detect criminal organizations involved with human smuggling at the source" (CBSA 2013-13161, 184; see also RCMP 2014-185). As a strategy to curtail migration "at the source," the project aimed to develop tangible skills of intelligence-led policing. While the securitizing game was driven by the professionals of politics, the section that follows illustrates how development of security knowledge practices is driven by security innovators. Funded through security assistance, the development of these security techniques are aimed at professionalizing and integrating SEA border police into transversal policing practices. As I highlight, the overriding objective is a reformatory effort to develop these deviant states, in effect making them "front line" surveillance and policing units of the Global North.

Developing Security Software

As a strategy to push the border out, Canada prepared twelve initial projects for capacity building border and police agencies in Southeast Asia. One of the first projects to be implemented from the $12 million allocated through the ACCBP was intended to develop Port Intelligence Units (PIUs).

The project had a geographic scope covering Cambodia, Indonesia, and Thailand, and worked with the UNODC to create multi-agency PIUs that would integrate local, regional, and international intelligence and policing practices. As outlined in a proposal from the CBSA to the ACCBP, the project was organized under three thematic areas. First was the building of infrastructure and establishment of physical space for the PIUs. Second was an effort at officer training and mentoring in intelligence and investigative skills. And the third theme comprised cooperation and coordination, attempting to link to "national, regional and international bodies for the purpose of effective intelligence sharing" (GAC 2013-2551, 3). Notably, the CBSA proposed working with the UNODC because it would complement other Australian-directed projects, in particular the Coordination and Analysis Unit (CAU) project, which "seeks to improve strategic level information sharing on migrant smuggling in Southeast Asia, and the PATROL project, which focuses on improving border security in the Greater Mekong Subregion" (ibid.). As I explain further below, the third pillar is an integral part of the project design to ensure its "sustainability." In particular, it allows recipient countries to become embedded in larger regional and international intelligence networks under the direction of the Global North, ensuring more reliable long-term enforcement of maritime mobility controls.

As a project starting "from scratch" (GAC 2013-2551, 37), the security aid included provisions for hardware in the form of equipment and infrastructure. This included office equipment and paint as well as "providing equipment such as vehicles, computers, surveillance items such as infra-red and photographic equipment, and the creation of standard operating procedures" (63). Other equipment, provided through CCC, included six sophisticated mobile phone ACESCQO field scanners. Described for use as "Digital Mobile Device Data Extraction" for "the purpose of intelligence gathering," the field scanners were procured for $8,000 each, and CBSA liaison officers trained Thai border police on how to use them (CBSA 2013-13161, 34). CCC also procured document examination kits that included 2,000 handheld blacklights, 8,000 batteries for the blacklights, and 2,000 TV-15 TriView magnifiers (71). Initially purchasing the exam kits for Thai border police, the CBSA officials also discussed purchasing kits to provide them through CBSA liaison officers to other countries. These kits were scheduled to be dispersed to Indonesia (200), Malaysia (200), Vietnam (200), and Singapore (1,000), and 400 to the IOM for donations (CBSA 2013-13161, 46). Canadian funds also purchased other "security hardware," such as a case management system, and Dell computers and routers to operationalize the PIUs.

The PIU training component comprised ninety officers (thirty from each country). Courses included a wide range of police sciences: smuggling of migrants investigation, interdiction techniques at seaports, crime scene investigation, money laundering, and criminal intelligence analysis (GAC 2013-2551, 13). Other components of the training included study visits for senior managers, operational intelligence analysis, profiling, investigation of migrant smuggling (including debriefing and interrogation techniques), informant handling, evidence and case preparation, statement taking, use of equipment, immersive (mock case) exercises, and technical support to investigations through mentoring (46). Underscoring the humanitarian sentiments of the programming, a human rights course was also provided.

Courses prepared for the PIU project were complemented by other ACCBP training to develop intelligence-led policing skills. An overview of a course given to Thai border police details that "course content focused on the Intelligence Cycle and enabled the participants to gain a comprehensive understanding of how to transform basic information, received from various sources, into actionable intelligence for criminal enforcement" (CBSA 2013-13161, 90). Modules included Introduction to Intelligence, Application of Intelligence, Intelligence Cycle, and Introduction to Basic Intelligence Analysis. The courses covered the basics of informant handling, documentation, risk assessment, managing and meeting informants, targeting and mitigating threats, contingency planning, identifying organized crime activities, and collecting, storing, and sharing information and intelligence products. An additional course on advanced document examination was offered to all PIU officers through attendance at the IOM document examination centre in Bangkok. A key objective of the project was described as building these capacities in combination with "the establishment of effective mechanisms for cooperation and coordination nationally, regionally and internationally, including MoUs where necessary to allow for intelligence sharing" (GAC 2013-2551, 44). Border police from all countries were also introduced and trained to use a Case Management Information System (CMIS) provided by Australia Federal Police.

Like those courses detailed above – which were provided to Pakistani, Iraqi, and Jordanian police – many of these capacity-building programs are stock offers from Canadian security innovators. As a strategy to have SEA border police work as reliable proxies for Canadian border management, the training program focused on long-term skill improvements. In designing the course, Canadian security experts warned about a "relative lack of willingness of organisations and departments to work closely together to tackle a crime issue, [large redaction]" (GAC 2013-2551, 37). To compensate for this perceived "lack of willingness," the need for "buy-in" from SEA recipients was emphasized. Stressing how "ownership" of the project would promote long-term success, one proposal advises, "Significant ownership of the PIUs has already been demonstrated by the beneficiary agencies, through their participation in the creation of SOPs, the identification of premises from within their existing estates, and the absorption of running costs within their regular budgets ... The best way to ensure sustainability and avoid waning of interest in the concept of the PIUs (intelligence-led, proactive investigations) is to make every effort to achieve operational success. This will motivate staff and encourage a sense of belonging to a special unit. Success will breed success, and ensure continued and enthusiastic support from the beneficiary agencies even after donor support is removed" (9).

Another aspect of a strategy of sustainability involves integration of SEA border police into local, regional, and international networks. For example, PIUs were designed on fusion-centre principles to include immigration officials, criminal police, and maritime police, as well as to liaise with the national navies. During development of the PIUs, the Canadian government paid for UNODC trainers to remain on-site to provide "tactical and strategic advice to the PIUs with a view to promoting a proactive, intelligence-led, human rights based approach with regard to detecting, disrupting and investigating migrant smuggling"

(GAC 2013-2551, 4). In addition to providing daily training and assistance to PIUs in an effort to "fuse" the various arms of maritime intelligence, the UNODC mentors would act as surveillance hubs for norm-maker donor countries. A START-GPSF project proposal indicates that UNODC mentors will be responsible for liaising with "the international law enforcement community present in the region (such as police and immigration officers from Australia, Canada, UK and the USA)" (GAC 2013-2551, 11). The note goes on to explain that the project's objective is "to facilitate and encourage to the extent possible law enforcement cooperation, including the conduct of joint investigations, not only between the PIUs in Cambodia, Indonesia and Thailand but also between the PIUs and the international law enforcement community" (ibid.).

Using the case management system provided by Australia, the PIUs were intended to be multi-agency intelligence hubs that provide surveillance for states of the Global North but could also receive intelligence to enforce border controls "at the source." In the annex to the project proposal, START-GPSF explain that Interpol data sets will be made available to at least one unspecified PIU through a direct Interpol connection. Establishing this direct virtual private network between the PIUs and Interpol involved the purchase of encrypted routers for each PIU. It was noted that "the data that will become available will give PIU officers access to information concerning travel document abuse, examples of specimen travel documents, Interpol's system of notices, alerts and warnings" (GAC 2013-2551, 5). In these integrated intelligence and border enforcement units, the design of the PIUs allowed for fluid surveillance sharing as well as integrating border agencies from SEA countries into an international enforcement system. One project summary explains, "The project will create Port Intelligence Units (PIUs) with a mobile operational capacity in Indonesia, Cambodia and Thailand, tactically situated in order to allow them to respond effectively to maritime migrant smuggling. Their reach will *extend well beyond their immediate locations* however, and through the channels for cooperation and coordination that will be established, the units will be able to respond to intelligence from international as well as national sources, from border control units at land, sea and air entry points, and from criminal police" (GAC 2013-2551, 44; emphasis added).

As a Canadian contribution to integrating SEA countries into the border management systems of prosperous countries, the ACCBP has been highly innovative and successful. One GAC document notes that "multi-agency intelligence units of the kind proposed here currently do not exist" in any of the recipient countries (GAC 2013-2551, 45). Building such systems of integrated surveillance – as well as ensuring that Northern/donor countries are embedded within these operations to provide "sustainability" – has involved a thorough effort to develop the capacities of donor countries. Starting with the identification of locations in each of the three countries, the project designed and built the PIU offices. Funded by Canadian security aid, the UNODC worked with the recipient countries to identify permanent staff for the program. Canadian security innovators then trained hundreds of staff in a range of disciplines connected to intelligence analysis and migrant smuggling investigations, developing much of the "software" of the recipient governments "from scratch."[8] Working with the recipient countries, Canada also produced a set of standard operating procedures for each PIU that normalized the "best practices" of risk-policing practices of the Global North. Using the ACBBP funds, PIUs were fully equipped, including with specialist case management and intelligence analysis software. Then, working to support Australian leadership, the PIUs were networked with local, regional, and international partners.

As a project to advance the interoperable practices of the transversal security community, the ACCBP programming has demonstrated how Canadian policing sciences and the "software" of security governance can develop security in deviant states of the Global South. Moreover, the project demonstrated considerable accomplishments in a short time. In creating an extraterritorial regime of border management, where recipient countries are to serve as front-line surveillance and enforcement, the PIU initiative has been a "successful" model. In fact, as I detail below, Canadian security innovators have been praised for the PIU model, and it has been suggested as a format to develop policing capacities in other "source" countries in efforts to globalize migration controls. However, before I detail the broader strategic benefits of the PIU project, I will examine how the PIU project has also encountered a number of barriers. While the effort of prosperous

8 Discussing the current capacities of border police in the SEA region, one briefing note highlights the "limited understanding of the benefits of an intelligence led approach to tackling crime" (GAC 2013-2551, 37).

donor countries to build a front-line system of border management in SEA is recounted as highly successful, it is important to demonstrate how "micropolitics" (Scott 1998) demonstrate the agency and resistance to global visions of control. As Scott (1998) details, micropolitics arise specifically in relation to efforts of utopian-transformers to implement practical, technical changes in the polities they seek to order. While these reforms are technically focused, antagonisms can surface. In security aid practice, these micropolitics expose the objectives of Canadian security innovation; they are not providing "assistance" to accommodate local knowledge and practices, but are there to transform policing and border practices according to a Northern ideal, and integrate these institutions into the transversal security community. Moreover, in detailing the barriers to implementation of these policing and surveillance techniques, the documents analysed below illustrate the rationalities of security development as an aim of reforming "deviant states."

Barriers to Security Techniques Development

Unlike the construction of prison walls or border stations, or the provision of policing equipment, the development of security techniques is animated by the knowledge practices that sustain them. Sophisticated systems of surveillance and social sorting are context specific, and efforts to embed them in the Global South, much like colonial efforts to develop Native administrations (Mitchell 2002; Scott 1999), produce conflictual and contradictory outcomes (Murakami Wood 2013). While the PIUs have been a model for quick and successful application of security "software" in the SEA region, linking these new intelligence nodes into efforts at transversal security governance, Canadian security innovators raised several challenges during the project.

Although "barriers" to security aid implementation are rarely detailed, certainly in contrast to the "successes," documents related to development of security software in the SEA region are notable for their discussions of operational challenges. In particular, the final narrative report of the PIU project contained a "lessons learned" section that described barriers encountered in the field. Items discussed included the lack of proper recruitment, unavailability of building supplies, and a general complaint with "speeds [at] which [some recipient agencies] move which are not consistent with high levels of project

Figure 5.2. First "Lesson Learned," Final Narrative Report from PIU Project in SEA (GAC 2013-2551, 37)

1. Law enforcement agencies were unhappy that agreement had been reached with the donor before agreement was reached with themselves concerning the project aims. In an ideal situation the needs of the beneficiary countries should shape the responses of the international community (both implementing agency and donor). In practice this is more likely to be a delicate balancing act in which donor and beneficiary aspirations are represented. This issue however resulted in considerable delay to project implementation while discussions were held concerning project aims and objectives.

implementation in short time frames" (GAC 2013-2551, 37). In addition, two other notable "obstacles" were listed. First was a grievance over the setting of project objectives (see figure 5.2).

The note reveals the first "obstacle": the program was designed *before* discussions with SEA border-policing agencies. Representing the SEA countries as "beneficiaries" of the security-aid package parallels altruistic tropes of development discourse, yet it fails to acknowledge that "migrant smuggling" is a problematization constructed by norm-maker of the transversal security community and parroted by Canadian political actors following the recent arrival of migrant ships. Representing SEA countries as "beneficiaries" is a sentiment of humanitarian governance, yet it masks the fact that the "aid" package is designed to benefit Canada and other prosperous countries. Importantly, the listing of this "obstacle" demonstrates that the "aid" recipients contested this relationship. While it is described as recalcitrance by "donors," countries of the global South have dynamic ways to resist the imposition of "best practices" from norm-makers. Though it is far from an "ideal situation," the interactions detailed by the note demonstrate that, while the recipients do participate in the externally designed development project, the symbolic "partnership" of security cooperation is expected to be maintained – and Canadian security innovators have to engage in symbolic repairs to carry on with *their* project.

After a redacted section of the document, the second declassified "obstacle" addressed the project funding. Specifically, a concern was raised about the "sustainability" of the project. However, it was a far cry from the "sustainability" concerns of the norm-maker countries (see figure 5.3).

In figure 5.3, the "degree of nervousness" pertains to "partner agencies," specifically the UNODC, who appear to be caught between donor

Figure 5.3. Second "Lesson Learned," Final Narrative Report from PIU Project in SEA (GAC 2013-2551, 38)

3. A degree of nervousness was often in evidence among some managers in partner agencies concerning the financial legacy the project would leave them with. In wishing to create meaningful and sustainable structures (rather than simply providing training and moving on) the project implied a degree of on-going commitment on the part of the beneficiary agencies. This resulted in some quarters in a reluctance to move forward until future implications were properly understood.

agencies and recipients.[9] Indeed, the prosperous countries supporting the project were explicit in their design to foster an *ongoing*, integrated system of maritime surveillance. The security aid was targeted precisely to deputize the SEA border policing agencies in the transversal security community and provide them with the "software" (literal and figurative) to engage in more sophisticated intelligence-led policing. Prosperous countries assumed that, with this security development, SEA recipients would take their newly developed policing sciences and contribute to transversal security. Yet, as demonstrated by figure 5.2, the PIU project was clearly designed by prosperous countries seeking firmed control over global mobilities – and the SEA border police were cognizant of this enterprise. In figure 5.3, we can see how the recipient countries did not want to fund a program for global border control; instead they wanted the prosperous countries to fund it. This note exposes a very different understanding of the "sustainability" of the project, in which the Global North emphasizes sustainability in continued reliability of intelligence and security practices, while the recipient countries are concerned about their abilities to fund a project that is essentially proxy policing for the Global North. Further, while we read this through Canadian translation, we can see that the UNODC were "nervous" about being the messenger.

An underlying point of this second bullet is that we should also reapply the funding grievance from the SEA countries to the project design

9 It is worth noting that documents show the UNODC had originally proposed a $5 million budget for the PIU project, yet Canadian funding from the ACCBP was limited to $2 million. In their final project report, the UNODC acknowledge the funding gap by detailing how the government offered a "scaled-back" version, which eliminated judicial reform and focused entirely on surveillance and intelligence (GAC 2013-2551, 83).

grievances from the first bullet. An important facet of the symbolic grievance and repair detailed in bullet one emphasized that SEA countries raised the design of the project precisely to underline the issue of ongoing funding. Whether this overture was noted by Canadian security innovators is unclear. Yet it reveals an important aspect of this security aid for border control that parallels the development trap: like development assistance used simply to manage poverty and maintain unequal wealth disparities (Turpin, Bobbette, and Miller 2013), security assistance is used to manage unease and maintain border regimes that protect wealth disparities.

Most of the documents detailing Canadian security aid to SEA for "migrant smuggling" emphasize the success of the project, though some documents do outline barriers to institutionalizing security governance regimes. Addressing the ongoing concern of donor countries about the "sustainability" of the project, the final narrative report for the PIU project contains an entry under the category "Risk":

> A risk that the overall impact of investment in training and procurement can be diluted by partners if they fail to fully understand or endorse the aims of the project in favour of a more perfunctory tick box approach to training and provision of equipment. Throughout the project this issue has arisen in each of the countries to a greater or lesser extent. Expectations are often shaped by previous experience, and the law enforcement agencies in some of the countries in the region have become accustomed to simple delivery of training and equipment that is not accompanied by *a requirement* to see lasting structures created as a result. These challenges have been overcome through extensive dialogue, persistence, diplomacy and, to an extent, compromise. (GAC 2013-2551, 38)

Stressing the expectation that the donor has more than "perfunctory tick box" training, the note articulates how this security aid comes attached with a "requirement to see lasting structures created as a result." A clear reflection of Canada's poor opinions about the enforcement practices of the SEA "partners" (as they are described here), the statement exposes the Janus-faced character of "migrant smuggling" aid, where the "partners" are expected to be surveillance functionaries and the "beneficiaries" are the norm-making donor countries. Notwithstanding the obstacles to moving forward with more security development in SEA, the note concludes, "To ensure that the progress made to date results in *concrete* operational outcomes, continued support in the form of training, mentoring, and reinforcing the sustainability of each PIU will be required" (GAC 2013-2551, 39; emphasis added).

Although Canada entered the field of migrant control relatively late compared with the norm-makers of the transversal security community, the note above underlines how Canadian norm-supporting comprises concrete, practical support for transversal security governance. Security aid is an important strategic avenue for Canada to fulfil its "place" as a norm-supporter, through these practical steps to develop the techniques of security in the Global South. Security innovators have been particularly effective at supporting the agendas of norm-makers, and the SEA region security aid reveals the strategic orientation of Canadian security innovation. In demonstrating how aid contributes to advancing the reputation of Canadian security innovation and to development of transversal policing, the security aid to SEA is characteristic of Canadian norm-supporting. Below, I unpack the strategic interests fulfilled by these security aid practices.

The "Anti-Human-Trafficking Agenda" and Canadian Strategic Interests

Like all security aid, the aid to SEA under the awkwardly titled "anti-human trafficking agenda" is rationalized by expressions of humanitarian government and animated by a desire to provide tangible contributions to the development of transversal security governance. Though the aid package can be presented as an effort to save migrants from dangerous travels, or the security of "the international community in general" (GAC 2013-2551, 93), the exploration of the documents offered in this chapter displays how the objective of the funding is to pre-emptively intercept "so many boats" from reaching Canadian shores. To do so *requires* that SEA security aid recipients participate in networked surveillance and policing to intercept "illegal" maritime mobilities "at the source."

As noted in one of the proposal documents for the SEA security aid project, "Canada and Canadian citizens benefit from this project in a number of ways" (GAC 2013-2551, 6). In addition to the benefit of keeping asylum-seekers away from Canadian shores, the development of security techniques in the SEA region furthers other strategic objectives. A first level of benefit is fulfilled by integration of SEA border police into the network of policing unwanted travellers. While this strengthens the practices of global mobilities control, there are specific benefits for Canadian security innovators who gain from accessing new sources of intelligence for "policing-at-a-distance" (Bigo 2006). As a memorandum of understanding between the CBSA and GAC explains, "By strengthening key areas of need, the [Royal Thai Police] Immigration Bureau will be better equipped to respond to Canadian requests for investigative and enforcement assistance to address two major Government of Canada priorities: Human Smuggling, and Organized Crime" (CBSA 2013-13161, 59). In developing "sustainable" practices of border migration in the SEA region, Canadian security agencies would benefit from an additional surveillance node. A GAC document emphasizes that the PIUs "represent an additional intelligence source that can be used by Canada should ventures be detected" (GAC 2013-2551, 13). Under the heading of "Strategic Value Added," another briefing underlines the point that "Canada is uniquely placed to benefit from the intelligence generated by these units" (GAC 2013-2551, 6).

A further strategic interest fulfilled by the security aid in the SEA region is the strengthening of relations between normative powers in the transversal security community. Not only do security assistance projects bring norm-takers into the transversal security community – though they offer institutional resistances – it allows a particular forum for norm-makers to interact and cooperate. As a norm-supporter, Canada plays an important strategic role in contributing particular, concrete, and tangible development programs to support the broader efforts of norm-makers to consolidate global networks of unregulated mobilities. As one document from the CBSA notes, "Providing this capacity building assistance will also generate support from our strategic allies such as the United States and Australia who are also working with the region to combat human smuggling" (CBSA 2013-13161, 21). Particularly in the SEA region, Australia's role as a significant norm-maker is noteworthy. Demonstrating that the categories of normative power are fluid, Australia provides a useful parallel to Canada as a "middle power" and norm-supporter. Yet Australia's geopolitical position and exceptional program of counter-migration shares far more parallels with the United States and the EU. In what they call "promoting visa integrity," Pickering and Weber (2013, 95–107) have detailed the external network of police, border agents, navy resources, and commercial entities in the SEA region who participate in pre-emptive and preventative border controls. Given Australia's "layered" efforts at pushing out their borders and working to establish a program of surveillance for norm-takers, Canadian security aid in SEA works under the Australian leadership and will "generate support" from the far more active Australian vision (and network) of transversal security governance.

In providing a technically oriented program of assistance, Canada can illustrate its security innovation in supporting the agenda of norm-makers. In a project initiation authorization signed by the minister of foreign affairs on 31 May 2013, for phase 2 of the PIU project, the memo emphasizes that "the contribution will also bolster Canada's reputation and its sustained commitment to enhancing the security of Thailand, Indonesia and Cambodia by supporting capacity building efforts for institutions that are on the front-lines of preventing human smuggling" (GAC 2013-2551, 14). As a key element of norm-supporting, the reputation of Canada as a trusted member of the transversal security community is of particular strategic value. With a focus on enhancing the integration and professionalism of SEA border police, Canadian security innovators have aimed to develop a "sustainable" program for the "front lines" of the transversal effort to manage "illegal" migration. Given that Canada has broad experience with developing tangible software of security, the SEA program has focused on these technical enhancements to maximize the capacities of the SEA recipients, which also maximizes the reputation of Canadian security innovators. With the goal of communicating Canadian contributions as a norm-supporter, a final level of strategic objectives can be demonstrated by the visibility strategy of Canada as a norm-supporter (as also seen in the Libyan and Haitian projects). Demonstrating that Canada emphasizes its communications strategies, project proposal forms always contain a subsection on "communications." In a typical but informative response, the section for the PIU project proposal stresses that "Canada will be properly credited at all events and in all publications through use of agreed logos etc. and Canada will be consulted prior to the publication of web stories or other public statements concerning the project" (GAC 2013-2551, 10).

Despite Canada's limited influence in the norm-making field of security governance, the security aid program in SEA demonstrates how expertise and innovation in policing can be mobilized strategically to enhance Canadian reputational value as a norm-supporter. The Canada "value added" from the project is demonstrated in the opening of the first PIU in Cambodia in May 2013. A press release from the UNODC recounts how "senior representatives of the Governments of Cambodia and Canada" partnered "in response to the threat" of migrant smuggling. The news release reported that the project, "funded by the

Government of Canada," will "form strong partnerships with key sections of the Cambodia National Police and with the international law enforcement community" (UNODC 2013). A photograph included in the press release demonstrated the prominent Government of Canada logos featured at the inauguration ceremony. With 100 guests attending, Martin Reeve, UNODC coordinator for the PIUs, described the long-term approach to integration and transversality: "For the PIUs to be effective, the international community will have to provide long-term support and create networks of trust and intelligence sharing with local law enforcement partners … PIU officers in Cambodia, Thailand and Indonesia will need to learn – over time – to cooperate with their local, regional and international counterparts" (ibid.).

As a reformatory effort to make deviant states from the Global South into more sustainable border-policing proxies, the ceremony emphasized the final commitments from countries of the Global North as well as the "buy-in" to enforcement from the Global South. Poised with the objectives of providing frontline intelligence on suspicious mobilities, the PIUs are networked through surveillance in what Bigo (2008, 19) describes as an "archipelago of policing" that "hold together the national police, military police, customs control, immigration, consulates, and even intelligence services and the military." Furthermore, PIUs themselves are "mobile" and epitomize "a dynamic conception of borders where borders are themselves on the move" (27). As a demonstration of the strategic interests fulfilled by security innovation, the PIUs underline Canadian contributions of norm-supporting. Technically oriented and tangible by design, they have enhanced the reputation of Canadian security innovators and, as I discuss below, have provided a venue for Canadian security aid to make innovative contributions to the aspirational control practices of the transversal security community.

Discussion: Security Aid and *Ban*optic Power

Canada has established itself as a reliable norm-supporter, as is especially evident from Canadian expertise in developing the professionalism and integration of policing entities from the Global South. "Capacity-building" programs have a broad scope of techniques of development, along with a large array of assistance recipients to enhance. While security-assistance regimes are often characterizable by an immediate focus on developing the techniques of particular recipients, I have argued that a broader objective of security aid is to assist in development of transversal security governance. A key aspect of this strategic objective is that the normative power of transversal surveillance has privileged collaborative, integrated efforts to protect and enhance the security of the "international community." Guided by an underlying humanitarian reason, these cooperative and transversal security-development projects are animated by a desire to control crime (i.e., crimmigration) and advance the rule of law.

Canada's security aid to SEA demonstrates how the threat of "illegal" migration has consolidated a cooperative and interoperable network of border policing and surveillance. As a program to develop security techniques, the aid funding has focused on "transferring" intelligence-led policing capacities of the Global North to the Global South, with an emphasis on making these practices "sustainable." Though barriers have arisen in Canada's effort to impose these requirements on recipient countries, the security aid project underlines how the transversal security community aspires to consolidate a regime of best practices under the normative imperative of "good" and "bad" circulations, while also demonstrating how the power relations of "assistance" regimes work to develop these best practice regimes in the jurisdictions of norm-takers. As a norm-supporter, Canada has demonstrated its security innovation by managing the delivery of capacity-building programs and helping to shepherd the deviant SEA countries into the transversal border policing network.

In a critical correlate to the presentation of policing efforts that target "illegal migration" as a cooperative regime of global crime control, scholars have cast aspersions on the altruistic humanitarian ideals presented by its advocates. Aas (2013, 30) has argued that the "Northern penal states" have reconfigured a punitive regime that, on one hand, aims to govern the threat of "illegal" migration through the criminal justice agencies but, on the other hand, has moved away from the pillars of procedural fairness that (should) comprise the criminal justice system. Moreover, unlike a "punitive" approach associated with the disciplinary regime of the criminal justice system, the character of the transversal governance of "illegal migration" is not centred on rehabilitation or incapacitation. As illustrated by Canada's effort to strip asylum-seekers of legal protections, Northern penal states are characterized by *exceptionalism* to the rule of law and an effort at spectacular deterrence (De Genova 2002, 436–9; Ericson 2007). Notably, Canadian efforts have paled in contrast to the exceptionalism of norm-makers in extraterritorial interception and detention. As a norm-supporter, Canada has advocated the consensus on exceptional punishment through political legitimization. The "anti-human smuggling" programs announced in SEA region represent a recent form of Canadian practices to support transversal policing with comprehensive development assistance. As demonstrated in chapter 2, Canadian technical assistance has been most clearly visible with efforts to govern drugs and transnational organized crime, particularly in Latin America. But the security aid program in the SEA region shows a new terrain of Canadian norm-supporting in combating "migration smuggling." Honing security innovation in the realm of risk policing and border management, Canadian security aid has supported efforts from norm-makers Australia, the EU, and the United States to address the "problem" of unauthorized migration in the SEA region. While Canada has only limited exposure to such unauthorized travel, norm-makers in the region have had prolonged interest in developing "sustainable" policing and surveillance in the region to filter "good" and "bad" circulations.

As an effort to develop the software of surveillance and security governance, Canadian security aid in the SEA region illustrates Didier Bigo's conceptualization of the banopticon. Bigo (2008, 32) writes that the dispositif of the "banopticon allows us to understand how a network of heterogeneous and transversal practices functions and makes sense as a form of (in)security at the transnational level" (ibid.). As Bigo has explained, numerous efforts at governing (in)security comprise banoptic regimes, including discourses of threat construction; institutional responses to threats of "illegal" migration; architectural structures of security governance (like the PIUs) that police and surveil threats; fields of expertise and expert practitioners who compete and collaborate in constructing/validating threats as well as guide security governance; technologies of laws that have been developed to order surveillance and interdiction on a transversal scale; and the vast array of techniques – particularly intelligence-led policing – that animate "best practices" to be developed in deviant states. Allowing us to appreciate the multi-scalar efforts to develop security, the banopticon does not present a "unified strategy" for understanding the control functions of norm-makers, but instead offers a complex and flexible understanding of "anonymous multiple struggles, which nevertheless contribute to a globalization of domination" (11). As a conceptual logic of transversal controls, the banopticon allows for the fields of (in)security to be appreciated in a rhizomatic fashion, accounting for coordinated security governance and competing fields of practice, as well as those not coordinated by complementary practices.

As a concept, banopticism is similar to normative power in that it helps explain how regimes of practice are not produced by a unified strategy of control, but instead based upon negotiated and contingent relations that derive from prescriptions to govern (in)security. Though norm-making typically articulates practices of control that have been rationalized – more often through humanitarian reasons – to privilege the Global North, these outcomes are procedural and cannot be counted as predetermined. They can be challenged, or they can fail. They can be reanimated or reconfigured, where their potential modulations are infinite. Yet, most commonly, they do not fail, not inasmuch as they are rationalized perfectly, but because of their critical mass. With an expansion of security expertise and the widening net of global (in)security – what has been called the "security trap" (CASE Collective 2006) – the rhizomatic production of transversal policing and surveillance "best practices" is a prolific field of transversal security governance where detections of failure are used only to justify further intervention, reform, and "assistance" from norm-makers.

Canadian efforts at security innovation are imbricated into these transversal modulations of security governance. And the ascension of security development programming into the realm of policing borders in the SEA region indicates Canadian norm-supporting. As a security innovator, the aid project demonstrates Canadian contributions to a global field of banoptic power, which is characterized by three dimensions. First are practices of exceptionalism and rules of emergency. This dimension is most clearly demonstrated by Northern penal states' proliferation of exceptional punishments, as scholars have demonstrated the deadly violence of these punitive regimes (Doty 2007; Krasmann 2007; Pickering 2010). Second are acts of profiling and bureaucracies that "screen" for risks, as evidenced by the training program in SEA that develop techniques of security. Finally, the third dimension is the "normative imperative of mobility" that privileges "good" flows and neutralizes "bad" flows (Bigo 2008, 32). Unlike the *pan*opticon that aims to surveil the population indiscriminately, the *ban*opticon is a targeted and discriminatory surveillance. In seeking out risks, the banopticon is not a reformatory project, but an expulsionary project: a *ban*ishment that keeps the unwanted travels away from a territorial interiority ("the shores"), yet simultaneously integrates "external" mechanisms (the border police) in the administration of this exclusion. Developing a transversal network of border policing Canada has contributed to a system of "inclusive exclusion" which "serves to include what is excluded" (Agamben 1998, 21).

As an effort of the transversal security community to establish a normative consensus on best practices of border management (see Muller 2010), the emerging transversal polity is fundamentally structured along the global disparities of wealth. As Canadian security innovators noted, "Smuggling of migrants by sea is a global and increasing phenomenon, where wealthy and advanced nations are inevitably targeted by migrants and the criminals who smuggle them" (GAC 2013-2551, 6). Various scholars have reformulated what the Canadian document referred to as the "large pool" of impoverished "would-be" migrants as a global surplus population (Pickering and Weber 2013) or a surplus humanity that is "structurally and biologically redundant to global accumulation and the corporate matrix" (Mahmud 2010, 11). In sorting entitled and unentitled global mobilities – what Duffield (2010) has detailed as the distinctions between insured and non-insured existence – surveillance functions operate according to what Aas (2011, 332) has described as "the changing modes of risk thinking and social exclusion [that] and are inscribed with specific notions of otherness and suspicion, essentially related to citizenship and global privilege." Nair (2010) has similarly highlighted the punitive characteristics of social exclusion of the neoliberal present by underlining its unique dimensions where racialized Others are at once expunged from the entitlements of citizenship, yet maintained within the social body in a liminal, transversal sovereign power.

As an affective dimension to Canada's membership in the transversal security community, policing and border controls have become more rigid, while the link between the excluded Others has become more explicitly associated with (in)security. While racial Othering has long animated settler governmentality in Canada (Crosby and Monaghan 2012; Monaghan 2013a, 2013b) as well as the imagination of Canada's postcolonial "multiculturalism" (Thobani 2007), the immediate post-9/11 period witnessed an intensification of racialized Othering. Government officials and mainstream media blamed Canada's refugee and immigration practices for enabling global security threats to enter the state (Sharma 2007, 135; see also Aiken 2007; Park 2013; Razack 2007; Thobani 2007). In relation to Canadian responses to 9/11, Razack (2007, 8) has demonstrated how, "in the 'war on terror,' race thinking accustoms us to the idea that the suspension of rights is warranted in the interests of national security." Moreover, racialized exceptionalism that banishes and inclusively excludes non-authorized travellers to the global peripheries is especially evident in an examination of the practices of transversal border policing.

Numerous scholars have developed Agamben's (1998) notion of "states of exception" (Doty 2007; Ericson 2007; Gregory 2006; Neal 2009; Razack 2007) in the global "war on terror" and, in furthering this analysis, Butler (2004, 56) has drawn out how "petty sovereigns abound." Demonstrating how sovereign decisions over life and death have proliferated to an array of micro-sites, Butler's formulation of "petty sovereigns" describes how "resurrected sovereignty is thus not the sovereignty of unified power under the conditions of legitimacy" (ibid.), but is instead simultaneously diffuse and concentrated, allowing for a broadened range of bureaucratic officials to engage in sovereign-like decisions. Applied to the transversal policing of migration, these anointed powers over life and death are "part of the apparatus of governmentality; their decision, the power they wield to 'deem' someone dangerous and constitute them effectively as such, is a sovereign power, a ghostly and forceful resurgence of sovereignty in the midst of governmentality" (59; see also Aas and Gundhus 2015; Fassin 2014; Huysmans 2011; Nair 2010). Contributing to Butler's insights, we can trace how security aid in the SEA region has accelerated a crimmigration control system that diffuses sovereign acts of "deeming" across increasingly dissipated fields.

While a traditional deeming of banishment would take place "at the shores" of Canada, border police in the SEA region have been trained with the objective (in theory) of identifying unauthorized "boats destined for Canada." Through the development of security techniques, Canadian authorities have attempted to impart the "act" of deeming across a spectrum of agencies associated with the PIUs, from immigration bureaucracies, to border police, criminal police, and national navies, and transnational groups like the UNODC and Interpol. As a strategy to incorporate deviant states into the transversal policing network, the techniques developed have focused on developing risk analysis and intelligence-led policing. Yet the risk calculations are not inclusively about suppressing the illegal, but sorting the flows between "good" and "bad" travellers. The efforts of Canadian security development are self-characterized as objective efforts to evaluate the truthfulness of travellers, where surveillance and intelligence functions of the transversal policing network are directed to sort authorized circulations from "illegal" ones. In deviating from Butler's framework, I contend that the development of security techniques moves away from discourse of exceptionalism and into discourses of objectivity and truthfulness. In particular, the sorting practices of border policing are not exclusive to an executive, but have been dispersed across an expanding array of actors: a transversal bureaucracy of petty sovereigns.

In the development of increasingly dispersed practices of surveillance, deeming, and transversal collaboration, we can highlight how the power to "inclusively exclude" is highly expansive and unbounded, operating through security assemblages and not territories (Huysmans 2014). In the context of "migrant smuggling," petty sovereigns maintain authority over lives that are "marked by precariousness and bareness" (Aas and Gundhus 2015, 18), yet practices of crimmigration control do not have the animating discourses of "war on terror" exceptional sovereignty. Like Canada's effort to develop security techniques in the SEA region, work to govern "illegal" migration is portrayed as more technocratic, and therefore more objective and scientific. Take one entry under "Human Rights," contained in the project proposal for PIU training the Thai border police (figure 5.4).

When highlighting that "very technical" practices of intelligence-led policing and surveillance capacities of the PIU are about testing truthfulness and sorting authorized and "illegal" travel objectively, the CBSA can omit the inherent violence of the bordering regime and conclude there "are no relevant gender or human rights concerns." Under its promotion as "assistance," the security aid regime presents itself as developing what Walters (2011) has called a "humanitarian border." Under Canadian security assistance, the SEA countries would benefit from professionalism, enhancing the rule of law and the objectivity of

Figure 5.4. Excerpt from ACCBP Project Proposal to Train Frontline Immigration and Law Enforcement of the Royal Thai Police (CBSA 2013-13161, 27)

12. Human Rights:

Please provide information regarding the proposed beneficiary's human rights record in the investment priority area. How would human rights considerations be integrated into project delivery? Also, will any specific gender considerations inform project design (in particular, how women and girls may be positively/negatively impacted by new/improved facilities or procedures)?

Although there are human rights issues in Thailand the concerns are minor and not so great as to prevent Canada from assisting and/or cooperating with the country through capacity building. The course material itself is very technical in nature and there are no relevant gender or human rights concerns. Improved professionalism through training and exposure to Canadian law enforcement methods and practices could have a positive impact on human rights and gender considerations. The CBSA will encourage the attendance of both male and female participants in the training courses.

crime control. Unlike practices of exceptionalism resting upon decisionism and a rupturing of the rule of law, Canadian security aid has aimed to develop a multi-agency, integrated, multi-scalar, globally integrated (and Northern penal state–directed) regime of border policing, premised on the promotion of the rule of law and a systematic approach to identify risks. Here, the rationalities of security assistance illustrate how petty sovereignty as practised in crimmigration control operates as a fully governmentalized and mobile sovereignty. It operates with a foregrounding of race-thinking endemic to the relationship between Northern penal states and the transversal. However, instead of discourses of bio-political war mobilized in other cases of migration control (Duffield 2008; Krasmann 2007; Phillips 2009), petty sovereignty is rationalized by technocratic routinization that implants the fantasies of "so many boats" storming Canadian shores into bureaucratic filaments of risk analysis wrapped in a prose of human rights. As an expression of the transversal security community, security aid is not an exceptionalism animated by existential threats or warring imaginaries, but an assemblage of "reasonable" and practical measures to govern the geographies of insecurity.

Conclusion(s)

Security techniques include a wide array of policing and surveillance practices to govern insecurities. Canada has established a reputation for surveillance and policing knowledge-practices, and security aid programs have become an avenue to develop these areas of expertise in the Global South. Rationalized by an animating logic of humanitarianism, Canada announces security aid programs to assist needy populations. Though some of these programs may help improve the human rights practices of recipient countries, their overriding objective is to integrate policing and surveillance agencies of the Global South into transversal security governance regimes. As demonstrated by the case study in Southeast Asia, the development of security is fraught with complications and barriers, though the aspirational character of these assistance practices ensures that failed efforts are redoubled in efforts to gain more "sustainable" security governance regimes.

The governance of mobility is a particularly visible site illustrating the broad scope of security techniques – as well as the underlying motives of norm-makers – to develop security governance practices in the Global South. Canada is not a norm-maker in the establishment of transversal mobility controls; however, this chapter demonstrates how Canadian security innovation can support broader transversal efforts to regulate the movements of undesirable populations. Given the transversality of contemporary border regimes, efforts to police the borders of prosperous Northern countries are increasingly de-territorialized and happen externally to border demarcations themselves. Such transversal policing is networked through surveillance and the search for suspicious identities, while maintaining "a veneer of scientific objectivity [that] is animated through the lens of prejudice" (McCulloch and Pickering 2009, 635). Most importantly, the regime of security aid provides a venue to reform the deviant states – those countries that source and transit unwanted mobilities – by integrating their policing and surveillance agencies into the transversal security community.

Though rationalized as humanitarian logic of wanting to help victims of human trafficking or assist migrants, the practices of policing transversal migration raise political and ethical questions about unequal divisions of wealth and the role of the Global North in maintaining these inequalities. Aas (2013, 34) argues that "the Northern penal state" has been created to maintain a "deeply stratified global order." Canadian security aid practices share in this global reality; however, instead of having an explicit purpose to maintain global inequalities, Canadian aid to develop security techniques is framed by humanitarian reasons. These projects are frequently animated by a desire to assist populations, and have no explicit intentions to incarcerate the world's poor. The humanitarian rationales of these programs express sympathy towards needy populations, as well as the desire to maintain a fair system of migration. Though an element of these programs appeals to a "domopolitics" (Walters 2004) that festers with anti-migration sentiments, those sentiments remain much less popular in Canada than in the EU or Australia. More importantly, the security innovators involved in these development regimes do not have a politics of containment as their objective. Their aims are to develope security techniques, which are framed as technical and apolitical. In framing security development as a technical endeavour to enhance policing and surveillance, Canadian security innovation contributes to transversal security governance regimes set by norm-makers, yet this narrow focus avoids the responsibilities of global inequalities that animate these trends.

Examining impacts from the stratification of global wealth, Sassen (2014) has highlighted how technological advances, themselves the product of brilliant and creative social thinking, have enabled a new social logic of expulsion. Although Sassen examines economic and environment techniques of governance, these logics are shared by the policing and surveillance techniques explored in this chapter. As Sassen (2014, 4) argues, the creativity behind new systems of "savage sorting" allows for countries of the Global North to make highly complex calculations and decisions, at rapid speeds, that tend towards a "brutal simplicity." Though the complexities in these techniques of governance are a result of creative and complex thinking, Sassen argues their impacts are increasingly simple: the world's poor are systematically sorted out and subjected to expulsion. As demonstrated by the techniques of security developed by security aid projects, the expulsion of these populations is not unconditional, but merely an expulsion from the spaces of global privilege. These populations remain inclusively excluded, and security agencies in the Global South have been increasingly – and this trend will only accelerate – tasked with the responsibilities of order maintenance and containment in these geographies of insecurity. While Canadian security aid regimes emphasize their technical and apolitical character, the aggregate contributions of these efforts at security development are to foster and enhance the transversal practices of security governance. By developing assistance projects that further these aspirational goals, Canadian security aid has enhanced the reputation of security innovation as a norm-supporting avenue for transversal policing, while refusing any political responsibilities for the injustices maintained by these new logics of expulsion. As opposed to "grand brutalities" conjuring political and ethical opposition, the petty brutalities of security aid have maintained a discursive commitment to assist needy populations, though working to ensure they remain excluded.

Conclusion(s): Security Aid in an Insecure World

Standing under the Peace Tower in front of the large crowd gathered for the annual Canada Day celebrations on Parliament Hill, Prime Minister Stephen Harper offered an assessment of Canada's place in the world: "Canada is not just any country, but a people determined to do right – a fact that makes me proud as we approach the one hundred fiftieth anniversary of our country ... [We are] compassionate neighbours, courageous warriors, and confident partners, a bastion of freedom in an un-free world, a standard-bearer of goodwill. In a time when too many choose to hate, [Canada is] a land of hope in a sea of uncertainty" (Canadian Press 2013). Harper's comments about an "un-free world" steeped in violence are rooted in a deeply conservative world view, one that combines realist internationalism with an Orientalist fear of the postcolonial Other. Yet the notion of an uncertain exterior world threatened by violence and insecurity is a popular trope, and one not held solely by the conservative-minded. Often these concerns about global insecurity are accompanied by genuine desires to help. Security aid appeals to this humanitarian sentiment and, precisely because of these sentiments, will continue to accelerate as a vehicle for promoting the development of security governance.

While not featuring prominently in the narratives and case studies that I have detailed, security aid can provide immediate safety and security to vulnerable populations. Assistance regimes are themselves expressions of a desire to provide immediate support and solidarity to those in need. Few would disagree with the immediate need to respond in some capacity to ISIL attacks on civilian populations in Iraq or Syria, or efforts to fund safety initiatives in refugee camps, or develop human rights protocols in countries like Colombia. Yet the humanitarian sentiments of "aid" do little to transform the underlying strains that produce insecurity. Fassin (2012, vii) has argued that "humanitarianism elicits the fantasy of a global moral community that may still be viable and the expectation that solidarity may have redeeming powers." Inasmuch as the humanitarian sentiments of security aid may stem from a "determination to do right," the means of practising solidarity with those in need has been limited to the narrow confines of developing security governance. The ability to enact a secular communion, a solidarity between the humanitarian sentiments and emancipatory transformation, remains merely a fantasy.

At the intersection of security governance and development theory, my arguments engage with, and contribute to, a diverse scholarship examining governing strategies in a global context of rising inequalities and insecurities. In presenting the conceptual arrangement of security aid to this much broader examination of global governance, my contributions demonstrate that security aid is fundamentally a balancing enterprise between the advancement of Canadian strategic interests and the collective interests of the transversal security community to reform deviant states of the Global South. While competition and disagreement are present among allies within this pursuit of collective interests, transversal security governance presents a field of shared interest and widespread collaboration between prosperous states and the phantom states they seek to govern through security reforms packaged as humanitarian aid.

While the reorientation of tradition development assistance – often through bureaucratic development agencies – comprises an aspect of this study, I stress that security aid is itself a distinct form of humanitarian governance. Security aid is a specific form of assistance rationalized as *the development regime of security*. Three specific types of assistance can be used to categorize how security aid is transmitted to recipient countries of the Global South. First is the category of security interventions, which refers to the expanding influence of the human security agenda to rationalize military-oriented interventions to protect and assist civilian populations in distress. As assistance missions to provide security, interventions act as a gateway to further security aid that aims to develop security capacities. The second type of aid is aimed at developing infrastructure, which is the "hardware" of security. As "techno fixes" (Haggerty 2004; Kearon 2013), this hardware includes materials, buildings, and machinery to allow security forces of the Global South to engage in systematic surveillance and policing. The third type of security aid is represented as techniques, a broad category to encompass the knowledge practices of governance associated with contemporary management of (in)security. These types of security aid are often complementary and conjoined, providing problem-solving approaches to stabilize and mitigate security governance quagmires associated with the geographies of insecurity in the Global South.

Much like traditional development practices, security aid is an expression of globalization processes that aspire to reform deviant states. As an aspirational design, security development is fraught with inconsistencies and contradictions, yet themes of failure are often projected as the responsibility of deviant states – particularly their poor practices of governance – and used to rationalize further calls for security development. With the likely continuation of global (in)security crises, Canadian norm-supporting will, regardless of political parties in government, continue to perform a technically oriented and practical role in the reformatory strategies of the transversal security community. Given the increasingly plural power structure of international geopolitics, where the monopoly of power held by the Global North is loosening, the role of security innovation in providing tangible and concrete support to develop capacities of recipient states will ensure a certain "niche" for Canadian security aid. Though the geopolitical role of Canadian internationalism will continue to diminish, areas to provide professionalized techniques and technologies to improve cooperation and interoperability of transversal security governance will ensure a strategic avenue for security aid programming. While these underlying strategic interests are rarely foregrounded in public discussions of security aid programming, the most powerful rationalization of security aid will remain its capturing of the humanitarian sentiments of Canadians "determined to do right" in these "seas of uncertainty" – as Mr Harper points out. Regrettably, the impacts of these assistance regimes will solidify the unequal relations of "aid" as opposed to addressing fundamental questions of justice.

Security Aid and Global Justice

Readers who have burrowed through my exploration of security aid practices have probably noticed the absence of terms like *justice* and *injustice*, particularly within my empirical data narrating the work of security innovators. In some instances, *justice* appears in the records of security aid projects, yet these mentions are almost exclusively related to discussions of criminal justice systems. The concept of justice (or injustice) is notably absent. Why?

Of course, justice is a polysemic concept. Notions of justice can range from the abstract to the technical, from individual to collective experiences, as well as procedural processes to immediate moments. In its most abstract meaning, justice reflects efforts to correct injustice. On a societal level, justice is perhaps most commonly associated with concepts of self-determination. Justice is a question of societies having the authority to make decisions about how they address social harms. It is therefore impossible or at the very least disingenuous to speak of justice when the capacities of self-determination are absent. Yet practices of security development within the transversal security community are antithetical to self-determination. Canadian efforts have the potential to provide immediate assistance to those in need, yet the underlying aspirations of these development ventures are to empower the policing and security forces of the Global South to enforce a vision of order designed by norm-makers of the Global North. Recipient countries receive "aid" funds that place explicit limits on their abilities to be self-determinant and, although these demands can be contested or resisted in part, the framework of transversal security cooperation entrenches a world of conditional sovereignties. While these limits on sovereignties are only extensions of globalization processes that have significantly constrained the self-determination of the postcolonial world, the integrated and interoperable designs of the transversal security community are particularly expressive of efforts by norm-makers to shape the practices of global security governance.

Canada's role in developing these transversal security governance practices have a particularly Janus-faced character. Although the sentiments of security aid have a resonance in the fantasy of a shared humanitarian communion, the practices of security aid work against these ideals on two fundamental levels, both of which help explain why discourses of justice and self-determination are absent in Canadian security aid practices. First is the explicit twinning of security aid to strategic interests. Second is the technical focus of Canadian norm-supporting. Below, I conclude by detailing how these two designs ensure a particular direction of security aid practices for the future.

Security Aid and Strategic Interests

Canadian norm-supporting is premised on two meanings of strategic interests: the improvement of security conditions that might adversely affect Canadians (or Canadian interests abroad), and a whole-of-government coordination aiming to leverage aid to increase Canadian prominence and profile in the transversal security community. These strategic interests are themselves expressions of an increasingly conservative-mindedness of government, where funds are expected to have immediate, tangible benefits for taxpayers. This culture of provincialism is not unique to Canada, nor is it unique to any one group of political partisans but presents an obvious contradiction between the romantic image of Canadians as international Boy Scouts and the self-interested workings of security development programming.

Tying assistance funding to strategic interests is not a new practice, but the prioritization of strategic security aid programming is specific to the formation of the security aid hubs. It is their mobilization of Canadian security innovation that pairs aid with a strategic aim to be seen as contributors who "punch above their weight," cultivating an image of prominence within the transversal security community. As I have detailed, the pursuit of Canadian strategic interests can take multiple forms. In a number of cases, the advancement of Canadian interests is crudely economic. The pursuit of economic interests is most evident with the security infrastructure projects and the activities of the Canadian Commercial Corporation, which has the singular purpose of supporting the sale of Canadian security technologies. Using its leverage and resources as a Crown corporation, CCC is a mercantilist-like entity that fuses private, corporate interests with the administration of aid projects. With the establishment of the Global Markets Action Plan, the Canadian government announced its intention to accelerate practices of tied-aid, which pair ODA assistance funds to explicit kickbacks for Canadian economic interests. While the future of the Action Plan is unknown, given the change of federal government, its influence on security aid through CCC was evident. Regardless of the explicitness of tied-aid policies with Canada's new federal government, the CCC remains a prominent security innovator and will likely have a continued role in selling Canadian "techno fixes" to security problems in the Global South. The prioritization of security and defence sectors sales has accelerated in the past five years, which has included a significant loosening of regulations on the export of these materials.[1] Given that private security actors are increasingly central to the proliferation of security governance (Abrahamsen and Williams 2009), CCC's role is of particular importance for future research on security aid, because it serves as a reminder of the continued (central) role of the state in facilitating "private" economies of security.

The CCC case study demonstrates a very explicit mercantilist element of security aid funding, and the exploration of Canadian engagements in Libya and Haiti add further depth to the economic interests that are twinned to assistance funding. In all of these cases, the security aid funding has a dual purpose when increasing the stability of recipient countries as a strategy of neoliberal development. While these findings confirm the trends within the security development nexus, they are inseparable from the relationships of inequality between donor and recipient countries, and conditionalities placed upon the self-determination of phantom states in the Global South that are expected to remould their governance practices according to the directives of the Global North.

In addition to the economic interests that are embedded in the strategic considerations of assistance funding, I have concentrated significant attention on the interest of promoting Canadian security innovation. Focusing on the role of expertise in security development, I argue that membership in the transversal security community is a significant site to understand Canada's "place in the world." The importance of security aid in developing an understanding of Canadian internationalism is rooted in Canada's position as a small, marginal player on the global stage. Although Canada is far from a global norm-maker, security aid has become a field of Canadian influence through the mobilization of

1 The Harper government has greatly expanded the number of countries eligible for arms sales. In an effort to expand arms and security trade to "non-traditional" markets, the Harper government has also removed more than half of the items on the "controlled-goods list" regulating these exports. A Canadian Press analysis of ten years of Industry Canada data on a class of exports made up of military weapons, guns, and ammunition – along with howitzers, mortars, flame throwers, grenades, and torpedoes – shows that annual exports in the sector averaged $257 million from 2003 to 2012, reaching $251 million in 2012 (Blanchfield 2013). The analysis shows a noticeable decline in exports to traditional allies such as the United Kingdom (down 10 per cent), Italy (37 per cent), the Netherlands (40 per cent), and Belgium (87 per cent). However, exports to countries such as Bahrain, Algeria, Iraq, Pakistan, Mexico, and Egypt have all increased substantially.

expertise in policing, security, prison management, and surveillance. With a number of security bureaucracies who hone these areas of expertise, Canadian security innovators have used assistance practices to increase their reputation in security governance. The advancement of Canadian expertise in security governance packages is the strategic interest fulfilled by security aid. And, as a norm-supporter of the transversal security community, Canada benefits from providing technical and concrete methods for developing global security cooperation and integration.

Within this domain of expertise, it is important to highlight that trends in global security governance are themselves largely divorced from the authorities of the political class, but driven by experts in security governance. While some political interests in advancing Canadian reputation and visibility are evident, the calculations and mobilizations of these knowledge practices are largely under the control of security innovators. Trends in security governance are wide-ranging, even paradigmatic. Security has become a defining rationale of contemporary governance, and these techniques of governance are driven by experts and security networks, not the professionals of politics (Bigo 2008). It is within these networks of security governance where the strategic interests of security aid are cultivated. Despite Canada's marginality on the world stage, the practical orientation of security aid has contributed to the character of Canadian security innovation as a reliable partner in the development of transversal security.

A final domain of strategic interests of security aid is the aspirational designs of the transversal security community and the desire to continually develop the security governance capacities of deviant states in the Global South. Where the Global South is increasingly presented as a source of insecurity to the Global North, the regimes of security development transfer the frontline practices of policing insecurities onto countries of the Global South. News media in the North frequently report on these insecurities: migrants fleeing crisis zones, communities engulfed in drug or resource conflicts, or civil uprisings stemming from political or economic instabilities. Though these crises are often described as problems created by the polities of the Global South and their inabilities to sufficiently suppress or control their populations, these threats are intertwined with the geopolitical activities of the Global North and – particularly in resources and drug use – the consumption of populations in the North. Far from an altruistic reaction to these insecurities, the response of the Global North has been to focus on development of security and policing capacities. As I explored with case studies in Haiti and Southeast Asia, the Canadian strategic interests for managing these insecurities at a distance are linked to objectives of restricting unwanted migrants from these localities, encouraging economic development, and minimizing disruptions to global trade circulations. This aggregate function of security aid is to manage global instability, maintain the status quo, and insulate the privileges of countries like Canada in the Global North from disruptions to business as usual – and, all the while, promote Canadian contributions to the efforts to cooperate and coordinate transversal security governance.

Though assistance regimes are animated by romantic and altruistic sentiments, the organizing logic of security aid is self-serving. Though Canada is only one of many countries that engage in security aid, I argue that the examination of Canadian security aid practices reveals a particular character – a character of norm-supporting – that harnesses assistance funding towards highly instrumental ends. As Mr Harper's comments demonstrate, the humanitarian sentiments of assistance enact an affective reality where Canadian aid provides "security" to those in need and fulfils national values as a beacon of hope. While this portrayal of aid speaks to a romantic representation of Canada's "place in the world," beneath these humanitarian tropes are aid practices that aim foremost to contain and manage instabilities rather than alleviate the strains that provoke these crises. Moreover, the recipients of security aid are not the civilians under duress, but the security governance agencies that are needed to manage these populations in need. Given that these development practices are technically focused upon integrating transversal agencies into global circuits of security governance, it would make little sense to speak of the justice attained by security aid. Instead, discourses of security aid respond to crisis with tropes of humanitarian governance that appeal to a Canadian imaginary of internationalism, while underlining the objectives of security and stability in the Global South. With the twinned discourses of "security" and "aid" animating Canadian responses to instabilities in the Global South, the underlying motives of advancing strategic interests are suppressed from public discussions. As I detail below, an additional layer of the Janus-faced design of security aid stems from technical-orientation of Canadian norm-supporting. As a norm-supporter, Canada has a limited – if not excluded – voice in the designing of the transversal. The expertise of security innovation is focused narrowly on implementation and practical development and, therefore, is buffered from political accountability when security aid efforts go awry.

Technical Norm-Supporting and De-politicization

Although professionals of politics like Stephen Harper mobilize grand sentiments of freedom/un-freedom and the global seas of uncertainty, the experts of security development rarely express the stakes in such weighty terms. Their accounts are far more modest. Particularly given Canada's role as a norm-supporter, security aid is sometimes referred to in grand narratives of democracy and human rights; however, the discursive attention of security innovators quickly moves to practical matters of capacity building, training, and contextual challenges. In descriptions of these difficulties, the objectives of security aid are frequently considered to be highly technical in orientation, very modest and incremental by design, aiming to immediate stabilization rather than political transformation. Most of all, the aspirational character strives for development of transversal security as an avenue to manage broader global securities. As points of frustration for security innovators who seek to implement apolitical and technical reforms to the security and policing practices of recipient countries, these barriers are expressions of the narrow and depoliticized focus of security aid practices.

David Chandler (2010, 2012) has commented on the dominance of "post-liberal" interventions. He argues that, unlike previous moments of internationalism, the dominant contemporary paradigm has abandoned the grand principles of liberalism that defined the initial post–Cold War moment. Imperatives of democracy and rights have been replaced with a prioritization of capacity building and, most importantly, a paradigm of resilience. Chandler (2012, 216) writes that the "resilience paradigm clearly puts the agency of those most in need of assistance at the centre, stressing a programme of empowerment and capacity-building." Yet the liberal internationalist paradigm "puts the emphasis upon the agency of external interveners, acting post hoc to protect or secure the victims of state-led or state-condoned abuses" (ibid.). Chandler has demonstrated how security discourses have shifted to bio-political strategies that seek to enact reformatory transformations in the conduct of populations (see also Duffield 2007; Dillon and Reid 2009). Particularly with the emergence of resilience discourses, the interventionist practices of the Global North are increasingly presented as "act[s] of empowerment rather than an act[s] of external power"

(Chandler 2012, 218). Chandler's work in particular shows how security governance has moved from a state-level to society-level practices.

While I believe the movement from liberal internationalism to resiliency paradigms might be overstating a singularity of security development practices, Chandler's argument is insightful for highlighting the selectivity of humanitarian governance practices. Regardless of whether the movement from internationalism to resilience is overstated (my contention is that these are layered, coexisting strategies), I would highlight that both paradigms are rationalized through humanitarian sentiments. The discursive formations of the Global North's interventions in the polities of the Global South have modulated, and Chandler (2010, 15) demonstrates how post-liberal interventions attempt to ignore or suppress fundamental questions of politics and accountability. Instead, they "seek to secure stability through balancing internal and external interests and concerns as matters of technical and administrative competence in the formulation of good governance." The central emphasis for humanitarian aid as emphasized by Chandler – and highly relevant to Canadian norm-supporting practices – are framed around technical norms of good governance and security. While corresponding with an increasingly interventionist assemblage of practices, the technical framing of security aid evades political questions of sovereignty, self-determination, and justice. Sovereignty is reduced to a technical skill set of managerial governance in which the integration into the transversal security community itself is an articulation of "building up" a notion of "domestic" governing capacities.

In contrast to a complete abandonment to the paradigm of liberal internationalism, I would stress that Canadian security aid retains a discursive commitment to an idealized liberal endgame. Yet there is a fundamental disjuncture between the discursive rationales that animate assistance projects and the practices of these development regimes. For the security aid projects that I have examined, Canadian assistance practices are conceptualized as a small, tangible aspect of an illusionary and elusive democratizing project. They are technical capacity-building projects where Canadian security innovators enter into projects established by norm-makers to provide immediate and concrete steps. Most importantly for Canadian security innovators, the broader goals of the democratizing project are set by norm-makers and become regarded as outside the control or domain of Canadian decision-making. In a context where Canadian security assistance projects defer to the authorities of norm-makers to frame the broader agenda, the narrow focus on technical capacity building also evades fundamental questions of political accountability. If the objectives of Canadian security aid are more narrowly focused on technical enhancements, the outcome means that measures of success are only a question of – as one participant put it – "as long as training is delivered, it's a success" (Interview 10).

Framing success around a narrow technical field, the moral imperative of providing immediate security forecloses questions of the "dark side" of security development. An unavoidable aspect of enhancing the capacities of security agencies is that these agencies will use the training and equipment donated by Canada to suppress their populations. While advocates of security development will argue that engagement with these security agencies is a necessity for incremental improvements, a consequence of these assistance practices is that recipients like the Haitian National Police will engage in far more illiberal practices than human rights–centred practices of policing. Neocleous (2008, 4) has argued that security is fundamentally "a means of modelling … society around a particular vision of order." Canadian security innovators provide a wide spectrum of interventions, infrastructures, and techniques for these political ordering processes and, as Olsson (2013) has argued, doing so grants a symbolic legitimacy for the violence that is encompassed in maintaining social order. Some critics of Northern interventionist practices in the Global South point out that developing the suppressive functions of these agencies is, in fact, the underlying design of security development. Outside of discursive commitments to freedom, as John Baird proclaimed in Libya, there is little evidence to contradict this criticism. On a strategic level, security aid is organized to advance the influence and interests of donor countries, and, on a practical level, these assistance regimes fortify governing regimes, often at the expense of broader transformations. As opposed to transformative change animated by principles of social justice, security aid functions to stabilize the status quo through the humanitarian appeal to security and stability. No issue can more clearly underline the role of security as an organizing logic of containment and cementing injustice than the transversal control of migration.

While completing the final pages of this book, the ongoing refugee tragedy has produced heated polemics on global insecurities, migration, and responses from countries of the Global North. More than 1.2,000 million refugees are claimed to have arrived in Europe during 2015, mostly by sea. In their attempts to travel across the Mediterranean, the IOM reports that more than 3,770 drowned en route. Many have died in large part as the result of decisions by EU governments to defund search-and-rescue practices for fear that the "reward" of maritime rescues would act as a "pull factor" to encourage more migration (Hodges 2015). In response to the increase in migration, the EU pledged a "comprehensive migration agenda" that, while discursively framed as a humanitarian response, would dramatically supplement border enforcement and preventive measures to disrupt departures (Sunderland and Frelick 2015). The proposed responses are highly similar to Canada's efforts to push the border out in Southeast Asia (detailed in chapter 5), yet the EU and its border-enforcement agency Frontex have long been norm-makers for these techniques of security governance (Topak 2014; also Aas and Gundhus 2015; Reid-Henry 2013). Although the refugee tragedy has received substantial media attention in Canada, there is a profound silence on the underlying causes of the migration surge. Nowhere has it been suggested that Canadian involvement (and then abandonment) in the 2011 intervention in Libya entails a direct responsibility for the ongoing crisis. With the "victory" celebration on Parliament Hill following the Libya intervention as a distant memory, Canada has deflected any notion of culpability.

The abandonment of Libya following the security intervention in 2011 illustrates the dark side of security aid. Canada was an eager norm-supporter, providing practical and visible contributions to the intervention. Canadian security innovators were quick to use the security intervention as a gateway for further security aid in the form of techniques and infrastructure. The political class and the bureaucracy worked quickly to advance strategic interests of commerce as well as the reliability and visibility of norm-supporting technical expertise. But when complications arose, the assistance regime was abandoned. While initially animated by grand narratives of freedom and democracy, the technical orientation of security aid practices had few "docking points" and even fewer prospects for the advancement of long-term strategic interests, and therefore could seamlessly rationalize a change of priority for reasons of technical and practical simplicity. As a technically oriented supporter of the efforts at political transformation, Canada cut and ran, with no lasting humanitarian sentimentalities. In demonstrating what is perhaps the most pernicious element of the technical orientation of Canadian norm-supporting, the depoliticization of Canadian involvement in security aid regimes buffers the practices of Canadian security development from their consequences. As a mere supporter of broader global trends, providing immediate and technical assistance, Canada can simply lament its lack of influence while simultaneously denigrating the Libyan people for their lack of "buy-in" or will to engage in "good" governance. But while the Canadian government turns away from Libya, those polities deemed as deviant states always remain inclusively excluded in the transversal. A further and currently unfolding dark consequence of the Libyan security intervention is that "abandonment" is rarely absolute. As the migrant crisis and instability from the region increase and again risk threatening the interests of countries in the Global North, a re-engagement with Libya becomes more likely. Though it is yet to be seen, Canada has begun new strategic planning to position itself in support of a re-engagement plan designed by norm-makers of the transversal security community aimed at developing the Libyan security state (CBC 2016). Notably, after years of abandonment and neglect of the well-being of Libyan civilians, the proposed aid will likely take the form of a military intervention, to consolidate the security forces and border policing of Libya authorities. Moreover, these efforts will not aim to help the migrants dying in the waters of the Mediterranean. Canadian assistance will be rationalized as a humanitarian venture, but its motives will be to advance the visibility of Canadian security innovation while providing practical, concrete support in fortifying the transversal policing capacities that aim to keep migrants away from the Global North.

Far from the mythologized image of Canadian do-good internationalism, these self-interested and punitive characteristics of security aid represent the rationalities that animate Canada's place in the world. Though liberal internationalists often lament that the world needs "more Canada," the self-interest and narrow-mindedness of Canadian internationalism as practised through security aid should raise the more appropriate question of whether the world would be better off with *less* Canada. This is particularly true of the "type" of Canada exemplified by the norm-supporting practices of security aid, where Canadian involvement in the international is one of technical support of norm-makers. Instead of what Liberal Foreign Affairs Minister Stéphane Dion calls a foreign policy of "responsible conviction," Canada wilfully ignores justice and purposefully cultivates an apolitical field of engagement. Keeping in mind that efforts to depoliticize are in fact efforts to re-politicize, it is Canada's practical efforts of security development that entrench the political designs of the transversal security community to maintain dramatic (and growing) global divisions of wealth and privilege. It is in these efforts that security aid manages the instabilities of global politics, rather than transforms them.

Inasmuch as they desire to assist populations in the seas of uncertainty, the practices of security aid support the aspirational designs of the transversal security community, which are increasingly discriminatory. Often the security governance regimes developed through these assistance projects aim to contain global populations, excluding a majority of the world from prosperous and wealthy countries and attempting to manage risks that could present security threats to donor countries. Given claims about Canada as a "bastion of freedom in an un-free world," the cumulative impact of these efforts towards interoperability and coordinated security governance is that a growing segment of the world's population is increasingly subjected to policing and control. Although the intent has been to develop an atmosphere of stability, the proliferation of security has had the opposite effect: the production of further insecurity.

As most criminological literature attests, safety is rarely provided by social control or security governance agencies. While these agencies can be helpful in using their monopoly of violence to provide immediate solutions to non-authorized violence, the most successful pathways for the cultivation of justice is through building social bonds, creating access to viable opportunities, and enabling the self-determination of communities to govern social harms. An overemphasis on security reproduces securitarian logics as a self-fulfilling prophecy. Given that security aid projects are rationalized within the humanitarian sentiments of assistance, it is a bleak irony that these projects – instead of supporting their humanitarian motives – result in more insecurity, violence, and injustice. Whether trends towards a world of more proliferate and resource-intensive policing and security apparatuses continue is, of course, subject to forces that we control. To transform these current trends, a fundamental recognition of global insecurity would have to shift from a humanitarian logic that cements inequalities towards a logic that seeks to diminish or eliminate global inequalities. Such a view would consider insecurity as a question of justice, not a practical consideration of security. Whether such a movement to curb the securitarian responses to insecurities can be successful is yet unknown.

References

Aas, Katja Franko. 2011. "'Crimmigrant' Bodies and Bona Fide Travelers: Surveillance, Citizenship and Global Governance." *Theoretical Criminology* 15 (3): 331–46. http://dx.doi.org/10.1177/1362480610396643.

– 2013. "The Ordered and the Bordered Society: Migration Control, Citizenship and the Northern Penal State." In *The Borders of Punishment: Migration, Citizenship, and Social Exclusion*, ed. Katja Franko Aas and Mary Bosworth, 21–39. Oxford: Oxford University Press.

Aas, Katja Franko, and Mary Bosworth, eds. 2013. *The Borders of Punishment: Migration, Citizenship, and Social Exclusion*. Oxford: Oxford University Press.

Aas, Katja Franko, and Helene Gundhus. 2015. "Policing Humanitarian Borderlands: Frontex, Human Rights and the Precariousness of Life." *British Journal of Criminology* 55 (1): 1–18. http://dx.doi.org/10.1093/bjc/azu086.

Abrahamsen, Rita. 2005. "Blair's Africa: The Politics of Securitization and Fear." *Alternatives* 30 (1): 55–80.

Abrahamsen, Rita, and Michael C. Williams. 2009. "Security beyond the State: Global Security Assemblages in International Politics." *International Political Sociology* 3 (1): 1–17.

Acharya, Amitav. 2011. "Norm Subsidiarity and Regional Orders: Sovereignty, Regionalism, and Rule⊠Making in the Third World." *International Studies Quarterly* 55 (1): 95–123. http://dx.doi.org/10.1111/j.1468-2478.2010.00637.x.

Adler, Emanuel. 2005. *Communitarian International Relations: The Epistemic Foundations of International Relations*. New York: Routledge.

Adler, Emanuel, and Michael Barnett, eds. 1998. *Security Communities*. New York: Cambridge University Press. http://dx.doi.org/10.1017/CBO9780511598661.

Adler, Emanuel, and Patricia Greve. 2009. "When Security Community Meets Balance of Power: Overlapping Regional Mechanisms of Security

Governance." *Review of International Studies* 35 (10): 59–84. http://dx.doi.org/10.1017/S0260210509008432.

Agamben, Giorgio. 1998. *Homo Sacer: Sovereign Power and Bare Life*. Palo Alto, CA: Stanford University Press.

– 2000. *Means without End: Notes on Politics*. Minneapolis: University of Minnesota Press.

Aiken, Sharryn. 2007. "From Slavery to Expulsion: Racism, Canadian Immigration Law, and the Unfulfilled Promise of Modern Constitutionalism." In *Interrogating Race and Racism*, ed. Vijay Agnew, 55–111. Toronto: University of Toronto Press. http://dx.doi.org/10.3138/9781442685444-004.

Albrecht, Peter, and Finn Stepputat. 2015. "The Rise and Fall of Security Sector Reform in Development." In *Handbook of International Security and Development*, ed. Paul Jackson, 150–64. Cheltenham, UK: Edward Elgar Publishing. http://dx.doi.org/10.4337/9781781955536.00017.

Alternative Chance. 2014. "Prison Conditions and Pre-Trial Detention in Haiti: Submission for the 112th Session of the United Nations Human Rights Committee." Boston College Law School. http://www.ijdh.org/wp-content/uploads/2014/09/HRC_Criminal-Justice-Sept-12.pdf.

Amnesty International. 2011. *Human Rights Concerns in Haiti: Amnesty International Submission to the UN Universal Periodic Review, October 2011*. http://tbinternet.ohchr.org/Treaties/CCPR/Shared%20Documents/HTI/INT_CCPR_NGO_HTI_105_8994_E.pdf.

– 2013. "Shut up we are the police." http://www.amnesty.ca/sites/default/files/pa20briefing20shut20up20we20are20the20police1.doc.

– 2014. "Haiti: Allegations of Excessive Use of Force during Demonstrations Must Be Thoroughly Investigated." News release, 15 December. http://reliefweb.int/report/haiti/haiti-allegations-excessive-use-force-during-demonstrations-must-be-thoroughly.

Amoore, Louise. 2006. "Biometric Borders: Governing Mobilities in the War on Terror." *Political Geography* 25 (3): 336–51. http://dx.doi.org/10.1016/j.polgeo.2006.02.001.

Amoore, Louise, and Marieke de Goede. 2008. "Introduction: Governing by Risk in the War on Terror." In *Risk and the War on Terror*, ed. Louise Amoore and Marieke de Goede, 5–20. New York: Routledge. http://dx.doi.org/10.1002/9780470721599.ch1.

Andreas, Peter, and Ethan Nadelmann. 2006. *Policing the Globe: Criminalization and Crime Control in International Relations*. Oxford: Oxford University Press.

Aradau, Claudia. 2014. "The Promise of Security: Resilience, Surprise and Epistemic Politics." *Resilience* 2 (2): 73–87. http://dx.doi.org/10.1080/21693293.2014.914765.

Aradau, Claudia, Jef Huysmans, Andrew Neal, and Nadine Voelkner, eds. 2015. *Critical Security Methods: New Frameworks for Analysis*. New York: Routledge.

Aradau, Claudia, and Rens Van Munster. 2007. "Governing Terrorism through Risk: Taking Precautions, (Un)Knowing the Future." *European Journal of International Relations* 13 (1): 89–115. http://dx.doi.org/10.1177/1354066107074290.

– 2008. "Taming the Future: The Dispositif of Risk in the War on Terror." In *Risk and the War on Terror*, ed. Louise Amoore and Marieke de Goede, 23–40. New York: Routledge.

Argomaniz, Javier. 2009. "When the EU Is the 'Norm-Taker': The Passenger Name Records Agreement and the EU's Internalization of US Border Security Norms." *Journal of European Integration* 31 (1): 119–36. http://dx.doi.org/10.1080/07036330802503981.

Arteaga Botello, Nelson. 2009. "The Mérida Initiative: Security-Surveillance Harmonization in Latin America." *European Review of Latin American and Caribbean Studies* 87:103–10.

– 2012. "Surveillance Studies: An Agenda for Latin America." *Surveillance & Society* 10 (1): 5–17.

Bachmann, Jan. 2014. "Policing Africa: The US Military and Visions of Crafting 'Good Order.'" *Security Dialogue* 45 (2): 119–36. http://dx.doi.org/10.1177/0967010614521267.

Ball, Kirstie. 2005. "Organization, Surveillance and the Body: Towards a Politics of Resistance." *Organization* 12 (1): 89–108. http://dx.doi.org/10.1177/1350508405048578.

Ball, Kirstie, and Laureen Snider, eds. 2013. *The Surveillance-Industrial Complex: A Political Economy of Surveillance*. New York: Routledge.

Banerjee, Subhabrata Bobby. 2008. "Corporate Social Responsibility: The Good, the Bad and the Ugly." *Critical Sociology* 34 (1): 51–79. http://dx.doi.org/10.1177/0896920507084623.

Baranyi, Stephen. 2014. "Canada and the Security-Development Nexus in Haiti: The 'Dark Side' or Changing Shades of Gray?" *Canadian Foreign Policy* 20 (2): 163–75. http://dx.doi.org/10.1080/11926422.2014.934858.

Barry-Shaw, Nikolas, and Dru Oja Jay. 2012. *Paved with Good Intentions: Canada's Development NGOs from Idealism to Imperialism*. Halifax: Fernwood Publishing.

Bascaramurty, Dakshana, and John Ibbitson. 2013. "Scarborough Tamils Elated about Harper's Commonwealth Boycott." *Globe and Mail*, 15 November. http://www.theglobeandmail.com/news/toronto/scarborough-tamils-elated-about-harpers-commonwealth-boycott/article15467105/.

Bauman, Zygmunt. 1998. *Globalization: The Human Consequences*. New York: Columbia University Press.
– 2004. *Wasted Lives: Modernity and Its Outcasts*. Cambridge: Polity.
Bayley, David H. 2005. "Police Reform as Foreign Policy." *Australian and New Zealand Journal of Criminology* 38 (2): 206–15. http://dx.doi.org/10.1375/acri.38.2.206.
Beck, Ulrich. 1992. *Risk Society: Towards a New Modernity*. London: Sage Publications.
– 2002. "The Terrorist Threat: World Risk Society Revisited." *Theory, Culture & Society* 19 (4): 39–55. http://dx.doi.org/10.1177/0263276402019004003.
Beeton, Dan. 2012. "Soldiers without a Cause: Why Are Thousands of UN Troops Still in Haiti?" *NACLA Report on the Americas* 45 (1): 6–11. http://dx.doi.org/10.1080/10714839.2012.11722105.
Bell, Colleen. 2011. *The Freedom of Security: Governing Canada in the Age of Counter-terrorism*. Vancouver: UBC Press.
– 2013. "Grey's Anatomy Goes South: Global Racism and Suspect Identities in the Colonial Present." *Canadian Journal of Sociology* 38 (4): 465–86.
Bellamy, Alex J., and Matt McDonald. 2002. "'The Utility of Human Security': Which Humans? What Security? A Reply to Thomas & Tow." *Security Dialogue* 33 (3): 373–7. http://dx.doi.org/10.1177/0967010602033003010.
Bellamy, Alex J., and Paul D. Williams. 2011. "The New Politics of Protection? Côte d'Ivoire, Libya and the Responsibility to Protect." *International Affairs* 87 (4): 825–50. http://dx.doi.org/10.1111/j.1468-2346.2011.01006.x.
Bigo, Didier. 2002. "Security and Immigration: Towards a Critique of the Governmentality of Unease." *Alternatives* 27 (S1): 63–92. http://dx.doi.org/10.1177/03043754020270S105.
– 2006. "Internal and External Aspects of Security." *European Security* 15 (4): 385–404. http://dx.doi.org/10.1080/09662830701305831.
– 2008. "Globalized (In)Security: The Field and the Ban-Opticon." In *Terror, Insecurity and Liberalism: Illiberal Practices of Liberal Regimes*, ed. Didier Bigo and Tsoukala Anastassia, 10–48. New York: Routledge. http://dx.doi.org/10.4324/9780203926765.ch2.
– 2011a. "Freedom and Speed in Enlarged Borderzones." In *The Contested Politics of Mobility: Borderzones and Irregularity*, ed. Vicki Squire, 31–50. New York: Routledge.
– 2011b. "Pierre Bourdieu and International Relations: Power of Practices, Practices of Power." *International Political Sociology* 5 (3): 225–58. http://dx.doi.org/10.1111/j.1749-5687.2011.00132.x.
– 2014. "The (In)Securitization Practices of the Three Universes of EU Border Control: Military/Navy – Border Guards/Police –

Database Analysts." *Security Dialogue* 45 (3): 209–25. http://dx.doi.org/10.1177/0967010614530459.

Bigo, Didier, and Elspeth Guild, eds. 2005a. *Controlling Frontiers: Free Movement into and within Europe*. Burlington, UK: Ashgate.

– 2005b. "Policing at a Distance: Schengen Visa Policies." In Didier and Guild, *Controlling Frontiers*, 233–63.

Bigo, Didier, and Rob B.J. Walker. 2007. "Political Sociology and the Problem of the International." *Millennium* 35 (3): 725–39. http://dx.doi.org/10.1177/03058298070350030401.

Björkdahl, Annika. 2005. "Norm-Maker and Norm-Taker: Exploring the Normative Influence of the EU in Macedonia." *European Foreign Affairs Review* 10 (2): 257–78.

– 2007. "Swedish Norm Entrepreneurship in the UN." *International Peacekeeping* 14 (4): 538–52. http://dx.doi.org/10.1080/13533310701427959.

– 2013. "Ideas and Norms in Swedish Peace Policy." *Swiss Political Science Review* 19 (3): 322–37. http://dx.doi.org/10.1111/spsr.12046.

Blanchfield, Mike. 2013. "Canada's Arms Industry Finds New Markets in Trouble Spots." *Edmonton Journal*, 9 December.

Blanton, Shannon L. 1999. "Instruments of Security or Tools of Repression? Arms Imports and Human Rights Conditions in Developing Countries." *Journal of Peace Research* 36 (2): 233–44. http://dx.doi.org/10.1177/0022343399036002006.

Bonelli, Laurent. 2008. "'Hidden in plain sight': Intelligence, Exception and Suspicion after 11 September 2001." In *Terror, Insecurity and Liberalism: Illiberal Practices of Liberal Regimes After 9/11*, ed. Didier Bigo and Anastassia Tsoukala, 100–20. New York: Routledge. http://dx.doi.org/10.4324/9780203926765.ch4.

Bouris, Dimitris, and Stuart Reigeluth. 2012. "Introducing the Rule of Law in Security Sector Reform: European Union Policies in the Palestinian Territories." *Hague Journal on the Rule of Law* 4 (1): 176–93. http://dx.doi.org/10.1017/S1876404512000103.

Bowling, Ben. 2010. *Policing the Caribbean: Transnational Security Cooperation in Practice*. Oxford University Press. http://dx.doi.org/10.1093/acprof:oso/9780199577699.001.0001.

Bowling, Ben, and James Sheptycki. 2011. "Policing Globopolis." *Social Justice* 38 (1–2): 184–202.

Breslin, Shaun, and George Christou. 2015. "Has the Human Security Agenda Come of Age? Definitions, Discourses and Debates." *Contemporary Politics* 21 (1): 1–10. http://dx.doi.org/10.1080/13569775.2014.993904.

Brewster, Murray. 2013. "Canada Geared Up for Mali in Spring, Documents Show." Canadian Press, 21 January. http://www.cbc.ca/news/politics/canada-geared-up-for-mali-in-spring-documents-show-1.1312613.

Brodeur, Jean-Paul. 2010. *The Policing Web*. Oxford University Press. http://dx.doi.org/10.1093/acprof:oso/9780199740598.001.0001.

Brodeur, Jean-Paul, and Benoît Dupont. 2006. "Knowledge Workers or 'Knowledge' Workers?" *Policing and Society* 16 (1): 7–26. http://dx.doi.org/10.1080/10439460500399304.

Brommesson, Douglas. 2010. "Normative Europeanization: The Case of Swedish Foreign Policy Reorientation." *Cooperation and Conflict* 45 (2): 224–44. http://dx.doi.org/10.1177/0010836710370246.

Bronson, Rachel. 2002. "When Soldiers Become Cops." *Foreign Affairs* 81 (6): 122–32.

Brown, Stephen. 2007. "Creating the World's Best Development Agency?: Confusion and Contradictions in CIDA's New Policy Blueprint." *Canadian Journal of Development Studies* 28 (2): 213–28.

– 2013. "Canada's Foreign Aid before and after CIDA: Not a Samaritan State." *International Journal: Canada's Journal of Global Policy Analysis* 68 (3): 501–12. http://dx.doi.org/10.1177/0020702013505730.

– 2014. "Undermining Foreign Aid: The Extractive Sector and the Recommercialization of Canadian Development Assistance." In *Rethinking Canadian Aid*, ed. Stephen Brown, Molly den Heyer, and David R. Black, 277–96. Ottawa: University of Ottawa Press.

Brown, Stephen, and Jörn Grävingholt, eds. 2016. *The Securitization of Foreign Aid*. London: Palgrave Macmillan. http://dx.doi.org/10.1007/978-1-137-56882-3.

Brown, Stephen, and John Sinclair. 2011. "Transparency and Canadian Foreign Aid." *Embassy*, 27 July.

Brunet-Jailly, Emmanuel, ed. 2007. *Borderlands: Comparing Border Security in North America and Europe*. Ottawa: University of Ottawa Press.

Burgess, J. Peter. 2009. "There Is No European Security, Only European Securities." *Cooperation and Conflict* 44 (3): 309–28. http://dx.doi.org/10.1177/0010836709106218.

Burgess, J. Peter, and Taylor Owen, eds. 2004. "Editors' Note." *Security Dialogue* 35 (3): 345–87. http://dx.doi.org/10.1177/0967010604047569.

Butler, Judith. 2004. *Precarious Life: The Powers of Mourning and Violence*. New York: Verso Books.

Buzan, Barry. 2004. "A Reductionist, Idealistic Notion That Adds Little Analytical Value." *Security Dialogue* 35 (3): 369–70. http://dx.doi.org/10.1177/096701060403500326.

Buzan, Barry, and Ole Wæver. 2003. *Regions and Powers: The Structure of International Security*. Cambridge University Press. http://dx.doi.org/10.1017/CBO9780511491252.

Byrne, Aisling. 2011. "Building a Police State in Palestine." Foreign Policy Blogs, 18 January. http://foreignpolicy.com/2011/01/18/building-a-police-state-in-palestine/.

Campion-Smith, Bruce. 2015. "Canadian Fighter Jets Strike Islamic State Targets in Iraq." *Toronto Star*, 15 January. http://www.thestar.com/news/canada/2015/01/15/canadian-fighter-jets-strike-islamic-state-targets-in-iraq.html.

Canada. 2004. *Securing an Open Society: Canada's National Security Policy*. Ottawa: Canada.

– 2011. *Beyond the Border: A Shared Vision for Perimeter Security and Economic Competitiveness*. Ottawa: Canada.

– 2012. "Canadian Prime Minister Announces Support to Enhance Security in the Americas." News release. http://www.canadainternational.gc.ca/guatemala/highlights-faits/2012/PM_Support_Soutient_Security.aspx?lang=en.

– 2013. *Global Markets Action Plan: The Blueprint for Creating Jobs and Opportunities for Canadians through Trade*. Ottawa: Canada.

– 2014. "Canada-Peru Defence Relations." News release, Prime Minister's Office, 10 April. http://news.gc.ca/web/article-en.do?nid=838279.

Canadian Council for Refugees (CCR). 2011. "Rights Advocates Decry Detention of Refugee Claimants from MV Sun Sea." News release, 10 February. http://ccrweb.ca/en/bulletin/11/02/10.

– 2013. "CCR Expresses Deep Concerns over Canadian Response to Sri Lankans Fleeing Human Rights Abuses." News release, 11 October. http://ccrweb.ca/en/public-statement/2013-10-11.

Canadian Press. 2011. "Libya Propaganda War: Canadian Planes Pitch In." *Huffington Post*, 29 July. http://www.huffingtonpost.ca/2011/07/29/libya-propaganda-war-canada_n_913343.html.

– 2013. "Spirit of Albertans during Floods Is What Makes Country Great, Harper Says at Canada Day Festivities." *National Post*, 1 July. http://news.nationalpost.com/news/canada/spirit-of-albertans-during-floods-is-what-makes-country-great-harper-says-at-canada-day-festivities.

– 2015. "Text of New Iraq Motion Expected Today in House of Commons." *Globe and Mail*, 24 March.

Caple James, Erica. 2004. "The Political Economy of 'Trauma' in Haiti in the Democratic Era of Insecurity." *Culture, Medicine and Psychiatry* 28 (2): 127–49, discussion 211–20. http://dx.doi.org/10.1023/B:MEDI.0000034407.39471.d4.

– 2010. *Democratic Insecurities: Violence, Trauma, and Intervention in Haiti*. Berkeley: University of California Press.

Carbone, Maurizio. 2013. "An Uneasy Nexus: Development, Security and the EU's African Peace Facility." *European Foreign Affairs Review* 18 (4): 103–23.

CASE Collective. 2006. "Critical Approaches to Security in Europe: A Networked Manifesto." *Security Dialogue* 37 (4): 443–87. http://dx.doi.org/10.1177/0967010606073085.

CBC. 2016. "Harjit Sajjan Hints at a Canadian Military Mission in Libya." *House*, 13 February. http://www.cbc.ca/radio/thehouse/tom-mulcair-takes-responsibility-for-ndp-s-extremely-cautious-campaign-1.3443873/harjit-sajjan-hints-at-a-canadian-military-mission-in-libya-1.3446865.

CCC (Canadian Commercial Corporation). 2009. *Confidence and Credibility: CCC Annual Report 2008–2009*. Ottawa: Canadian Commercial Corporation.

– 2010. *Leadership and Growth: CCC Annual Report 2009–2010*. Ottawa: Canadian Commercial Corporation.

– 2011. *Enhancing Canadian Competitiveness on a Global Scale: CCC Annual Report 2010–2011*. Ottawa: Canadian Commercial Corporation.

– 2012. *A Valued Partner in Competitive World Markets: CCC Annual Report 2011–2012*. Ottawa: Canadian Commercial Corporation.

– 2013. *Leveraging Canada's Strengths to Access New Opportunities: CCC Annual Report 2012–2013*. Ottawa: Canadian Commercial Corporation.

– 2014. *Powering Export Growth: CCC Annual Report 2013–2014*. Ottawa: Canadian Commercial Corporation.

CCIC (Canadian Council for International Cooperation). 2005. "CCIC Briefing Note: The Stabilization and Reconstruction Taskforce (START) and the Global Peace and Security Fund (GPSF)." Ottawa: Canadian Council for International Cooperation. http://www.ccic.ca/_files/en/what_we_do/002_human_2005-11_gpsf_start_briefing_note.pdf.

Chandler, David. 2006. *Empire in Denial: The Politics of State-Building*. London: Pluto.

– 2007. "The Security–Development Nexus and the Rise of 'Anti-Foreign Policy.'" *Journal of International Relations and Development* 10 (4): 362–86. http://dx.doi.org/10.1057/palgrave.jird.1800135.

– 2010. "The Uncritical Critique of 'Liberal Peace.'" *Review of International Studies* 36 (S1): 137–55. http://dx.doi.org/10.1017/S0260210510000823.

– 2012. "Resilience and Human Security: The Post-Interventionist Paradigm." *Security Dialogue* 43 (3): 213–29. http://dx.doi.org/10.1177/0967010612444151.

– 2016. "New Narratives of International Security Governance: The Shift from Global Interventionism to Global Self-Policing." *Global Crime* 17 (3–4): 264–80.

Charbonneau, Bruno, and Wayne S. Cox. 2008. "Global Order, US Hegemony and Military Integration: The Canadian–American Defence Relationship."

International Political Sociology 2 (4): 305–21. http://dx.doi.org/10.1111/j.1749-5687.2008.00053.x.

Charbonneau, Bruno, and Geneviève Parent. 2010. "Managing Life in Afghanistan: Canadian Tales of Peace, Security." In *Locating Global Order: American Power and Canadian Security after 9/11*, ed. Bruno Charbonneau and Wayne S. Cox, 87–107. Vancouver: UBC Press.

Charbonneau, Louis. 2011. "Haiti's Preval to U.N.: We Need Bulldozers, Not Tanks." Reuters, 6 April. http://www.reuters.com/article/2011/04/06/us-haiti-un-idUSTRE7356DP20110406.

Chin, Gregory. 2009. "Shifting Purpose: Asia's Rise and Canada's Foreign Aid." *International Journal: Canada's Journal of Global Policy Analysis* 64 (4): 989–1009. http://dx.doi.org/10.1177/002070200906400409.

Christie, Ryerson. 2012. "The Pacification of Soldiering, and the Militarization of Development: Contradictions Inherent in Provincial Reconstruction in Afghanistan." *Globalizations* 9 (1): 53–71. http://dx.doi.org/10.1080/14747731.2012.627720.

Clark, Campbell. 2011. "Baird Brings Big Business on Trip to Libya." *Globe and Mail*, 11 October. http://www.theglobeandmail.com/news/politics/baird-brings-big-business-on-trip-to-libya/article1356075/.

Coaffee, Jon, and David Murakami Wood. 2006. "Security Is Coming Home: Rethinking Scale and Constructing Resilience in the Global Urban Response to Terrorist Risk." *International Relations* 20 (4): 503–17. http://dx.doi.org/10.1177/0047117806069416.

Cockayne, James. 2014. "The Futility of Force? Strategic Lessons for Dealing with Unconventional Armed Groups from the UN's War on Haiti's Gangs." *Journal of Strategic Studies* 37 (5): 736–69. http://dx.doi.org/10.1080/01402390.2014.901911.

Cohen, Andrew. 2003. *While Canada Slept: How We Lost Our Place in the World*. Toronto: McClelland & Stewart.

Coleman, Mathew. 2007. "A Geopolitics of Engagement: Neoliberalism, the War on Terrorism, and the Reconfiguration of US Immigration Enforcement." *Geopolitics* 12 (4): 607–34. http://dx.doi.org/10.1080/14650040701546087.

Combined Maritime Forces. 2015. "Combined Maritime Forces." Main page. http://combinedmaritimeforces.com/.

Contessi, Nicola P. 2010. "Multilateralism, Intervention and Norm Contestation: China's Stance on Darfur in the UN Security Council." *Security Dialogue* 41 (3): 323–44. http://dx.doi.org/10.1177/0967010610370228.

Cornwall, Andrea. 2007. "Buzzwords and Fuzzwords: Deconstructing Development Discourse." *Development in Practice* 17 (4–5): 471–84. http://dx.doi.org/10.1080/09614520701469302.

Cornwall, Andrea, and Karen Brock. 2005. "What Do Buzzwords Do for Development Policy? A Critical Look at 'Participation,' 'Empowerment' and 'Poverty Reduction.'" *Third World Quarterly* 26 (7): 1043–60. http://dx.doi.org/10.1080/01436590500235603.

Côté-Boucher, Karine. 2008. "The Diffuse Border: Intelligence-Sharing, Control and Confinement along Canada's Smart Border." *Surveillance & Society* 5 (2): 142–65.

Cousineau, Sophie, and Greg McArthur. 2013. "Former SNC-Lavalin Executive Funnelled $160-Million to Gadhafi Son, RCMP says." *Globe and Mail*, 25 January. http://www.theglobeandmail.com/news/national/former-snc-lavalin-executive-funnelled-160-million-to-gadhafi-son-rcmp-says/article7865504/.

Cowen, Deborah. 2014. *The Deadly Life of Logistics: Mapping Violence in Global Trade*. Minneapolis: University of Minnesota Press. http://dx.doi.org/10.5749/minnesota/9780816680870.001.0001.

Cowen, Michael, and Robert W. Shenton. 1996. *Doctrines of Development*. London: Routledge. http://dx.doi.org/10.4324/9780203392607.

Craft, Cassady, and Joseph P. Smaldone. 2002. "The Arms Trade and the Incidence of Political Violence in Sub-Saharan Africa, 1967–97." *Journal of Peace Research* 39 (6): 693–710. http://dx.doi.org/10.1177/0022343302039006003.

Crosby, Andy, and Jeffrey Monaghan. 2012. "Settler Governmentality and the Algonquins of Barriere Lake." *Security Dialogue* 43 (5): 421–38. http://dx.doi.org/10.1177/0967010612457972.

Curle, Clinton Timothy. 2007. *Humanité: John Humphrey's Alternative Account of Human Rights*. Toronto: University of Toronto Press. http://dx.doi.org/10.3138/9781442684447.

d'Adesky, Anne-christine. 2012. *Beyond Shock: Charting the Landscape of Sexual Violence in Post-Quake Haiti: Progress, Challenges & Emerging Trends 2010–2012*. Port-au-Prince. PotoFanm+Fi coalition. https://potofi.files.wordpress.com/2012/12/beyond-shock-abridged-version-haiti-gbv-progress-report-nov-2012.pdf.

Dafnos, Tia. 2012. "Beyond the Blue Line: Researching the Policing of Aboriginal Activism Using Access to Information." In *Brokering Access: Power, Politics, and Freedom of Information Process in Canada*, ed. Mike Larsen and Kevin Walby, 209–32. Vancouver: UBC Press.

Daly, Brian. 2012. "Former SNC-Lavalin CEO Pierre Duhaime Arrested." *Toronto Sun*, 28 November. http://www.torontosun.com/2012/11/28/former-snc-lavalin-ceo-pierre-duhaime-arrested/

Dauvergne, Catherine. 2008. *Making People Illegal: What Globalization Means for Migration and Law*. Cambridge University Press. http://dx.doi.org/10.1017/CBO9780511810473.

Davis, Diane. 2006. "Undermining the Rule of Law: Democratization and the Dark Side of Police Reform in Mexico." *Latin American Politics and Society* 48 (1): 55–86.

Day, Graham, and Christopher Freeman. 2003. "Policekeeping Is the Key: Rebuilding the Internal Security Architecture of Postwar Iraq." *International Affairs* 79 (2): 299–313. http://dx.doi.org/10.1111/1468-2346.00309.

Dean, Mitchell. 2006. "Military Intervention as 'Police' Action?" In *The New Police Science*, ed. Markus Dubber and Mariana Valverde, 185–206. Palo Alto, CA: Stanford University Press.

Deflem, Mathieu. 2002. *Policing World Society: Historical Foundations of International Police Cooperation*. Oxford: Oxford University Press.

De Genova, Nicholas. 2002. "Migrant 'Illegality' and Deportability in Everyday Life." *Annual Review of Anthropology* 31 (1): 419–47. http://dx.doi.org/10.1146/annurev.anthro.31.040402.085432.

De Larrinaga, Miguel, and Marc Doucet. 2010. *Security and Global Governmentality: Globalization, Governance and the State*. Oslo: PRIO.

Del Biondo, Karen, Stefan Oltsch, and Jan Orbie. 2013. "Security and Development in EU External Relations: Converging, but in Which Direction?" In *The Routledge Handbook of European Security*, ed. Sven Biscop and Richard Whitman, 126–41. London: Routledge.

de Mesquita, Bruce Bueno, and Alastair Smith. 2007. "Foreign Aid and Policy Concessions." *Journal of Conflict Resolution* 51 (2): 251–84. http://dx.doi.org/10.1177/0022002706297696.

Denney, Lisa. 2015. "Operationalizing the Development Nexus: Security Sector Reform and Its Implications." In Jackson, *Handbook of International Security and Development*, 135–49. http://dx.doi.org/10.4337/9781781955536.00016.

Department of National Defence. 2014. "Minister Nicholson Announces Canada's Donation of Non-Lethal Equipment to Ukraine." News release, 26 November. http://news.gc.ca/web/article-en.do?nid=909109.

– 2015. "Minister Nicholson Commits Military Gear to the Iraqi Security Forces, Departs for London for High Level Discussions on ISIL." News release, 20 January. http://news.gc.ca/web/article-en.do?nid=923599.

Derouen, Karl, Jr, and Uk Heo. 2004. "Reward, Punishment or Inducement? US Economic and Military Aid, 1946–1996." *Defence and Peace Economics* 15 (5): 453–70. http://dx.doi.org/10.1080/1024269042000222392.

Desrosiers, Marie-Eve, and Philippe Lagassé. 2009. "Canada and the Bureaucratic Politics of State Fragility." *Diplomacy and Statecraft* 20 (4): 659–78. http://dx.doi.org/10.1080/09592290903455774.

Deutsch, Karl, Sidney Burrell, Robert Kann, Maurice Leg, Jr, Martin Lichterman, Raymond Lindgren, Francis Loewenheim, and Richard Van

Wagenen. 1957. *Political Community and the North Atlantic Area*. Princeton, NJ: Princeton University Press.

Dillon, Michael. 1996. *Politics of Security: Towards a Political Philosophy of Continental Thought*. New York: Routledge.

– 2007. "Governing Terror: The State of Emergency of Biopolitical Emergence." *International Political Sociology* 1 (1): 7–28. http://dx.doi.org/10.1111/j.1749-5687.2007.00002.x.

Dillon, Michael, and Luis Lobo-Guerrero. 2008. "Biopolitics of Security in the 21st Century: An Introduction." *Review of International Studies* 34 (2): 265–92. http://dx.doi.org/10.1017/S0260210508008024.

Dillon, Michael, and Julian Reid. 2009. *The Liberal Way of War: Killing to Make Life Live*. New York: Routledge.

Dorn, Walter. 2009. "Intelligence-Led Peacekeeping: The United Nations Stabilization Mission in Haiti (MINUSTAH), 2006–07." *Intelligence and National Security* 24 (6): 805–35. http://dx.doi.org/10.1080/02684520903320410.

Doty, Roxanne. 2007. "States of Exception on the Mexico-U.S. Border: Security, 'Decisions,' and Civilian Border Patrols." *International Political Sociology* 1 (2): 113–37. http://dx.doi.org/10.1111/j.1749-5687.2007.00008.x.

Dubber, Markus. 2006. "The New Police Science and the Police Power Model of the Criminal Process." In *The New Police Science*, ed. Markus Dubber and Mariana Valverde, 107–44. Palo Alto, CA: Stanford University Press.

Duffield, Mark. 2001. *Global Governance and the New Wars: The Merging of Development and Security*. London: Zed Books.

– 2005. "Getting Savages to Fight Barbarians: Development, Security and the Colonial Present: Analysis." *Conflict Security and Development* 5 (2): 141–59. http://dx.doi.org/10.1080/14678800500170068.

– 2007. *Development, Security, and Unending War*. Cambridge: Polity.

– 2008. "Global Civil War: The Non-Insured, International Containment and Post-Interventionary Society." *Journal of Refugee Studies* 21 (2): 145–65. http://dx.doi.org/10.1093/jrs/fem049.

– 2010. "The Liberal Way of Development and the Development–Security Impasse: Exploring the Global Life-Chance Divide." *Security Dialogue* 41 (1): 53–76. http://dx.doi.org/10.1177/0967010609357042.

– 2012. "Challenging Environments: Danger, Resilience and the Aid Industry." *Security Dialogue* 43 (5): 475–92. http://dx.doi.org/10.1177/0967010612457975.

Duffield, Mark, and Vernon Hewitt, eds. 2013. *Empire, Development and Colonialism: The Past in the Present*. Suffolk, UK: Boydell & Brewer.

Duffield, Mark, and Nicholas Waddell. 2004. "Human Security and Global Danger: Exploring a Governmental Assemblage." http://citeseerx.ist.psu.edu/viewdoc/download?doi=10.1.1.116.141&rep=rep1&type=pdf.

Dupuy, Alex. 2007. *The Prophet and the Power: Jean-Bertrand Aristide, the International Community, and Haiti*. Lanham, MD: Rowman and Littlefield.

Edmonds, Kevin. 2013. "Beyond Good Intentions: The Structural Limitations of NGOs in Haiti." *Critical Sociology* 39 (3): 439–52. http://dx.doi.org/10.1177/0896920512437053.

Edwards, Kevin. 2012. "Signs Point toward Controversial Renewal of MINUSTAH's Mandate in Haiti." *NACLA*, 13 September.

Egnell, Robert. 2010. "The Organised Hypocrisy of International State-Building." *Conflict Security and Development* 10 (4): 465–91. http://dx.doi.org/10.1080/14678802.2010.500523.

Egnell, Robert, and Peter Haldén. 2009. "Laudable, Ahistorical and Overambitious: Security Sector Reform Meets State Formation Theory: Analysis." *Conflict Security and Development* 9 (1): 27–54. http://dx.doi.org/10.1080/14678800802704903.

Eisenstadt, S.N., and René Lemarchand. 1981. *Political Clientelism, Patronage and Development*. London: Sage Publications.

Engler, Yves, and Anthony Fenton. 2005. *Canada in Haiti: Waging War on the Poor Majority*. Black Point, NS: Fernwood Publications.

Ericson, Richard. 2007. *Crime in an Insecure World*. Cambridge: Polity.

Ericson, Richard, and Kevin Haggerty. 1997. *Policing the Risk Society*. Oxford: Oxford University Press.

Eriksen, Stein Sundstøl. 2011. "'State Failure' in Theory and Practice: The Idea of the State and the Contradictions of State Formation." *Review of International Studies* 37 (1): 229–47. http://dx.doi.org/10.1017/S0260210510000409.

Eriksson, Johan, and Mark Rhinard. 2009. "The Internal-External Security Nexus Notes on an Emerging Research Agenda." *Cooperation and Conflict* 44 (3): 243–67. http://dx.doi.org/10.1177/0010836709106215.

Escobar, Arturo. 1995. *Encountering Development: The Making and Unmaking of the Third World*. Princeton, NJ: Princeton University Press.

Eski, Yarin. 2011. "'Port of Call': Towards a Criminology of Port Security." *Criminology & Criminal Justice* 11 (5): 415–31. http://dx.doi.org/10.1177/1748895811414593.

Essex, Jamey. 2013. *Development, Security, and Aid: Geopolitics and Geoeconomics at the US Agency for International Development*. Athens: University of Georgia Press.

Fantino, Julian. 2013. "We will meet our obligations." *Charlottetown Guardian*, 16 April.

Farmer, Paul. 2011. "Partners in Help: Assisting the Poor over the Long Term." *Foreign Affairs*, 29 July. http://www.foreignaffairs.com/articles/68002/paul-farmer/partners-in-help.

Fassin, Didier. 2012. *Humanitarian Reason: A Moral History of the Present*. Berkeley: University of California Press.

– 2014. "Petty States of Exception: The Contemporary Policing of the Urban Poor." In *The Anthropology of Security: Perspectives from the Frontline of Policing, Counter-terrorism and Border Control*, ed. Mark Maguire, Catarina Frois, and Nils Zurawski, 104–18. London: Pluto.

Fatton, Robert. 2002. *Haiti's Predatory Republic: The Unending Transition to Democracy*. Boulder, CO: Lynne Reiner Publishers.

– 2007. *The Roots of Haitian Despotism*. Boulder, CO: Lynne Rienner Publishers.

Fekete, Liz. 2009. *A Suitable Enemy: Racism, Migration and Islamophobia in Europe*. London: Pluto.

Fenton, Anthony, and John Elmer. 2013. "Building an Expeditionary Force for Democracy Promotion." In *Empire's Ally: Canada and the War in Afghanistan*, ed. Jerome Klassen and Greg Albo, 306–38. Toronto: University of Toronto Press.

Finnemore, Martha, and Kathryn Sikkink. 1998. "International Norm Dynamics and Political Change." *International Organization* 52 (4): 887–917. http://dx.doi.org/10.1162/002081898550789.

Forst, Michel. 2012. *Report of the Independent Expert on the Situation of Human Rights in Haiti*. New York: United Nations. http://ijdh.org/wordpress/wp-content/uploads/2012/06/Report-of-the-Independent-Expert-on-the-situation-of-human-rights-in-Haiti-Michel-Forst.pdf.

– 2013. *Report of the Independent Expert on the Situation of Human Rights in Haiti*. New York: United Nations. http://reliefweb.int/sites/reliefweb.int/files/resources/Report%20of%20the%20independent%20expert%20on%20the%20situation%20of%20human%20rights%20in%20Haiti%20Michel%20Forst%20A-HRC-22-65.pdf.

Foucault, Michel. 1978. *The History of Sexuality: An Introduction*. Vol. 1. New York: Vintage.

– 2003. *"Society must be defended": Lectures at the College de France 1975–1976*. New York: Picador.

– 2007. *Security, Territory Population: Lectures at the College de France*. New York: Picador.

Foucault, Michel, with Graham Burchell, Colin Gordon, and Peter Miller, eds. 1991. *The Foucault Effect: Studies in Governmentality*. Chicago: University of Chicago Press.

Gallón, Gustavo. 2016. *Report of the Independent Expert on the Situation of Human Rights in Haiti.* Human Rights Council, Thirty-First Session. Geneva: United Nations.

Gill, Lesley. 2004. *The School of the Americas: Military Training and Political Violence in the Americas.* Durham, NC: Duke University Press. http://dx.doi.org/10.1215/9780822386001.

Girard, Philippe. 2010. *The Tumultuous History: From Pearl of the Caribbean to Broken Nation.* New York: Palgrave Macmillan.

Global Affairs Canada (GAC). 2007. *Formative Evaluation of Canada's Global Peace and Security Fund – Sudan: Final Report. Office of the Inspector General (ZID).* Ottawa: Department of Foreign Affairs and International Trade.

– 2011. "Minister Baird Concludes Fact-Finding Mission to Libya." News release. http://www.international.gc.ca/media/aff/news-communiques/2011/183.aspx?lang=eng.

– 2012. *Departmental Performance Report 2011–12: Supplementary Information Tables.* Ottawa: Department of Foreign Affairs and International Trade. http://www.international.gc.ca/department-ministere/plans/dpr-rmr/dpr-rmr_1112_sup.aspx?lang=eng.

– 2013a. "Canada Concerned by Lawlessness in Libya." News release, 3 May. http://www.canadainternational.gc.ca/libya-libye/highlights-faits/2013/2013-05-03_lawlessness-anarchie.aspx?lang=en.

– 2013b. "Canada Condemns Violence in Tripoli." News release, 16 November. http://www.international.gc.ca/media/aff/news-communiques/2013/11/16a.aspx?lang=eng.

– 2013c. "Counter-Terrorism Capacity Building Assistance." http://www.international.gc.ca/crime/ctcb-rcat.aspx?lang=eng.

– 2014a. "Canada Congratulates Libya on Destruction of Chemical Weapons." News release, 4 February. http://www.international.gc.ca/media/aff/news-communiques/2014/02/04b.aspx?lang=eng.

– 2014b. "Canada Temporarily Withdraws Staff from Libya." News release, 29 July. http://www.international.gc.ca/media/aff/news-communiques/2014/07/29a.aspx?lang=eng.

Goldsmith, Andrew, and James Sheptycki. 2007. "Introduction." In *Crafting Transnational Policing: Police Capacity-Building and Global Policing Reform,* ed. Andrew Goldsmith and James Sheptycki, 1–28. Portland, OR: Hart Publishing.

Gordon, Todd. 2010. *Imperialist Canada.* Winnipeg: Arbeiter Ring Publications.

Graham, Stephen. 2011. *Cities under Siege: The New Military Urbanism.* London: Verso Books, 2011.

Gregory, Derek. 2006. "The Black Flag: Guantánamo Bay and the Space of Exception." *Geografiska Annaler. Series B, Human Geography* 88 (4): 405–27. http://dx.doi.org/10.1111/j.0435-3684.2006.00230.x.

Grewcock, Michael. 2009. *Border Crimes: Australia's War on Illicit Migrants*. Sydney: Institute of Criminology.

Guild, E. Elspeth. 2009. *Security and Migration in the 21st Century*. Cambridge: Polity.

Guzik, Keith. 2013. "Security a la Mexicana: On the Particularities of Security Governance in México's War on Crime." *Theory and Society* 42 (2): 161–87. http://dx.doi.org/10.1007/s11186-013-9189-9.

Ha, Tu Thanh. 2011. "How High-Tech Canadian Drones Gave Libyan Rebels a Boost." *Globe and Mail*, 23 August. http://www.theglobeandmail.com/news/world/how-high-tech-canadian-drones-gave-libyan-rebels-a-boost/article591547/.

Haggerty, Kevin. 2004. "Technology and Crime Policy: Reply to Michael Jacobson." *Theoretical Criminology* 8 (4): 491–7. http://dx.doi.org/10.1177/1362480604046661.

Hallams, Ellen. 2010. *The United States and NATO since 9/11: The Transatlantic Alliance Renewed*. New York: Routledge.

Hallsworth, Simon, and John Lea. 2011. "Reconstructing Leviathan: Emerging Contours of the Security State." *Theoretical Criminology* 15 (2): 141–57. http://dx.doi.org/10.1177/1362480610383451.

Hallward, Peter. 2007. *Damming the Flood: Haiti, Aristide, and the Politics of Containment*. New York: Verso Books.

– 2009. "Lyonel Trouillot, or the Fictions of Formal Democracy." *Small Axe* 30 (3 30): 174–85. http://dx.doi.org/10.1215/07990537-2009-038.

Hameed, Yavar, and Jeffrey Monaghan. 2012. "Accessing Dirty Data: Methodological Strategies for Social Problems Researchers." In *Brokering Access: Politics, Power and Freedom of Information in Canada*, ed. Mike Larsen and Kevin Walby, 142–68. Vancouver: UBC Press.

Hamilton, Graeme, and Nicolas Van Praet. 2014. "Former SNC-Lavalin Executive Riadh Ben Aissa Pleads Guilty to Corruption Charges." *Financial Post*, 1 October. http://business.financialpost.com/2014/10/01/snc-riadh-ben-aissa-pleads-guilty/.

Hardt, Michael, and Antonio Negri. 2000. *Empire*. Cambridge, MA: Harvard University Press.

Hart, Michael. 2008. *From Pride to Influence: Towards a New Canadian Foreign Policy*. Vancouver: UBC Press.

HealthRoots. 2011. *MINUSTAH: Keeping the Peace, or Conspiring against It?* Harvard School of Public Health. http://ijdh.org/wordpress/wp-content/uploads/2011/10/MINUSTAH-White-Paper1.pdf.

Heinbecker, Paul. 2011. *Getting Back in the Game: A Foreign Policy Playbook for Canada*. Toronto: Dundurn.

Heng, Yee-Kuang, and Kenneth McDonagh. 2011. "After the 'War on Terror': Regulatory States, Risk Bureaucracies and the Risk-Based Governance of Terror." *International Relations* 25 (3): 313–29. http://dx.doi.org/10.1177/0047117811415484.

Hettne, Björn. 2010. "Development and Security: Origins and Future." *Security Dialogue* 41 (1): 31–52. http://dx.doi.org/10.1177/0967010609357040.

Hettne, Björn, and Fredrik Söderbaum. 2005. "Civilian Power or Soft Imperialism? EU as a Global Actor and the Role of Interregionalism." *European Foreign Affairs Review* 10 (4): 535–52.

Hills, Alice. 2009. "Security as a Selective Project." *Studies in Social Justice* 3 (1): 79–97.

– 2010. "The Unavoidable Ghettoization of Security in Iraq." *Security Dialogue* 41 (3): 301–21. http://dx.doi.org/10.1177/0967010610370224.

– 2012. "Lost in Translation: Why Nigeria's Police Don't Implement Democratic Reforms." *International Affairs* 88 (4): 739–55. http://dx.doi.org/10.1111/j.1468-2346.2012.01099.x.

– 2013. "Policing, Good-Enough Governance and Development: The Evidence from Mogadishu." *Conflict Security and Development* 13 (3): 317–37. http://dx.doi.org/10.1080/14678802.2013.811051.

Hobbing, Peter. 2010. "Tracing Terrorists: The European Union–Canada Agreement on Passenger Name Record (PNR) Matters." In *Mapping Transatlantic Security Relations: The EU, Canada, and the War on Terror*, ed. Mark B. Salter, 73–97. New York: Routledge.

Hodges, Dan. 2015. "The 900 Refugees Drowned in the Mediterranean Were Killed by British Government Policy." *Telegraph* (UK), 20 April. http://www.telegraph.co.uk/news/general-election-2015/politics-blog/11549721/The-900-refugees-dead-in-the-Mediterranean-were-killed-by-British-government-policy.html.

Hoijtink, Marijn. 2014. "Capitalizing on Emergence: The 'New' Civil Security Market in Europe." *Security Dialogue* 45 (5): 458–75. http://dx.doi.org/10.1177/0967010614544312.

Holmqvist, Caroline. 2014. *Policing Wars: On Military Intervention in the Twenty-First Century*. New York: Palgrave Macmillan. http://dx.doi.org/10.1057/9781137323613.

Hoogvelt, Ankie. 1997. *Globalization and the Postcolonial World: The New Political Economy of Development*. Baltimore, MD: Johns Hopkins University Press. http://dx.doi.org/10.1007/978-1-349-25671-6.

Horgby, Anna, and Mark Rhinard. 2015. "The EU's Internal Security Strategy: A Historical Perspective." *Security Journal* 28 (3): 309–21.

Howell, Jude, and Jeremy Lind. 2009a. "Changing Donor Policy and Practice in Civil Society in the Post-9/11 Aid Context." *Third World Quarterly* 30 (7): 1279–96. http://dx.doi.org/10.1080/01436590903134924.

– 2009b. "Manufacturing Civil Society and the Limits of Legitimacy: Aid, Security and Civil Society after 9/11 in Afghanistan." *European Journal of Development Research* 21 (5): 718–36. http://dx.doi.org/10.1057/ejdr.2009.40.

Human Rights Watch (HRW). 2014. "Haiti." In *World Report 2014: Haiti,* 255–260 http://www.hrw.org/world-report/2014/country-chapters/haiti.

Huysmans, Jef. 2002. "Shape-Shifting NATO: Humanitarian Action and the Kosovo Refugee Crisis." *Review of International Studies* 28 (3): 599–618. http://dx.doi.org/10.1017/S0260210502005995.

– 2006. *The Politics of Insecurity: Fear, Migration and Asylum in the EU.* New York: Routledge.

– 2011. "What's in an Act? On Security Speech Acts and Little Security Nothings." *Security Dialogue* 42 (4–5): 371–83. http://dx.doi.org/10.1177/0967010611418713.

– 2014. *Security Unbound: Enacting Democratic Limits*. New York: Routledge.

Hyndman, Jennifer. 2009. "Acts of Aid: Neoliberalism in a War Zone." *Antipode* 41 (5): 867–89. http://dx.doi.org/10.1111/j.1467-8330.2009.00700.x.

– 2015. "The Securitisation of Sri Lankan Tourism in the Absence of Peace." *Stability: International Journal of Security & Development* 4 (1): 1–16. http://dx.doi.org/10.5334/sta.fa.

Ibbitson, John. 2011. "The Harper Doctrine: Conservative Foreign Policy in Black and White." *Globe and Mail,* 12 June 12. http://www.theglobeandmail.com/news/politics/ottawa-notebook/the-harper-doctrine-conservative-foreign-policy-in-black-and-white/article615115/.

Ibrahim, Maggie. 2005. "The Securitization of Migration: A Racial Discourse." *International Migration (Geneva)* 43 (5): 163–87. http://dx.doi.org/10.1111/j.1468-2435.2005.00345.x.

Ignatieff, Michael. 2003. *Empire Lite: Nation Building in Bosnia*. Kosovo: Random House.

Ilcan, Suzan, and Anita Lacey. 2011. *Governing the Poor: Exercises of Poverty Reduction, Practices of Global Aid*. Montreal and Kingston: McGill-Queen's University Press.

Institute for Justice and Democracy in Haiti. 2014. "The U.S. Should Support Fair and Inclusive Elections in Haiti." News release, 20 February.

http://www.ijdh.org/wp-content/uploads/2013/05/IJDH-Election-handout-Feb-19-2014.pdf.

Ives, Kim. 2011. "Wikileaks Points to US Meddling in Haiti." *Guardian (UK)*, 21 January. http://www.theguardian.com/commentisfree/cifamerica/2011/jan/21/haiti-wikileaks.

Jackson, Paul. 2011. "Security Sector Reform and State Building." *Third World Quarterly* 32 (10): 1803–22. http://dx.doi.org/10.1080/01436597.2011.610577.

Jefferson, Andrew. 2007. "Prison Officer Training and Practice in Nigeria: Contention, Contradiction and Re-imagining Reform Strategies." *Punishment & Society* 9 (3): 253–69. http://dx.doi.org/10.1177/1462474507077494.

Johnston, Jake, and Mark Weisbrot. 2011. *Haiti's Fatally Flawed Election*. Washington DC: Center for Economic and Policy Research. http://www.cepr.net/documents/publications/haiti-2011-01.pdf.

Joya, Angela. 2013. "Failed States and Canada's 3D Policy in Afghanistan." In *Empire's Ally: Canada and the War in Afghanistan*, ed. Jerome Klassen and Greg Albo, 277–305. Toronto: University of Toronto Press.

Kaldor, Mary. 2003. "The Idea of Global Civil Society." *International Affairs* 79 (3): 583–93. http://dx.doi.org/10.1111/1468-2346.00324.

– 2007. *Human Security: Reflections on Globalization and Intervention*. Malden, MA: Polity.

– 2013. "In Defence of New Wars." *Stability: International Journal of Security and Development* 2 (1): 1–16. http://dx.doi.org/10.5334/sta.at.

Kang, David. 2002. *Crony Capitalism: Corruption and Development in South Korea and the Philippines*. Cambridge: Cambridge University Press. http://dx.doi.org/10.1017/CBO9780511606175.

Kaplan, Martha. 1995. "Panopticon in Poona: An Essay on Foucault and Colonialism." *Cultural Anthropology* 10 (1): 85–98. http://dx.doi.org/10.1525/can.1995.10.1.02a00040.

Kauppi, Niilo, and Mikael R. Madsen. 2014. "Fields of Global Governance: How Transnational Power Elites Can Make Global Governance Intelligible." *International Political Sociology* 8 (3): 324–30. http://dx.doi.org/10.1111/ips.12060.

Kaussen, Valerie. 2009. "Violence and Methodology: Reading Aristide in the Aftermath of 2004." *Small Axe* 30 (3 30): 148–60. http://dx.doi.org/10.1215/07990537-2009-036.

Kavalski, Emilian. 2013. "The Struggle for Recognition of Normative Powers: Normative Power Europe and Normative Power China in Context." *Cooperation and Conflict* 48 (2): 247–67. http://dx.doi.org/10.1177/0010836713485386.

Kearon, Tony. 2013. "Surveillance Technologies and the Crises of Confidence in Regulatory Agencies." *Criminology & Criminal Justice* 13 (4): 415–30. http://dx.doi.org/10.1177/1748895812454747.

Keenan, Jeremy. 2009a. *The Dark Sahara: America's War on Terror in Africa*. London: Pluto.

– 2009b. *The Dying Sahara: US Imperialism and Terror in Africa*. London: Pluto.

Kempin, Ronja, and Jocelyn Mawdsley. 2013. "The Common Security and Defence Policy as an Act of American Hegemony." *European Security* 22 (1): 55–73. http://dx.doi.org/10.1080/09662839.2012.726221.

Kenkel, Kai. 2010. "South America's Emerging Power: Brazil as Peacekeeper." *International Peacekeeping* 17 (5): 644–61. http://dx.doi.org/10.1080/13533312.2010.516958.

Kersavage, Kathryn. 2014. "The 'Responsibility to Protect' Our Answer to 'Never Again'? Libya, Syria and a Critical Analysis of R2P." *International Affairs Forum* 5 (1): 23–41. http://dx.doi.org/10.1080/23258020.2014.933057.

Kessler, Oliver, and Christopher Daase. 2008. "From Insecurity to Uncertainty: Risk and the Paradox of Security Politics." *Alternatives* 33 (2): 211–32. http://dx.doi.org/10.1177/030437540803300206.

Kinsman, Gary, Dieter Buse, and Mercedes Steedman. 2000. *Whose National Security?: Canadian State Surveillance and the Creation of Enemies*. Toronto: Between the Lines.

Kinsman, Gary, and Patrizia Gentile. 2010. *The Canadian War on Queers: National Security as Sexual Regulation*. Vancouver: UBC Press.

Kitchen, Veronica. 2009. "Argument and Identity Change in the Atlantic Security Community." *Security Dialogue* 40 (1): 95–114. http://dx.doi.org/10.1177/0967010608100849.

– 2010a. *The Globalisation of NATO: Intervention, Security and Identity*. New York: Routedge.

– 2010b. "NATO's Out-of-Area Norm from Suez to Afghanistan." *Journal of Transatlantic Studies* 8 (2): 105–17. http://dx.doi.org/10.1080/14794011003760269.

Kitchen, Veronica, and Karthika Sasikumar. 2009. "Canada (En)Counters Terrorism: US-Canada Relations and Counter-terrorism Policy." *Terrorism and Political Violence* 21 (1): 155–73. http://dx.doi.org/10.1080/09546550802587572.

Klassen, Jerome. 2013. "Empire, Afghanistan, and Canadian Foreign Policy." In *Empire's Ally: Canada and the War in Afghanistan*, ed. Jerome Klassen and Greg Albo, 3–43. Toronto: University of Toronto Press. http://dx.doi.org/10.1007/978-3-642-32141-2_1.

Klein, Naomi. 2004. "Baghdad Year Zero." *Harper's*, September.

Koschut, Simon. 2014. "Transatlantic Conflict Management Inside-Out: The Impact of Domestic Norms on Regional Security Practices." *Cambridge Review of International Affairs* 27 (2): 339–61. http://dx.doi.org/10.1080/09557571.2013.840561.

Krahmann, Elke. 2003. "Conceptualizing Security Governance." *Cooperation and Conflict* 38 (1): 5–26. http://dx.doi.org/10.1177/0010836703038001001.

– 2013. "The United States, PMSCs and the State Monopoly on Violence: Leading the Way towards Norm Change." *Security Dialogue* 44 (1): 53–71. http://dx.doi.org/10.1177/0967010612470292.

Krasmann, Susanne. 2007. "The Enemy on the Border Critique of a Programme in Favour of a Preventive State." *Punishment & Society* 9 (3): 301–18. http://dx.doi.org/10.1177/1462474507077496.

Krause, Volker. 2004. "Hazardous Weapons? Effects of Arms Transfers and Defense Pacts on Militarized Disputes, 1950–1995." *International Interactions* 30 (4): 349–71. http://dx.doi.org/10.1080/03050620490884038.

Laffey, Mark, and Suthaharan Nadarajah. 2012. "The Hybridity of Liberal Peace: States, Diasporas and Insecurity." *Security Dialogue* 43 (5): 403–20. http://dx.doi.org/10.1177/0967010612457974.

Lancaster, Carol. 2007. *Foreign Aid: Diplomacy, Development, Domestic Politics*. Chicago: University of Chicago Press.

Larner, Wendy, and Nina Laurie. 2010. "Travelling Technocrats, Embodied Knowledges: Globalising Privatisation in Telecoms and Water." *Geoforum* 41 (2): 218–26. http://dx.doi.org/10.1016/j.geoforum.2009.11.005.

Larsen, Mike, and Justin Piché. 2009. "Exceptional State, Pragmatic Bureaucracy, and Indefinite Detention: The Case of the Kingston Immigration Holding Centre." *Canadian Journal of Law and Society* 24 (2): 203–29. http://dx.doi.org/10.1017/S0829320100009911.

Larsen, Mike, and Kevin Walby, eds. 2012. *Brokering Access: Power, Politics, and Freedom of Information Process in Canada*. Vancouver: UBC Press.

Leech, Philip. 2015. "Who Owns 'the Spring' in Palestine? Rethinking Popular Consent and Resistance in the Context of the 'Palestinian State' and the 'Arab Spring.'" *Democratization* 22 (6): 1011–29. http://dx.doi.org/10.1080/13510347.2014.899584.

Levitz, Stephanie. 2015. "Canada Should Have Handled Afghan Aid Program Differently, Audit Concludes." Canadian Press, 16 March. http://www.cbc.ca/news/politics/canada-should-have-handled-afghan-aid-program-differently-audit-concludes-1.2996713.

Lisle, Debbie. 2013. "Frontline Leisure: Securitizing Tourism in the War on Terror." *Security Dialogue* 44 (2): 127–46. http://dx.doi.org/10.1177/0967010613479426.

Loughlan, Victoria, Christian Olsson, and Peer Schouten. 2015. "Mapping." In *Critical Security Methods: New Frameworks for Analysis*, ed. Claudia Aradau, Jef Huysmans, Andrew Neal, and Nadine Voelkner, 23–56. New York: Routledge.

Luscombe, Alex, and Kevin Walby. 2014. "High Policing and Access to Information." *Police Practice and Research* 16 (6): 485–98. http://dx.doi.org/10.1080/15614263.2014.958487.

Lyon, David. 2006. "Surveillance, Power and Everyday Life." In *Oxford Handbook of Information and Communication Technologies*, ed. Robin Mansell, C. Avgenrou, and R. Silverstone, 449–72. Oxford: Oxford University Press.

– 2009. *Identifying Citizens: ID Cards as Surveillance.* Cambridge: Polity.

– 2010. "Liquid Surveillance: The Contribution of Zygmunt Bauman to Surveillance Studies." *International Political Sociology* 4 (4): 325–38. http://dx.doi.org/10.1111/j.1749-5687.2010.00109.x.

Macaulay, Fiona. 2007. "Knowledge Production, Framing and Criminal Justice Reform in Latin America." *Journal of Latin American Studies* 39 (3): 627–51. http://dx.doi.org/10.1017/S0022216X07002866.

Mack, Andrew. 2002. "The Human Security Report Project: Background Paper." Vancouver: Human Security Centre, Liu Institute for Global Issues, University of British Columbia.

Mackrael, Kim. 2013. "Fantino to Talk Foreign Aid with Miners." *Globe and Mail*, 2 March.

MacLean, Sandra, David Black, and Timothy Shaw, eds. 2006. *A Decade of Human Security: Global Governance and New Multilateralisms*. Burlington, VT: Ashgate.

Maguire, Edward R., and William R. King. 2013. "Transferring Criminal Investigation Methods from Developed to Developing Nations." *Policing and Society* 23 (3): 346–61. http://dx.doi.org/10.1080/10439463.2013.818097.

Mahmud, Tayyab. 2010. "'Surplus Humanity' and the Margins of Legality: Slums, Slumdogs, and Accumulation by Dispossession." *Chapman Law Review* 14 (1): 1–74.

Manners, Ian. 2002. "'Normative Power Europe: A Contradiction in Terms?" *Journal of Common Market Studies* 40 (2): 235–58. http://dx.doi.org/10.1111/1468-5965.00353.

– 2006. "European Union 'Normative Power' and the Security Challenge." *European Security* 15 (4): 405–21. http://dx.doi.org/10.1080/09662830701305880.

Marriage, Zoë. 2010. "Congo Co: Aid and Security." *Conflict Security and Development* 10 (3): 353–77. http://dx.doi.org/10.1080/14678802.2010.484200.

Martin, Mary, and Taylor Owen. 2010. "The Second Generation of Human Security: Lessons from the UN and EU Experience." *International Affairs* 86 (1): 211–24. http://dx.doi.org/10.1111/j.1468-2346.2010.00876.x.

Mawdsley, Emma. 2007. "The Millennium Challenge Account: Neo-liberalism, Poverty and Security." *Review of International Political Economy* 14 (3): 487–509. http://dx.doi.org/10.1080/09692290701395742.

McCulloch, Jude, and Sharon Pickering. 2009. "Pre-Crime and Counter-terrorism: Imagining Future Crime in the 'War on Terror.'" *British Journal of Criminology* 49 (5): 628–45. http://dx.doi.org/10.1093/bjc/azp023.

– eds. 2013. *Borders and Crime: Pre-Crime, Mobility and Serious Harm in an Age of Globalization*. New York: Palgrave Macmillan.

McKay, Ian, and Jamie Swift. 2012. *Warrior Nation: Rebranding Canada in an Age of Anxiety*. Toronto: Between the Lines.

Mcleod, Paul. 2012. "MacKay Defends $800,000 Flyover." *Halifax Chronicle-Herald*, 14 March. http://thechronicleherald.ca/novascotia/73374-mackay-defends-800000-flyover.

Melossi, Dario, Máximo Sozzo, and Richard Sparks. 2011. "Criminal Questions: Cultural Embeddedness and Global Mobilities." In *Travels of the Criminal Question*, ed. Dario Melossi, Máximo Sozzo, and Richard Sparks, 1–16. Oxford: Hart Publishing.

Miles, William. 2012. "Deploying Development to Counter Terrorism: Post-9/11 Transformation of U.S. Foreign Aid to Africa." *African Studies Review* 55 (3): 27–60. http://dx.doi.org/10.1017/S0002020600007198.

MINUSTAH and UN. 2016. *Annual Report on the Situation of Human Rights in Haiti: Executive Summary and Recommendations, 1 July 2014–30 June 2015*. Geneva: Office of the High Commissioner of Human Rights. https://minustah.unmissions.org/sites/default/files/2014-2015_haiti-annual_report_summary.pdf.

Mitchell, Katharyne. 2010. "Ungoverned Space: Global Security and the Geopolitics of Broken Windows." *Political Geography* 29 (5): 289–97. http://dx.doi.org/10.1016/j.polgeo.2010.03.004.

Mitchell, Timothy. 2002. *Rule of Experts: Egypt, Techno-Politics, Modernity*. Berkeley, CA: University of California Press.

Moffette, David, and Shaira Vadasaria. 2016. "Uninhibited Violence: Race and the Securitization of Immigration." *Critical Studies on Security*, 24 November. http://dx.doi.org/10.1080/21624887.2016.1256365.

Monaghan, Jeffrey. 2013a. "Mounties in the Frontier: Circulations, Anxieties, and Myths of Settler Colonial Policing in Canada." *Journal of Canadian Studies / Revue d'études canadiennes* 47 (1): 122–48.

– 2013b. "Settler Governmentality and Racializing Surveillance in Canada's North-West." *Canadian Journal of Sociology* 38 (4): 487–508.

– 2015a. "Criminal Justice Policy Transfer and Prison Counter-Radicalization: Examining Canadian Participation in the Roma-Lyon Group." *Canadian Journal of Law and Society* 30 (3): 381–400. http://dx.doi.org/10.1017/cls.2015.11.

– 2015b. "Four Barriers to Access to Information: Perspectives of a Frequent User." In *Access to Information and Social Justice*, ed. Jamie Brownlee and Kevin Walby, 53–74. Winnipeg: Arbiter Ring.

– 2015c. "Security Aid: The Development Regime of Surveillance and Social Control." PhD diss., Queen's University.

– 2016. "Security Development and the Palestinian Authority: An Examination of the 'Canadian Factor.'" *Conflict Security and Development* 16 (2): 125–43.

Monture-Angus, Patricia. 2011. "The Need for Radical Change in the Canadian Criminal Justice System: Applying a Human Rights Framework." In *Visions of the Heart: Canadian Aboriginal Issues*, ed. David Alan Long and Olivia Patricia Dickason, 3rd ed., 238–57. Oxford: Oxford University Press.

Moore, Dawn. 2011. "The Benevolent Watch: Therapeutic Surveillance in Drug Treatment Court." *Theoretical Criminology* 15 (3): 255–68. http://dx.doi.org/10.1177/1362480610396649.

Moore, Rebecca. 2007. *NATO's New Mission: Projecting Stability in a Post–Cold War World*. Westport, CT: Greenwood Publishing Group.

Morrison, David. 1998. *Aid and Ebb Tide: A History of CIDA and Canadian Development Assistance*. Waterloo, ON: Wilfrid Laurier University Press.

Morrissey, John. 2011. "Closing the Neoliberal Gap: Risk and Regulation in the Long War of Securitization." *Antipode* 43 (3): 874–900. http://dx.doi.org/10.1111/j.1467-8330.2010.00823.x.

Mountz, Alison. 2010. *Seeking Asylum: Human Smuggling and Bureaucracy at the Border*. Minneapolis: University of Minnesota Press. http://dx.doi.org/10.5749/minnesota/9780816665372.001.0001.

Muggah, Robert. 2010. "The Effects of Stabilisation on Humanitarian Action in Haiti." *Disasters* 34 (S3): S444–63. http://dx.doi.org/10.1111/j.1467-7717.2010.01205.x.

Muller, Benjamin. 2010. *Security, Risk and the Biometric State: Governing Borders and Bodies*. New York: Routledge.

Müller, Markus-Michael. 2012. *Public Security in the Negotiated State*. Basingstoke, UK: Palgrave Macmillan.

Mulroney, David. 2015. *Middle Power, Middle Kingdom: What Canadians Need to Know about China in the 21st Century*. Toronto: Allen Lane.

Murakami Wood, David. 2013. "What Is Global Surveillance? Towards a Relational Political Economy of the Global Surveillant Assemblage." *Geoforum* 49:317–26. http://dx.doi.org/10.1016/j.geoforum.2013.07.001.

Nair, Sheila. 2010. "Sovereignty, Security, and Migrants: Making Bare Life." In *International Relations and States of Exception: Margins, Peripheries, and Excluded Bodies*, ed. Shampa Biswas and Sheila Nair, 95–115. New York: Routledge.

Neal, Andrew. 2009. *Exceptionalism and the Politics of Counter-Terrorism: Liberty, Security and the War on Terror*. London: Routledge.

Neocleous, Mark. 2008. *Critique of Security*. Montreal and Kingston: McGill-Queen's University Press. http://dx.doi.org/10.3366/edinburgh/9780748633289.001.0001.

– 2011. "The Police of Civilization: The War on Terror as Civilizing Offensive." *International Political Sociology* 5 (2): 144–59. http://dx.doi.org/10.1111/j.1749-5687.2011.00126.x.

– 2014. *War Power, Police Power*. Edinburgh: Edinburgh University Press. http://dx.doi.org/10.3366/edinburgh/9780748692361.001.0001.

Nesbitt, Nick. 2009. "Aristide and the Politics of Democratization." *Small Axe* 30 (3 30): 137–47. http://dx.doi.org/10.1215/07990537-2009-035.

Nossal, Kim Richard. 1988. "Mixed Motives Revisited: Canada's Interest in Development Assistance." *Canadian Journal of Political Science* 21 (1): 35–56. http://dx.doi.org/10.1017/S0008423900055608.

– 1989. *The Politics of Canadian Foreign Policy*. 2nd ed. Scarborough, ON: Prentice-Hall Canada.

– 2010. "Rethinking the Security Imaginary: Canadian Security and the Case of Afghanistan." In *Locating Global Order: American Power and Canadian Security after 9/11*, ed. Bruno Charbonneau and Wayne S. Cox, 107–25. Vancouver: UBC Press.

Oelsner, Andrea. 2009. "Consensus and Governance in Mercosur: The Evolution of the South American Security Agenda." *Security Dialogue* 40 (2): 191–212. http://dx.doi.org/10.1177/0967010609103086.

Ojeda, Diana. 2013. "War and Tourism: The Banal Geographies of Security in Colombia's 'Retaking.'" *Geopolitics* 18 (4): 759–78. http://dx.doi.org/10.1080/14650045.2013.780037.

Oliveira, Gilberto Carvalho. 2013. "'New Wars' at Sea: A Critical Transformative Approach to the Political Economy of Somali Piracy." *Security Dialogue* 44 (1): 3–18. http://dx.doi.org/10.1177/0967010612470294.

Olsson, Christian. 2013. "'Legitimate Violence' in the Prose of Counterinsurgency: An Impossible Necessity?" *Alternatives* 38 (2): 155–71. http://dx.doi.org/10.1177/0304375413486332.

O'Reilly, Conor. 2010. "The Transnational Security Consultancy Industry: A Case of State-Corporate Symbiosis." *Theoretical Criminology* 14 (2): 183–210. http://dx.doi.org/10.1177/1362480609355702.

Orford, Anne. 1999. "Muscular Humanitarianism: Reading the Narratives of the New Interventionism." *European Journal of International Law* 10 (4): 679–711. http://dx.doi.org/10.1093/ejil/10.4.679.

Papillon, Isabelle. 2014. "Death Squads Sow Terror in Port-au-Prince's Poor Neighborhoods." *Haïti Liberté* 8 (7). http://www.haiti-liberte.com/archives/volume8-7/Death%20Squads%20Sow%20Terror.asp.

Park, Augustine. 2010. "Peacebuilding, the Rule of Law and the Problem of Culture: Assimilation, Multiculturalism, Deployment." *Journal of Intervention and Statebuilding* 4 (4): 413–32. http://dx.doi.org/10.1080/17502971003700977.

– 2013. "Racial-Nationalism and Representations of Citizenship: The Recalcitrant Alien, the Citizen of Convenience and the Fraudulent Citizen." *Canadian Journal of Sociology* 38 (4): 579–600.

Patrick, Stewart. 2011. *Weak Links: Fragile States, Global Threats, and International Security*. Oxford: Oxford University Press.

Patrick, Stewart, and Kaysie Brown. 2007. *Greater Than the Sum of Its Parts? Assessing "Whole of Government" Approaches to Fragile States*. New York: International Peace Academy.

Pawlak, Patryk. 2009. "Network Politics in Transatlantic Homeland Security Cooperation." *Perspectives on European Politics and Society* 10 (4): 560–81. http://dx.doi.org/10.1080/15705850903314833.

Payton, Laura. 2015. "David Mulroney Warns Canada Should Apply Afghanistan's Lessons to Iraq." CBC News, 20 March. http://www.cbc.ca/news/politics/david-mulroney-warns-canada-should-apply-afghanistan-s-lessons-to-iraq-1.3002692.

Phillips, Kristen. 2009. "Interventions, Interceptions, Separations: Australia's Biopolitical War at the Borders and the Gendering of Bare Life." *Social Identities* 15 (1): 131–47. http://dx.doi.org/10.1080/13504630802693570.

Pickering, Sharon. 2010. *Women, Borders, and Violence: Current Issues in Asylum, Forced Migration, and Trafficking*. New York: Springer Science & Business Media.

– 2014. "Floating Carceral Spaces: Border Enforcement and Gender on the High Seas." *Punishment & Society* 16 (2): 187–205. http://dx.doi.org/10.1177/1462474513517018.

Pickering, Sharon, and Leanne Weber, eds. 2006. *Borders, Mobility and Technologies of Control*. New York: Springer Netherlands. http://dx.doi.org/10.1007/1-4020-4899-8.

– 2013. "Policing Transversal Borders." In *The Borders of Punishment: Migration, Citizenship, and Social Exclusion*, ed. Katja Franko Aas and Mary Bodsworth, 93–110. Oxford: Oxford University Press. http://dx.doi.org/10.1093/acprof:oso/9780199669394.003.0006.

Podur, Justin. 2012. *Haiti's New Dictatorship: The Coup, the Earthquake and the UN Occupation*. Toronto: Between the Lines.

Pommier, Bruno. 2011. "The Use of Force to Protect Civilians and Humanitarian Action: The Case of Libya and Beyond." *International Review of the Red Cross* 93 (884): 1063–83. http://dx.doi.org/10.1017/S1816383112000422.

Pouliot, Vincent. 2007. "Pacification without Collective Identification: Russia and the Transatlantic Security Community in the Post–Cold War Era." *Journal of Peace Research* 44 (5): 605–22. http://dx.doi.org/10.1177/0022343307080858.

– 2010. *International Security in Practice: The Politics of NATO-Russia Diplomacy*. Cambridge: Cambridge University Press. http://dx.doi.org/10.1017/CBO9780511676185.

Price, Richard. 2004. "Emerging Customary Norms and Anti-Personnel Landmines." In *The Politics of International Law*, ed. Christian Reus-Smit, 106–30. New York: Cambridge University Press. http://dx.doi.org/10.1017/CBO9780511491641.006.

Prime Minister's Office. 2013. "Statement by the Prime Minister of Canada." News release, 7 October.

– 2014. "Canada Completes First Delivery of Military Supplies to Forces Fighting ISIL." News release, 29 August. http://news.gc.ca/web/article-en.do?nid=880329.

Puar, Jasbir. 2007. *Terrorist Assemblages: Homonationalism in Queer Times*. Durham, NC: Duke University Press. http://dx.doi.org/10.1215/9780822390442.

Puar, Jasbir, and Amit Rai. 2002. "Monster, Terrorist, Fag: The War on Terrorism and the Production of Docile Patriots." *Social Text* 20 (3): 117–48. http://dx.doi.org/10.1215/01642472-20-3_72-117.

Public Safety Canada. 2012. "Backgrounder – Overview: Ending the Abuse of Canada's Immigration System by Human Smugglers." Ottawa: Public Safety Canada. http://www.cic.gc.ca/english/department/media/backgrounders/2012/2012-06-29i.asp.

Pugh, M. 2001. "The Challenge of Civil-Military Relations in International Peace Operations." *Disasters* 25 (4): 345–57. http://dx.doi.org/10.1111/1467-7717.00183.

Pugliese, David. 2014. "Out of Afghanistan: A Legacy under Construction." *Ottawa Citizen*, 16 February. http://www.ottawacitizen.com/news/Afghanistan+legacy+under+construction/9517124/story.html.

Quan, Douglas. 2013. "Immigration Lawyers Call for Review of All Failed MV Sun Sea Refugee Claims." Postmedia News, 11 October. http://o.canada.

com/news/world/immigration-lawyers-call-for-a-review-of-all-failed-mv-sun-sea-refugee-claims.

– 2014. "Canadian Forces Donate Surplus Military Hardware to Police Agencies." Postmedia News, 29 August. http://o.canada.com/news/national/rcmp-defends-acquisition-of-surplus-military-hardware.

Rasiulis, Andrew. 2001. "The Military Training Assistance Program (MTAP): An Instrument of Military Diplomacy." *Canadian Military Journal* (Autumn): 63–4.

Ratcliffe, Jerry. 2008. *Intelligence-Led Policing*. Portland, OR: Willan Publishing.

Razack, Sherene. 2004. *Dark Threats and White Knights: The Somalia Affair, Peacekeeping, and the New Imperialism*. Toronto: University of Toronto Press.

– 2007. "'Your client has a profile': Race and National Security in Canada after 9/11." *Studies in Law, Politics, and Society* 40:3–40. http://dx.doi.org/10.1016/S1059-4337(06)40001-6.

Redfield, Peter. 2005. "Doctors, Borders, and Life in Crisis." *Cultural Anthropology* 20 (3): 328–61. http://dx.doi.org/10.1525/can.2005.20.3.328.

Rees, Wyn. 2008. "Inside Out: The External Face of EU Internal Security Policy." *Journal of European Integration* 30 (1): 97–111. http://dx.doi.org/10.1080/07036330801959515.

Reid-Henry, Simon. 2013. "An Incorporating Geopolitics: Frontex and the Geopolitical Rationalities of the European Border." *Geopolitics* 18 (1): 198–224. http://dx.doi.org/10.1080/14650045.2012.691139.

Rose, Nikolas. 1999. *Powers of Freedom: Reframing Political Thought*. New York: Cambridge University Press. http://dx.doi.org/10.1017/CBO9780511488856.

– 2000. "Government and Control." *British Journal of Criminology* 40 (2): 321–39. http://dx.doi.org/10.1093/bjc/40.2.321.

Rosga, AnnJanette. 2010. "The Bosnian Police, Multi-ethnic Democracy, and the Race of 'European Civilization.'" *Ethnic and Racial Studies* 33 (4): 675–95. http://dx.doi.org/10.1080/01419870903362605.

Rotmann, Philipp, Gerrit Kurtz, and Sarah Brockmeier. 2014. "Major Powers and the Contested Evolution of a Responsibility to Protect." *Conflict Security and Development* 14 (4): 355–77. http://dx.doi.org/10.1080/14678802.2014.930592.

Sabaratnam, Meera. 2013. "Avatars of Eurocentrism in the Critique of the Liberal Peace." *Security Dialogue* 44 (3): 259–78. http://dx.doi.org/10.1177/0967010613485870.

Salter, Mark. 2008. "Imagining Numbers: Risk, Quantification, and Aviation Security." *Security Dialogue* 39 (2–3): 243–66. http://dx.doi.org/10.1177/0967010608088777.

– 2010. *Mapping Transatlantic Security Relations: The EU, Canada and the War on Terror*. New York: Routledge.

Salter, Mark, and Can E. Mutlu, eds. 2012. *Research Methods in Critical Security Studies: An Introduction*. New York: Routledge.

Samara, Tony Roshan. 2010. "Policing Development: Urban Renewal as Neo-Liberal Security Strategy." *Urban Studies (Edinburgh)* 47 (1): 197–214. http://dx.doi.org/10.1177/0042098009349772.

Sanyal, Kalyan. 2007. *Rethinking Capitalist Development: Primitive Accumulation, Governmentality and Post-colonial Capitalism*. New York: Routledge.

Sassen, Saskia. 2014. *Expulsions*. New Haven, CT: Harvard University Press.

Sayigh, Yezid. 2009. "'Fixing Broken Windows': Security Sector Reform in Palestine, Lebanon, and Yemen." *Carnegie Papers*, no. 17, October.

Scherrer, Amandine. 2009. *G8 against Transnational Organized Crime*. Burlington, VT: Ashgate Publishing.

Scherrer, Amandine, and Benoit Dupont. 2010. "Noeuds ou champs?: Analyse de l'expertise internationale sur la criminalité transnationale organisée et le terrorisme." *Canadian Journal of Criminology and Criminal Justice* 52 (2): 147–72.

Schuller, Mark. 2010. *Unstable Foundations: Impact of NGOs on Human Rights for Port-au-Prince's Internally Displaced People*. http://www.ijdh.org/2010/10/topics/housing/unstable-foundations-impact-of-ngos-on-human-rights-for-port-au-princes-internally-displaced-people-mark-schuller/.

– 2012. *Killing with Kindness: Haiti, International Aid, and NGOs*. City: Rutgers University Press.

Scoffield, Heather. 2011. "Libya Won't Go from 'Gadhafi to Thomas Jefferson,' Baird Concedes." *Globe and Mail*, 27 July. http://www.theglobeandmail.com/news/politics/libya-wont-go-from-gadhafi-to-thomas-jefferson-john-baird-concedes/article4261886/.

Scott, David. 1999. *Refashioning Futures: Criticism after Postcoloniality*. Princeton: Princeton University Press. http://dx.doi.org/10.1515/9781400823062.

Scott, James. 1998. *Seeing Like a State: How Certain Schemes to Improve the Human Condition Have Failed*. New Haven, CT: Yale University Press.

Scott, Michael. 2000. *Problem-Oriented Policing: Reflections on the First 20 Years*. Washington, DC: US Department of Justice, Office of Community Oriented Policing Services. http://www.popcenter.org/library/reading/pdfs/reflectionsfull.pdf, retrieved 16 April 2015.

Serrano, Monica, and Thomas G. Weiss. 2013. "R2P's Unfinished Journey." In *The International Politics of Human Rights*, ed. Monica Serrano and Thomas G. Weiss, 228–53. London: Routledge.

Shamsie, Yasmine. 2009. "Export Processing Zones: The Purported Glimmer in Haiti's Development Murk." *Review of International Political Economy* 16 (4): 649–72. http://dx.doi.org/10.1080/09692290802477670.

Shannon, Róisín. 2009. "Playing with Principles in an Era of Securitized Aid: Negotiating Humanitarian Space in Post-9/11 Afghanistan." *Progress in Development Studies* 9 (1): 15–36. http://dx.doi.org/10.1177/146499340800900103.

Shapiro, Michael. 2007. "The New Violent Cartography." *Security Dialogue* 38 (3): 291–313. http://dx.doi.org/10.1177/0967010607081511.

Sharma, Nandita. 2007. "White Nationalism, Illegality and Imperialism: Border Controls as Ideology." In *(En)Gendering the War on Terror: War Stories and Camouflaged Politics*, ed. Krista Hunt and Kim Rygiel, 121–43. Burlington, VT: Ashgate.

Shaw, Timothy. 2010. "Canada, Africa, and 'New' Multilateralisms for Global Governance: Before and After the Harper Regime in Ottawa?" In *Locating Global Order: American Power and Canadian Security after 9/11*, ed. Bruno Charbonneau and Wayne S. Cox, 219–34. Vancouver: UBC Press.

Sheptycki, James. 1995. "Transnational Policing and the Makings of a Postmodern State." *British Journal of Criminology* 35 (4): 613–35.

– 2005. "Transnational Policing." *Canadian Review of Policing Research* 1. http://crpr.icaap.org/index.php/crpr/article/viewArticle/31/48.

Sidaway, James D. 2012. "Subaltern Geopolitics: Libya in the Mirror of Europe." *Geographical Journal* 178 (4): 296–301. http://dx.doi.org/10.1111/j.1475-4959.2012.00466.x.

Snyder, Mark. 2010. *Selling Subordination as Stabilization*. http://ijdh.org/wordpress/wp-content/uploads/2010/11/Selling_Subordination_as_Stabilization.pdf.

Sovacool, Benjamin, and Saul Halfon. 2007. "Reconstructing Iraq: Merging Discourses of Security and Development." *Review of International Studies* 33 (2): 223–43. http://dx.doi.org/10.1017/S0260210507007486.

Spicer, Keith. 1966. *A Samaritan State? External Aid in Canada's Foreign Policy*. Toronto: University of Toronto Press.

Squire, Vicki, ed. 2010. *The Contested Politics of Mobility: Borderzones and Irregularity*. New York: Routledge.

Sriskandarajah, Anuppiriya. 2014. "Bounding Motherhood: The Case of Sri Lankan Tamil Refugees in Canada." *Women's Studies* 43 (7): 911–29. http://dx.doi.org/10.1080/00497878.2014.938190.

Stein, Janice Gross, and J. Eugene Lang. 2007. *The Unexpected War: Canada in Kandahar*. Toronto: Viking Canada.

Stern, Maria, and Joakim Öjendal. 2010. "Mapping the Security-Development Nexus: Conflict, Complexity, Cacophony, Convergence?" *Security Dialogue* 41 (1): 5–29. http://dx.doi.org/10.1177/0967010609357041.

Studnicki-Gizbert, Daviken, and Fabiola Bazo. 2013. "The Emergence of Transnational 'Natural Commons' Strategies in Canada and Latin America." *Canadian Journal of Development Studies* 34 (1): 71–8. http://dx.doi.org/10.1080/02255189.2013.767193.

Stumpf, Juliet. 2006. "The Crimmigration Crisis: Immigrants, Crime, and Sovereign Power." *American University Law Review* 56:367–419.

Sullivan, Patricia L., Brock F. Tessman, and Xiaojun Li. 2011. "US Military Aid and Recipient State Cooperation." *Foreign Policy Analysis* 7 (3): 275–94. http://dx.doi.org/10.1111/j.1743-8594.2011.00138.x.

Sunderland, Judith, and Bill Frelick. 2015. "EU's Approach to Migrants: Humanitarian Rhetoric, Inhumane Treatment." *Open Democracy*, 15 April. https://www.opendemocracy.net/beyondslavery/judith-sunderland-bill-frelick/eu%E2%80%99s-approach-to-migrants-humanitarian-rhetoric-inhuman.

Swanson, Kate. 2007. "Revanchist Urbanism Heads South: The Regulation of Indigenous Beggars and Street Vendors in Ecuador." *Antipode* 39 (4): 708–28. http://dx.doi.org/10.1111/j.1467-8330.2007.00548.x.

Sylvan, David, and Stephen Majeski. 2009. *U.S. Foreign Policy in Perspective: Clients, Enemies and Empire*. New York: Routledge.

Taber, Jane. 2011. "Ambrose and Raitt Deftly Manage Difficult Files for Harper." *Globe and Mail*, 24 October. http://www.theglobeandmail.com/news/politics/ottawa-notebook/ambrose-and-raitt-deftly-manage-difficult-files-for-harper/article618504/.

Tartir, Alaa. 2015. "Securitised Development and Palestinian Authoritarianism under Fayyadism." *Conflict Security and Development* 15 (5): 479–502. http://dx.doi.org/10.1080/14678802.2015.1100016.

Taylor, Marcus. 2009. "Displacing Insecurity in a Divided World: Global Security, International Development and the Endless Accumulation of Capital." *Third World Quarterly* 30 (1): 147–62. http://dx.doi.org/10.1080/01436590802622441.

Thakur, Ramesh, and Thomas G. Weiss. 2009. "R2P: From Idea to Norm – and Action?" *Global Responsibility to Protect* 1 (1): 22–53. http://dx.doi.org/10.1163/187598409X405460.

Thobani, Sunera. 2007. *Exalted Subjects: Studies in the Making of Race and Nation in Canada*. Toronto: University of Toronto Press.

Topak, Özgün. 2014. "The Biopolitical Border in Practice: Surveillance and Death at the Greece-Turkey Borderzones." *Environment and Planning. D, Society and Space* 32 (5): 815–33. http://dx.doi.org/10.1068/d13031p.

Treasury Board of Canada Secretariat. 2015. "Global Peace and Security Fund (GPSF). http://www.tbs-sct.gc.ca/hidb-bdih/plan-eng.aspx?Org=0&Hi=27&Pl=451.

Trenton, Daniel. 2011. "Document Details Martelly Plan for New Haiti Army." *Boston Globe*, 27 September. http://www.ijdh.org/2011/09/topics/politics-democracy/document-details-martelly-plan-for-new-haiti-army-boston-globe/.

Trouillot, Lyonel. 2009. "Hallward, or the Hidden Face of Racism." *Small Axe* 30 (3 30): 128–36. http://dx.doi.org/10.1215/07990537-2009-034.

Tsoukala, Anastassia. 2008. "Defining the Terrorist Threat in the Post-September 11 Era." In *Terror, Insecurity and Liberty: Illiberal Practices of Liberal Regimes after 9/11*, ed. Didier Bigo and Anastassia Tsoukala, 49–99. New York: Routledge. http://dx.doi.org/10.4324/9780203926765.ch3.

Turpin, Etienne, Adam Bobbette and Meredith Miller, eds. 2013. *Jakarta: Architecture + Adaptation*. Jakarta: Universitas Indonesia Press.

UN. 2015. "MINUSTAH." http://www.un.org/en/peacekeeping/missions/minustah/facts.shtml.

UNODC (United Nations Office on Drugs and Crime). 2013. "Intelligence Unit Opens in a Key Cambodian Seaport to Combat Migrant Smuggling." News release, 3 June. http://www.unodc.org/southeastasiaandpacific/en/cambodia/2013/06/migrant-smuggling/story.html.

U.S. Department of State. 2013. *Haiti 2013 Human Rights Report*. http://www.state.gov/documents/organization/220661.pdf.

Valverde, Mariana. 2001. "Governing Security, Governing through Security." In *The Security of Freedom: Essays on Canada's Anti-Terrorism Bill*, ed. Ronald Daniels, Patrick Macklem, and Kent Roach, 83–92. Toronto: University of Toronto Press. http://dx.doi.org/10.3138/9781442682337-007.

– 2011. "Questions of Security: A Framework for Research." *Theoretical Criminology* 15 (1): 3–22. http://dx.doi.org/10.1177/1362480610382569.

van Liempt, Ilse, and Stephanie Sersli. 2013. "State Responses and Migrant Experiences with Human Smuggling: A Reality Check." *Antipode* 45 (4): 1029–46. http://dx.doi.org/10.1111/j.1467-8330.2012.01027.x.

Veltmeyer, Henry. 2013. "The Political Economy of Natural Resource Extraction: A New Model or Extractive Imperialism?" *Canadian Journal of Development Studies* 34 (1): 79–95. http://dx.doi.org/10.1080/02255189.2013.764850.

Wæver, Ole. 1995. "Securitization and Desecuritization." In *On Security*, ed. Ronnie D. Lipschutz, 46–86. New York: Columbia University Press.

– 1998. "Security, Insecurity, and Asecurity in the West European Non-War Community." In *Security Communities*, ed. Emanuel Adler and Michael Barnett, 69–118. New York: Cambridge University Press. http://dx.doi.org/10.1017/CBO9780511598661.003.

Walby, Kevin, and Jeffrey Monaghan. 2011. "'Haitian Paradox' or Dark Side of the Security-Development Nexus? Canada's Role in the Securitization of Haiti, 2004–2009." *Alternatives* 36 (4): 273–87. http://dx.doi.org/10.1177/0304375411431760.

Waldie, Paul. 2011. "SNC-Lavalin Defends Libyan Prison Project." *Globe and Mail*, 24 February. http://www.theglobeandmail.com/globe-investor/snc-lavalin-defends-libyan-prison-project/article568518/.

Walker, R.B.J. 1993. *Inside/Outside: International Relations as Political Theory*. Cambridge: Cambridge University Press.

Walters, William. 2004. "Secure Borders, Safe Haven, Domopolitics." *Citizenship Studies* 8 (3): 237–60. http://dx.doi.org/10.1080/1362102042000256989.

– 2008. "Putting the Migration-Security Complex in Its Place." In *Risk and the War on Terror*, ed. Louise Amoore and Marieke de Goede, 158–77. New York: Routledge.

– 2011. "Foucault and Frontiers: Notes on the Birth of the Humanitarian Border." In *Governmentality: Current Issues and Future Challenges*, ed. Ulrich Bröckling, Susanne Krasmann, and Thomas Lemke, 138–64. New York: Routledge.

Watson, Scott. 2011. "The 'Human' as Referent Object? Humanitarianism as Securitization." *Security Dialogue* 42 (1): 3–20. http://dx.doi.org/10.1177/0967010610393549.

Weber, Leanne. 2013. "Policing a World in Motion." In *Borders and Crime: Pre-Crime, Mobility and Serious Harm in an Age of Globalization*, ed. Jude McCulloch and Sharon Pickering, 35–54. New York: Palgrave Macmillan.

Weber, Leanne, and Benjamin Bowling. 2008. "Valiant Beggars and Global Vagabonds: Select, Eject, Immobilize." *Theoretical Criminology* 12 (3): 355–75. http://dx.doi.org/10.1177/1362480608093311.

Weisbrot, Mark. 2012. "Is This Minustah's 'Abu Ghraib Moment' in Haiti?" *Guardian*, 3 September. http://www.theguardian.com/commentisfree/cifamerica/2011/sep/03/minustah-un-haiti-abuse.

Weiss, Thomas G. 2012. "On R2P, America Takes the Lead." *Current History (New York)* 111 (748): 322–4.

Weizman, Eyal. 2011. *The Least of All Possible Evils: Humanitarian Violence from Arendt to Gaza*. New York: Verso Books.

Welsh, Jennifer. 2004. *At Home in the World: Canada's Global Vision for the 21st Century*. Toronto: HarperCollins Publishers.

– 2012. "The Responsibility to Protect: Dilemmas of a New Norm." *Current History (New York)* 111 (748): 291–8.

– 2013. "Norm Contestation and the Responsibility to Protect." *Global Responsibility to Protect* 5 (4): 365–96. http://dx.doi.org/10.1163/1875984X-00504002.

Wherry, Aaron. 2015. "Stephen Harper on the Legality of Bombing Syria: LOL." *Maclean's*, 26 March. http://www.macleans.ca/politics/stephen-harper-on-the-legality-of-bombing-syria-lol/.

WikiLeaks. 2008. "Haiti: The Centerpiece of Canada's Latin America Strategy." 7 April. http://www.wikileaks.org/plusd/cables/08OTTAWA467_a.html.

– 2011. "Why We Need Continuing MINUSTAH Presence in Haiti." 1 October. https://wikileaks.org/plusd/cables/08PORTAUPRINCE1381_a.html.

Wilkinson, Cai. 2015. "The Securitization of Development." In *Handbook of International Security and Development*, ed. Paul Jackson, 33–46. Cheltenham, UK: Edward Elgar Publishing.

Wong, Diana. 2005. "The Rumor of Trafficking: Border Controls, Illegal Migration, and the Sovereignty of the Nation-State." In *Illicit Flows and Criminal Things: States, Borders, and the Other Side of Globalization*, ed. Willem van Schendel and Itty Abraham, 69–100. Bloomington: Indiana University Press.

Youngs, Richard, and Hélène Michou. 2011. *Assessing Democracy Assistance: Palestine*. N.p.: Foundation for the Future, May 2011.

Zanotti, Jim. 2010. *U.S. Security Assistance to the Palestinian Authority*. Washington: Congressional Research Service.

Zanotti, Laura. 2008. "Imagining Democracy, Building Unsustainable Institutions: The UN Peacekeeping Operation in Haiti." *Security Dialogue* 39 (5): 539–61. http://dx.doi.org/10.1177/0967010608096151.

– 2010. "Cacophonies of Aid, Failed State Building and NGOs in Haiti: Setting the Stage for Disaster, Envisioning the Future." *Third World Quarterly* 31 (5): 755–71. Medline:20821882http://dx.doi.org/10.1080/01436597.2010.503567.

Zedner, Lucia. 2007. "Pre-Crime and Post-Criminology?" *Theoretical Criminology* 11 (2): 261–81. http://dx.doi.org/10.1177/1362480607075851.

Zibechi, Raul. 2014. *The New Brazil: Regional Imperialism and the New Democracy*. Trans. Ramor Ryan. Oakland, CA: AK Press.

Zureik, Elia. 2010. "Colonialism, Surveillance, and Population Control: Israel/Palestine." In *Surveillance and Control in Israel/Palestine: Population, Territory and Power*, ed. Elia Zureik, David Lyon, and Yasmeen Abu-Laban, 3–46. New York: Routledge.

Access to Information Act Requests Cited

CBSA 2010-1481
CBSA 2010-4262
CBSA 2013-13161
CCC 2012-55
CCC 2012-66
CCC 2014-127
CCC 2014-142
CCC 2014-146
CIDA 2009-97
CIDA 2010-330
CIDA 2010-338
CIDA 2011-177
CIDA 2011-191
CIDA 2012-532
CSC 2011-172
CSC 2012-450
CSIS 2012-194
DND 2010-1284
DND 2011-914
DND 2011-1137
DND 2011-1138
DND 2011-1218
DND 2012-325
DND 2012-547
DND 2012-621
DND 2012-866
DND 2012-981
DND 2012-1782
DND 2012-1828
DND 2012-1828
DND 2012-1962
DND 2013-169
DND 2013-486
DND 2013-590
DND 2013-701
DND 2013-702
DND 2013-1000
DND 2013-1006
DND 2013-1292
DND 2013-1523
DND 2013-1963
DND 2014-708
DND 2014-715
DoJ 2010-1638
DoJ 2012-2148
Durham Police FOI 2011-331
GAC 2008-274
GAC 2008-275
GAC 2010-540
GAC 2010-549
GAC 2010-2423
GAC 2010-2427
GAC 2010-2429
GAC 2011-489

GAC 2011-492
GAC 2011-959
GAC 2011-1215
GAC 2011-1216
GAC 2011-1370
GAC 2011-1371
GAC 2011-1372
GAC 2011-1373
GAC 2011-1374
GAC 2011-1380
GAC 2011-1498
GAC 2011-1560
GAC 2011-1609
GAC 2011-2067
GAC 2011-2068
GAC 2011-2465
GAC 2012-49
GAC 2012-1740
GAC 2012-1956
GAC 2012-2009
GAC 2012-3104
GAC 2012-3267
GAC 2012-3329
GAC 2013-330
GAC 2013-1571
GAC 2013-1691
GAC 2013-2551
GAC 2013-2554
GAC 2014-778
GAC 2014-847
GAC 2014-1571
Montreal Police FOI 11-570
OPP CSCS-20111447
PCO 2010-558
PSC 2012-466
PSC 2014-78
RCMP 2009-5894
RCMP 2011-805
RCMP 2011-2021
RCMP 2011-3711
RCMP 2012-3277
RCMP 2014-99
RCMP 2014-185

Index

Page numbers with (f) refer to figures.